D1568286

They
Walked with God

They
Walked with God:

St. Bernadette Soubirous
St. John Vianney
St. Damien of Molokai
St. André Bessette
Bl. Solanus Casey

By Diane Allen

A saint is a little looking glass of God.

– John Ashcough

Table of Contents

Chapter 1

Saint Bernadette Soubirous

Bernadette (Bernarde Marie) Soubirous was born at the Boly Flour Mill on January 7, 1844 in Lourdes, France. Lourdes at that time was a town of five thousand inhabitants, situated in the foothills of the Pyrénées on the Gave River. Bernadette was baptized at the local parish church of St. Peter's on January 9, just two days after her birth. She was the eldest of the four surviving children born to Louise and François Soubirous. Five of Bernadette's other siblings died in childhood.

Louise Soubirous had an accident when Bernadette was just ten months old. She was holding a candle and standing by the fireplace when a spark caught the bodice of her dress on fire, burning her chest. As a consequence, she was no longer able to nurse Bernadette.

Louise made arrangements for Bernadette to stay in Bartrès, a village three miles away, at the home of family friends, Marie and Basile Lagües who had just lost their first baby. Caring for Bernadette and nursing her would distract Marie from her grief. Louise would also pay Marie for her services. Bernadette stayed with Marie and Basile for almost a year and the arrangement worked out very well.

As a child, Bernadette was frail and sickly. From the time she was six years old, her health was in a state of decline. When she was eleven years old, she contracted cholera which stunted her growth. As an adult, she stood only 4'6" tall. She also suffered from severe asthma attacks which would plague her throughout her life.

Even as a child, Bernadette showed a remarkable piety and love for the religious life. However, it was an ordinary piety for it was not unlike the piety of many of the girls her age in Lourdes.

Bernadette's father, François Soubirous, was employed at the Boly Mill in Lourdes. He and Louise were very kind to their customers and would advance flour to those who were in need. Out of charity, they used to cancel certain debts at the mill for their customers who were experiencing hardship. One resident of Lourdes described the Soubirous family as "discreet, polite and quiet."

For ten years the mill prospered, but as time went by the business began to suffer one setback after another. In time, the equipment needed repair but François did not have the money to pay for it. In addition, many other mills were springing up in Lourdes which had a negative impact on the business. The family was on the verge of bankruptcy. At this time, François had an accident in which he lost his left eye. Finally, it became impossible for him to pay the rent at the Boly Mill and the Soubirous family was evicted. Bernadette was twelve years old at the time.

After moving from one place to another, the Soubirous family finally wound up on the street with nothing more than a few simple possessions and the cloths on their back. When the Soubirous family had lived and worked at the Boly Mill they were well-respected among the citizens of Lourdes but after losing everything, they were looked down upon and shunned as undesirables.

François begged Louise's cousin, André Sajous (Uncle Sajous), to let them live in a property he owned, the former Lourdes jail, known by the ominous name – "the cachot" (dungeon). André did not want to agree to the request. He had a wife and five children and like François, he was also poor. André's wife was very compassionate and he knew that she would be sharing the little bread they had with François's four children. However, André felt that he could not refuse the request and allowed the Soubirous family to move in.

The dungeon was a dark and wretched one room cell where criminals had once been imprisoned. The iron bars still remained on one of the windows. The damp and dingy jail cell was considered so unsanitary that it was finally banned from holding prisoners. Bernadette's asthma was aggravated by the damp living quarters and she was often sick.

The yard next to the Soubirous' new living quarters was used to keep livestock and on the other side of the yard was a stinking manure pile which Uncle Sajous had dumped there because he was certain no one would ever occupy the dungeon again. A terrible stench was always present in and around the Soubirous' new dwelling.

The dungeon was only big enough to hold the family's three beds and a cupboard. The fireplace was used for cooking. The only decorations were a Crucifix and a Rosary that hung above the fireplace. Uncle Sajous allowed the family to stay there rent-free.

André Sajous and his wife and children lived just across the way from the Soubirous family. His house could be reached by walking through a small yard and up a rickety old staircase. André could hear the Soubirous family praying the Rosary every evening without fail. He was impressed by their strong faith, which had not wavered in their desperate situation. The family was close-knit and deeply devoted to each other. There was never so much as a bitter or harsh word spoken between François and Louise.

André was also impressed by the Soubirous children. He never heard them ask for anything even though he knew that many times, they went hungry. The children had been brought up to accept their lot without complaint and they were well-behaved and polite to everyone.

After losing the mill, Louise and François worked at odd jobs as day laborers and did seasonal work in Lourdes. François found employment in a stable caring for a proprietor's horses and from time to time a local baker hired him to transport flour and bread to a nearby town. Louise worked as a harvester in the fields and found employment as a housecleaner and laundress for middle-class and upper-class families. She also gathered wood in the forest which she sold to buy bread for her family.

While her parents went out to work for the day, twelve-year-old Bernadette stayed at home and cared for her brother Jean-Marie who was five-years-old and her brother Justin who was almost two-years-old. Bernadette's younger sister Toinette attended school, an opportunity that was not available to Bernadette since she had to care for her siblings.

Bernadette proved to be very responsible at a young age and had numerous household duties. Her mother could leave her in charge of the children without the slightest anxiety. When Bernadette and Toinette had time, they would collect scrap iron and bones and would sell them for money for the family's needs.

With her parents and sister away during the day, Bernadette often took Jean-Marie and Justin to St. Peter's parish with her where she loved to go into a dark and quiet corner of the church to pray. The little ones liked to gaze at the lovely gold statue of Our Lady of the Miraculous Medal. Bernadette would hold her brothers on her lap and pray before the beautiful statue of the Virgin.

One bitterly cold day, Bernadette and her brother Justin, who was then only two years old, were taking a walk in Lourdes. Justin was barefooted and neither he nor Bernadette had winter coats on. Mrs. Jacomet, the Police Commissioner's wife, and her daughter Armanda were taking a walk as well. Armanda had recently learned how to knit and had a pair of socks with her that she has just made. "Mother, I want to give these socks to the poorest child I see on the street today," Armanda said. When Armanda saw little Justin, she handed the socks to him, and with great delight he immediately put them on.

Once, little Jean-Marie walked to the nearby church of St. Peter's by himself. Mrs. Emmanuelite Estrade had gone to the church that day to pray and noticed Jean-Marie in the shadows.

He had on very poor clothing and his face was emaciated, showing all the signs of malnutrition. At the time, he was so hungry that he was scraping the candle wax off the floor and eating it. Emmanuelite felt so sorry for him that she took him to her home and gave him something to eat. After that, she often invited Jean-Marie to her home for a good meal.

One day, two police officers called at the Soubirous home. The previous night, two sacks of flour had disappeared from the bakery that François worked at. François's boss suspected him of the theft because of his extreme poverty. François denied the charges and invited the police to search his home. The police officers searched but found no evidence of the missing flour.

While the police were looking around his home, they noticed a single wood plank propped up against the wall. It looked suspicious to them. François admitted that he had taken the piece of wood but said that he took it because it appeared to have been discarded. Besides, it was an object without any monetary value. He planned to use it for firewood to warm his family's home. The police were aware that no one had reported the piece of wood as missing.

Nevertheless, François was arrested and taken to the office of the Commissioner of Police, Dominique Jacomet. Afterward, he was charged with larceny and locked up in the Baous prison where he remained for nine days. When he was released, he had no bitterness regarding the injustice that had been done to him. He was simply overjoyed to be back with his family. Likewise, Louise was thrilled to be reunited with her husband.

When Bernadette was fourteen years old, arrangements were made for her to go to the village of Bartrès and live with Marie and Basile Lagües and their five children. Marie had cared for Bernadette when she was a baby.

Marie agreed to send Bernadette to school in Bartrès so that she could finally learn how to read and write. She would also arrange for Bernadette to attend catechism class so that she could prepare for her first Holy Communion. When Bernadette was not in school, she would help care for Marie's five children, assist with the housework and take the sheep to pasture. Bernadette would not receive any wages, but she would be given free room and board. She would sleep in the servant's quarters.

François and Louise saw the advantages to the arrangement. They were so poor that they did not have the means to provide their children with sufficient food or clothing. They loved their daughter dearly, but there were many nights when the entire family went to bed hungry. With Bernadette in Bartrès, there would be one less mouth to feed. In addition, in Bartrès, Bernadette would have the opportunity to prepare for her first Holy Communion. For a long time, she had been asking her parents to allow her to do so.

In Bartrès, Bernadette had numerous duties from sun up to sundown. In the morning, she bathed and dressed Marie's children and did the housework. After that, she took Marie's lambs and sheep out to pasture for the better part of the day. In the hours of solitude in the fields, Bernadette prayed her Rosary and did her knitting and mending. However, the long and silent hours in the fields were lonely and wearisome and she became very homesick for her family.

Marie observed that Bernadette seemed to have a special talent for looking after the sheep and she asked herself, "If Bernadette is away at school and catechism classes, who will take my sheep out to pasture?" Marie decided to teach Bernadette the catechism herself but she did not have the ability or the patience to give her proper instruction.

Marie could barely read or write and Bernadette could not do so at all. In addition, the catechism was in French and Bernadette spoke only the local dialect, Patois. Also, in the evenings, after a long day of work, Bernadette was too exhausted to concentrate or to study. She said later that with Marie as her teacher, she learned nothing. The promises that Marie made to François and Louise regarding Bernadette's education were never fulfilled.

Marie was very fond of Bernadette and felt that in many ways, she was a model child. She never complained about anything and did whatever she was asked to do. There was never a rude or sassy remark from her lips. She was a joy to have in the home and she got along well with everyone. In addition, she was an excellent and responsible worker. Marie became very attached to her.

Nevertheless, Bernadette was unhappy in Bartrès and her sadness and loneliness seemed to increase with each passing day. She had been told she would be prepared for her first Holy Communion while living with Marie but it had not happened. Bernadette was very disappointed and told a visitor to relay to her parents that she wanted to return home. She waited but they did not come to pick her up. Later, when a friend was going to Lourdes, Bernadette said to her, "Please tell my parents I am tired of being here. Tell them to come and get me and take me home." Finally, Bernadette took matters into her own hands. She told Marie Lagües that she had decided to go back to Lourdes and proceeded to walk the three miles back to her home.

Bernadette was fourteen years old when she returned to Lourdes, but due to her small stature she looked more like a child of ten or eleven years old. Almost immediately after returning home, Bernadette signed up to attend the Hospice School run by the Sisters of Charity and Christian Instruction of Nevers. Five hundred girls were enrolled in the school. On one side of the building was a hospital which the Sisters owned and operated and on the other side was the school.

Bernadette was put in the class with the "charity cases," girls whose parents were not able to pay for their tuition. The charity cases were only allowed to attend the school until they made their first Holy Communion. After that, they were expected to go to work.

In addition to the charity cases, day students as well as boarders also attended the Hospice School. They were girls who were in a much more comfortable financial situation and they would have the opportunity to continue their education at the school after making their first Holy Communion.

The classes to prepare the girls for their first Holy Communion were given by Father Bertrand Marie Pomian, the assistant priest at the parish of St. Peter's. At the school, Bernadette would also be taught how to read, write, and sew.

Bernadette was very excited to be enrolled in the Hospice School and she was very glad to be back with her family. One morning, she and Toinette decided to go out in search of wood which could then be sold to buy bread for the family. Their good friend Jeanne Abadie went along with them. Since it was a very cold and drizzly day, Louise made Bernadette put on a hooded cloak before leaving the house. Louise worried about her daughter's asthma, especially during the winter months. Louise often had Bernadette wear a chest protector, but it was so heavy and ill-fitting that she seemed to breathe with even greater difficulty when wearing it.

On that day, the three girls walked to Massabielle, an obscure area with a steep and rocky cliff, hollowed out by a grotto, at the edge of the Gave River. The girls had never been there before but it seemed like a good place to hunt for wood. As Jeanne and Toinette crossed a shallow stream, they let out a squeal as their feet touched the icy water, which was actually melted snow. A heavy mist was falling and the temperature seemed to be dropping.

While her companions went on ahead, Bernadette stopped momentarily to take off her shoes and stockings before crossing the stream. Stockings at that time were an unheard of luxury for the poor and Bernadette's mother insisted that she wear them because of her fragile health.

Suddenly, Bernadette heard a blast which sounded to her like a strong gust of wind. Strangely enough, the air was calm, with no sign of wind anywhere. She started to take off her other stocking when she heard the blast once again.

Bernadette looked across the meadow and noticed that the leaves on the poplar trees were completely still. Above the grotto of Massabielle, there was a small niche-like cavity in the rocky cliff. The bushes and brambles that were near the niche began to quiver and shake.

The dark niche suddenly grew bright as if someone had shined a light on it. An exceedingly beautiful young woman appeared who was standing with bare feet on the moss inside the niche. Over her right arm hung a Rosary and on each foot was a yellow rose. She smiled at Bernadette in greeting and stretched out her arms slightly while opening her hands.

Bernadette described the lady as "alive and very young." She was illuminated with a soft light that neither "hurt nor dazzled the eyes." She was also small, no taller than Bernadette. She was wearing a white dress with a blue sash and a white veil covered her head.

Bernadette rubbed her eyes, thinking that her eyes were playing tricks on her, but the lady was still there. She wanted to call out to Toinette and Jeanne but was not able to do so. She knelt down and took out her Rosary but was not able to lift her hand to make the sign of the cross. Not knowing what was happening, she was seized with fear.

The lady took her own Rosary in her hand and made the sign of the cross with it and suddenly Bernadette was able to do so as well. At that moment, all of her fear disappeared. As Bernadette prayed the Rosary, the lady passed the Rosary through her fingers but dd not move her lips. The lady's Rosary, which was only a five-decade Rosary, had large white beads that were widely spaced and attached to a yellow chain. It was larger than any of the Rosaries that were sold in Lourdes. When they had completed the Rosary, the lady bowed slightly, smiled at Bernadette and then disappeared. The niche in the rocky cliff became dark and the brambles and bushes around it grew still once again.

Toinette and Jeanne caught sight of Bernadette as they were making their way back toward the grotto. She was on her knees and looking toward the niche in the rocky cliff. They called to her but she did not answer nor did she turn her head to look at them. Her body was completely still. Toinette and Jeanne became afraid when they saw how pale and unresponsive Bernadette was. Toinette feared that she was dead but Jeanne said that if she was dead, she would not be in a kneeling position.

When Bernadette came back to herself, she saw her companions and crossed the stream in order to reach them. She was surprised to find that the icy water no longer seemed cold. Rather, it felt warm, "like dishwater" as she described it. Toinette and Jeanne were jumping about trying to keep warm and they were surprised to see that the cold water did not seem to bother Bernadette in the least.

Bernadette asked the girls if they had seen anything unusual at the grotto and they said they had not. Later, when walking home, Bernadette told Toinette about the beautiful young lady she had seen. She asked Toinette not to tell anyone and Toinette gave her word that she would keep the secret. Bernadette wished that she could go back to the grotto and look up at the niche once again but they had to return home.

That evening, Toinette blurted out the secret to her mother regarding the lady Bernadette had seen at the grotto. Bernadette had referred to her as "Aqueró," which means "that." Louise was certain that the story was a product of Bernadette's imagination. "Your eyes were playing tricks on you!" Louise said to Bernadette. "You probably saw a white rock." Bernadette explained that it was not a white rock but a young lady – a beautiful lady who was surrounded by light. Louise made Bernadette promise to never go to the grotto again. That night, as the Soubirous family gathered for evening prayer, Bernadette began to cry. She was overwhelmed by the events and the emotions of the day. Her mother asked her more questions about the happenings at the grotto but she was not able to reply.

The following day, Bernadette told her mother that she felt like something was pushing her to go to Massabielle, but her mother would not allow it. On Saturday, Bernadette went to the parish to talk to Father Pomian about what she had seen at the grotto. What struck Father Pomian more than anything else was Bernadette's description of the sound she heard which was like "a gust of wind."

Father Pomian was well aware that the wind and the sound of wind is a Biblical symbol of the presence of the Holy Spirit. The book of Acts in the New Testament describes the day of Pentecost when the Holy Spirit came like the "sound of a mighty wind" and descended on the Apostles while they were in the Upper Room. In the book of Kings, the Holy Spirit came to the prophet Elijah in the form of a gentle breeze. In the book of Job, scripture says that God spoke to Job in the midst of a wind storm.

Father Pomian asked Bernadette if it would be all right for him to share her story with the pastor of St. Peter's, Father Dominique Peyramale, and she agreed to it. That very evening, Father Pomian told Father Peyramale all that Bernadette had said to him regarding the beautiful lady she had seen at the grotto. Father Peyramale was not the least bit interested in the matter and found it too farfetched to give any credence to.

On Sunday after Mass, a number of Bernadette's friends from the Hospice School, all charity cases just like herself, walked with her to her home. Toinette had told them about the beautiful lady at Massabielle and they wanted Bernadette to take them there. Bernadette asked her mother if she could go to Massabielle with her friends and her mother said she would need to get permission from her father.

Bernadette then went to the horse stable where her father worked. He told Bernadette he would not give his permission for he feared that something evil was lurking at the grotto. His employer, Mr. Cazenave overheard the conversation and urged François to allow Bernadette to go. "If the lady she sees is holding a Rosary, she cannot be evil," he said to François. The permission was then granted.

Bernadette and her classmates filled a bottle of holy water at the parish before leaving. The ten girls walked through the woods until they came to a slippery and sloping foot path that led to the grotto. When Bernadette approached the foot path, she broke out into a run. Her friends went down the steep slope slowly, grabbing onto the nearby shrubs and bushes for support. When they caught up with her, she was kneeling and praying the Rosary. At the end of the second decade she said, "There is the light. There is the lady. She is looking at all of you!" Bernadette sprinkled holy water in the direction of the apparition saying, "If you come from God, stay here, but if you do not come from God, depart." The lady smiled at her and bowed her head. The more Bernadette sprinkled her with holy water, the more she smiled.

Bernadette's eyes remained glued to the niche and she soon became oblivious to everything around her. Transported out of herself, she was in a state of ecstasy. All of the color drained out of her face and she became deathly pale. Her friends shouted her name and shook her but she was not aware of any of it. They grew frightened and began to cry. They wanted to carry her away from the grotto but they would have to take her back up the steep slope and they could not budge her. For some strange reason, Bernadette suddenly became very heavy, too heavy to move.

Several of the girls ran to the nearby Savy Mill to get help. They came upon Mrs. Nicolau, the miller's wife who was taking a walk with her sister near the mill. When the girls explained that Bernadette was deathly ill, the two women rushed to the grotto and tried to move her but were not able to do so. Mrs. Nicolau then went to get her twenty-eight-year-old son Antoine, a very strong and sturdy young man, and he quickly followed her back to the grotto.

Antoine described what happened and said:

> Bernadette Soubirous, they told me, is at the grotto of Massabielle. We don't know what she sees. We can't drag her away. Come and help us.
>
> Bareheaded and without a jacket, I, at once, followed my mother and aunt, and went down by the

wretched little path to the grotto. On arriving there, I saw three or four poor girls, Toinette Soubirous and Bernadette.

The latter was on her knees, deathly pale, her eyes wide open and fixed on the niche. She had her hands joined and her beads between her fingers. Tears were streaming from both her eyes. She was smiling and her face was lovely, lovelier than anything I've ever seen. It made me feel both happy and sad, and all day long my heart was moved at the thought of it.

I remained for a time motionless, watching her. The girls were watching her like I was. My mother and aunt were also spellbound. . . In spite of her smile, I was grieved to see her so pale. At length I went up to her, for my mother said to me, "Take hold of her and we'll bring her home with us."

I took her by the right arm. She struggled to stay. Her eyes remained fixed upwards. Not a murmur. But after the struggles, a somewhat hurried breathing. I lifted her by one arm, then by the other. My mother took one arm. While lifting her, I wiped her eyes and put my hand in front of her to prevent her seeing. I tried also to make her bend her head but she raised it again and reopened her eyes, with a smile. . .

We had great difficulty in getting her to climb the path, my mother holding one hand and I, the other, both of us pulling in front, and my aunt and the girls following behind. She was trying hard to go down again, without however saying a word. It took a great effort to drag her along. Strong as I am, it would have been heavy work had I been alone.

All the way up, her face remained deathly pale, and her eyes were still wide open and fixed upwards. I was sweating when we reached the top. We went down by the wood road as far as the mill, leading the child in the same manner, my mother and I together. Mother questioned her and so did I. She made no answer. . .I was sad and afraid. Her face and eyes remained the same as at the grotto. Tears trickled down her face continuously. I again put my hand now and then in front of her eyes and dried her tears. She never stopped smiling until she reached the mill.

As we went in, on the very threshold, she lowered her eyes and head and the color came back to her face. We took her into the kitchen and made her sit down. The girls had come in with us. When she was seated, I said to her, "What do you see in that hole? Do you see something not very nice?" She said, "Oh no! I see a very lovely lady. She has a Rosary on her arm and her hands are joined." While saying this, Bernadette pressed the palms of her hands together.

As Antoine observed, Bernadette, upon coming out of her ecstasy, was astonished to find herself at the Savy Mill. Antoine and his mother were worried about Bernadette and laid her on a bed to rest. Soon Bernadette's mother arrived and began to scold her severely. "What has possessed you to make everyone run after you?" her mother asked. She had a stick in her hand and looked like she was about to give her daughter a good thrashing. Jeanne Abadie was there and noticed that Bernadette remained calm even as her mother grew angrier. Mrs. Nicolau was indignant. "Louise, what are you doing?" Mrs. Nicolau said. "Your daughter is an angel from heaven. Do not hit her!"

Once back at home, Louise told Bernadette to never go back to the grotto again. "What is happening to you there is a fantasy. It is a figment of your imagination!" Louise said sternly.

When Bernadette arrived at the Hospice School on Monday morning, it was obvious that everyone there had learned about the events which had taken place the previous day at the grotto of Massabielle. Bernadette was summoned to the office of Mother

Ursule Fardes, the Mother Superior, who questioned her about what she had experienced. "What you have seen is an illusion, a dream," Mother Ursule said to her. "You must stop thinking about it altogether!" she added.

That afternoon when Bernadette left school, forty-year-old Sophie Pailhasson, a resident of Lourdes, walked up to her and slapped her across the face. "What a clown you are!" Sophie said sarcastically. A number of the school girls gathered around Bernadette and made cruel remarks to her, taunting her.

The next day Bernadette was told that Mrs. Jeanne-Marie Milhet wanted to see her. Mrs. Milhet was a woman of means and was one of the few residents in Lourdes who was willing to give work to Bernadette's mother. Mrs. Milhet asked Bernadette a number of questions about the apparition at the grotto and told her that she and her friend, Antoinette Peyret, wanted to accompany her there. "My parents have forbidden me to go there," Bernadette replied.

Mrs. Milhet spoke to Louise and told her that she wanted to go to the grotto with Bernadette. Along with Antoinette, they would leave before daybreak and nobody would even know. She assured Louise that there was nothing at all to worry about. Louise felt she had to comply because Mrs. Milhet regularly gave her work and she very much needed to keep the job.

Mrs. Milhet and Antoinette were at Bernadette's house the next morning at 5:30 a.m. They brought a blessed candle with them. Mrs. Milhet wanted Bernadette to ask the lady her name. Mrs. Milhet brought a pen, a piece of paper and an ink pot. Bernadette was to hand the paper and pen to the lady so that she could write down her name.

Mrs. Milhet and Antoinette believed that the beautiful lady was Elisa Latapie who had been the president of the Children of Mary and had died some time ago. Perhaps she had come from Purgatory with a message. But Bernadette was convinced that the lady was not Elisa because there was not the slightest resemblance between the two.

At the grotto of Massabielle, Bernadette, Mrs. Milhet, and Antoinette knelt down and began the Rosary. It a short time, Bernadette saw the lady standing in the niche. Without taking a step, the lady gently floated down to the inner hollow of the grotto. Bernadette stepped forward with paper and pen in hand and asked her to write down her name. The lady began to laugh and said, "It is not necessary." That was the first time that she had spoken to Bernadette and her voice was delicate, soft and very beautiful. It was an audible voice but Bernadette said that she also seemed to hear the voice within her heart.

"Would you have the kindness to come here for fifteen days?" the lady asked Bernadette and she agreed to do so. "I do not promise to make you happy in this world, only in the next," the lady added. She then gently glided back up to the niche in the cliff and disappeared. Bernadette said later, "She vanished like a cloud." A soft light remained in the niche for a short time after.

The apparition had lasted less than half an hour. Although Mrs. Milhet and Antoinette saw and heard nothing, they were convinced that the apparition was real. For one thing, during the apparition, Bernadette's countenance changed completely. An angelic smile was on her lips, her eyes shone with a beautiful light and an indefinable grace spread over her whole being. "The lady looked at you for a long time and she smiled at you," Bernadette told Antoinette.

Mrs. Milhet wanted to do something special for Bernadette. It hurt her to think of Bernadette living in that damp and unsanitary jail cell. She told Louise that she wanted Bernadette to stay at her house. She would have a warm and comfortable bed to sleep in as well as plenty of good food to eat, as much as she wanted, and she would be able to enjoy Mrs. Milhet's lovely home. Louise agreed to it.

The morning of the fourth apparition, the weather was bitterly cold. At daybreak, Bernadette and her mother left for the grotto. Aunt Bernarde who was going with them for the first time, brought a blessed candle. During the apparition, Bernadette held the blessed candle in her left hand.

On the way back home, Bernadette talked to her mother and to her Aunt Bernarde about what she had experienced at the grotto that day. She heard screaming and other terrible noises coming from the Gave River but strangely, when she looked in the direction of the Gave, no one was there. It sounded like an angry mob of people in a terrible brawl. Bernadette believed they were evil spirits. When she heard them shout, "Get out of here!" she felt that all of their anger was directed at the beautiful lady. The beautiful lady looked in the direction of the Gave River where the sinister noises were coming from. Her single gaze reduced the invisible mob to complete silence.

The apparition lasted half an hour. When it was over, Louise held her daughter in her arms. Bernadette said that she felt temporarily blinded until her eyes adjusted once again to the earth.

The fifth apparition occurred on the following day, February 20. Word had spread quickly and about thirty people were present for the fifth apparition. The beautiful lady appeared and taught Bernadette a prayer that was meant for her alone. She was to say the prayer every day for the rest of her life. Bernadette never revealed the words of the prayer but faithfully prayed it each day.

A group of public officials including Mayor Lacadé, Imperial Prosecutor Jacques-Vital Dutour, Major Renault, Magistrate Clément Rives and Police Commissioner Dominique Jacomet had heard about the happenings at Massabielle. They scheduled a meeting in the Town Hall in order to exchange their views on the situation.

After a lengthy discussion at the Town Hall meeting, the public officials agreed that the gatherings at the grotto had to be stopped. For one thing, it was a dangerous and sloping path that led down to the grotto and people could easily get hurt.

In addition, with the increasing number of people who were going to the grotto regularly, fistfights and skirmishes were a real possibility. However, people came to the grotto prayerfully and respectfully and left in silence. There was no hint of trouble and the public officials knew it.

But more than any other consideration, the authorities wanted to put a stop to the gatherings at the grotto because they hated to see the people of Lourdes being duped by a fourteen-year-old girl who was probably mentally ill. They also suspected that Bernadette's parents, paupers that they were, would try to profit financially from the crowds who were now coming to the grotto. That was considered fraud and it was against the law.

It was decided that the best course of action would be to intimidate and frighten Bernadette by putting her through a lengthy interrogation. They were certain that it would be easy to find inconsistencies in her testimony and to expose her for the liar and the opportunist that she was. Once that was accomplished, they would demand that she never go back to the grotto again and the whole matter would be over. Mr. Jacomet stepped forward to say that he could accomplish the task easily.

Approximately one hundred people stood at the edge of the Gave River in order to be present for the sixth apparition. Bernadette was at the grotto early in the morning when the beautiful lady appeared.

That afternoon after Vespers, Mr. Callet, a police officer, grabbed Bernadette by the hood of her cloak and told her that the Commissioner of Police, Dominique Jacomet needed to speak to her. Mr. Jacomet was standing nearby and he escorted Bernadette to his office.

Bernadette recognized Mr. Jacomet at once. He was the man who had arrested her father under false charges a year before, claiming that he had stolen a sack of flour. Mr. Jacomet held a position of great power and authority in Lourdes and he was feared by the local people.

Mr. Jacomet began questioning Bernadette in detail. "Is it true that you saw the Blessed Virgin Mary?" he asked. "I saw a young woman but she did not tell me her name," Bernadette replied. Mr. Jacomet asked Bernadette if she knew who the lady was and she said she did not. "Is this young woman beautiful?" Mr. Jacomet asked. "Oh, yes," Bernadette replied. "She is very beautiful." "Is she as beautiful as Mrs. Pailhasson or Mrs. Dufo?" Mr. Jacomet inquired. Mrs. Pailhasson and Mrs. Dufo were considered to be the two most beautiful ladies in Lourdes. "She is much more beautiful. There is no comparison," Bernadette replied.

After lengthy questioning, Mr. Jacomet said to Bernadette, "You are a liar. If you do not confess to making up the story about the apparitions, I am going to take you to court!" He expected then that she would begin to cry, but strangely, she did not. With great self-possession she answered, "Do whatever you have to do." He was completely taken aback by her reply.

Mr. Jacomet then read his notes back to Bernadette but he had distorted all the facts. "You saw a young woman who was twenty years old," Mr. Jacomet said. "I said she was young," Bernadette replied. "I did not say she was twenty years old." "You saw a young woman who was as beautiful as Mrs. Pailhasson," Mr. Jacomet said. "No," Bernadette replied. "I said that she was much more beautiful than Mrs. Pailhasson." Bernadette pointed out every error that Mr. Jacomet had made as he read her testimony back to her. "You have changed everything that I told you," she said boldly. By now, Mr. Jacomet had been questioning her for over an hour.

During the interview Bernadette remained calm and self-possessed. Later when she looked back on her meeting with Mr. Jacomet she said, "I was no longer myself. I was not afraid. There was something within me which enabled me to overcome everything."

Mr. Jacomet told Bernadette that everyone in Lourdes was laughing at her and that she must never go back to the grotto again. She explained that she could not obey his orders because she had promised the lady that she would go to the grotto for fifteen days. "If that is the way you want it, I will now send for the police and you will go to jail," Mr. Jacomet exclaimed.

Outside in the street, a crowd was forming in front of Mr. Jacomet's office. They began shouting and banging on the door and the window shutters. "Let Bernadette go!" they cried. "Let her come out!"

When François Soubirous was summoned, the angry group of men told him that Mr. Jacomet was interrogating his daughter and he had no right to do so. They entreated François to go into Mr. Jacomet's office and put a stop to it. "If you are a man, go in there and get Bernadette!" they exclaimed as they pushed François toward the door. Their anger ignited his own anger and gave him the courage he needed to confront Mr. Jacomet.

Once inside Mr. Jacomet's office, François' anger quickly turned to fear and he began to lose his courage. Mr. Jacomet recognized him at once as the ruined miller that he had dealt with in the past. Mr. Jacomet said to him, "François, you have already served time in jail for larceny. I do not want to send you back to jail again but if you continue to allow your daughter to go to the grotto, I will have no other choice!" François promised that he would not let Bernadette go to the grotto again.

Bernadette had been calm during the interrogation by Mr. Jacomet and she remained calm as she and her father walked back to their home. She was even lighthearted. She remembered how flustered Mr. Jacomet became during the interview. He was so nervous that he began shaking which caused the tassel on his hat to continuously pop up and down. It struck Bernadette as funny and when she told her father about it, she began to laugh. Later, someone asked Bernadette, "Weren't you afraid when Mr. Jacomet told you he would put you in jail?" "No, I couldn't have cared less," she replied.

When the citizens of Lourdes learned of Mr. Jacomet's harsh treatment of Bernadette, they turned against him. They saw him as an enemy and an adversary and refused to have anything more to do with him. As time passed, he was never able to reconcile with the townspeople or to redeem himself, although he wanted to. He was so disturbed by the hostility and the ill-will toward him that it was thought to have shortened his life. He died at the relatively young age of fifty-two years.

On the morning of February 22, Bernadette told her parents that she felt very sad. She had made a promise to the beautiful lady that she would go back to the grotto for fifteen days and she wanted with all her heart to keep the promise. However, her father had promised Mr. Jacomet that she would not return to the grotto. "I must either disobey you or disobey the lady," Bernadette said to her parents.

François was convinced that he was doing the right thing by forbidding his daughter to go to the grotto and he refused to reconsider. That morning, he told Bernadette to go straight to school. When she entered the school grounds, the Sisters let her know that they were very unhappy with her. They felt she had given a bad name to their school by being brought before the Commissioner of Police. The Mother Superior showed her disapproval by speaking very harshly to her. Bernadette remained calm and made no reply.

At one o'clock in the afternoon, Bernadette felt an irresistible force drawing her to Massabielle and she left the Hospice School and headed toward the grotto. Two policemen noticed that she was leaving school and they began to follow her. Approximately one hundred people had gathered at the grotto that day in order to be present at the apparition.

At the grotto, Bernadette knelt and began the Rosary. The police sergeant began taunting Bernadette, calling her a liar and an idiot. The beautiful lady did not appear that day.

Bernadette was distraught because she felt that she had somehow failed the lady, otherwise, she reasoned, she would have appeared at the grotto. In the evening, she went to Father Pomian's confessional and told him all that had transpired that day. From the beginning of the apparitions, Father Pomian had given Bernadette a listening ear and had treated her with respect. "Nobody has the right to stop you from going to the grotto!" he said to her.

François began to rethink his decision about forbidding Bernadette from going to the grotto. He reasoned that if she was drawn there by an irresistible force, who was he to try to stop her. He was also thinking about what Father Pomian had said to her - "Nobody has the right to stop you from going to the grotto." François told Bernadette that he had changed his mind and he now gave her his permission to go to the grotto whenever she wanted to. Meanwhile, the mayor and other city officials were plotting together to bring legal action against her.

The seventh apparition took place on February 23. The crowd that gathered at Massabielle had been growing at each apparition. During the seventh apparition, the lady told Bernadette three secrets which she was to reveal to no one. She kept the secrets for the rest of her life.

People in Lourdes began to wonder if the beautiful lady was in fact, the Blessed Virgin Mary. However, many believed that it was impossible that the Blessed Virgin would appear in Massabielle. The grotto at Massabielle was a place where garbage was often dumped and where herds of pigs were sometimes pastured. Some ventured to say that if the Blessed Virgin was to appear in France, she would most likely appear in the Paris Cathedral or to a member of a respectable and upstanding family and not to the likes of the Soubirous family.

As time passed, Uncle Sajous noticed the increase in visitors to the dungeon. He did not want people to see the utter destitution that the Soubirous family was living in and he especially did not want them to see the stinking manure pile that was right beside their home. He told Bernadette that she could receive her guests in a room upstairs at his house and she agreed to do so.

The eighth apparition occurred on February 24th. The lady came down to talk to Bernadette in the interior cavity of the grotto. On this day, the beautiful lady said to Bernadette, "Penance, Penance, Penance. Pray to God for sinners." The lady's face was sad and Bernadette too felt the deepest sadness. "Would it bother you to get down on your knees and to kiss the ground as a penance for sinners?" the lady asked. Bernadette immediately prostrated herself and kissed the ground, ready to do whatever the lady asked her to do. "The sad thing here on earth is sin," the lady explained in the eighth apparition.

The ninth apparition occurred on February 25 with three hundred people assembled at the grotto. During the apparition, which Bernadette alone could see, the lady told her to drink from the spring and to wash in it. Bernadette did not see a spring so she walked toward the nearby Gave River. The lady called her back and pointed to the interior of the grotto. However, there was no spring where the lady was pointing, only rocks, gravel and mud.

Bernadette dug at the ground where the lady was pointing and gathered only mud in her hand. However, she tried two more times and the third time she was able to gather a small amount of dirty water in the hollow of her hand. It was hard to swallow, but she forced herself to do so.

Next, the lady told her to eat of the grass. When Bernadette plucked some of the nearby grass and ate it, it made a terrible impression on the people who were watching. They jeered and laughed at her mockingly. "She is out of her mind!" some yelled. When the apparition was over, her Aunt Bernarde hurriedly used her handkerchief to clean Bernadette's cheeks that were stained with mud. Bernadette and her aunt then walked quickly home.

Bernadette was not embarrassed or upset by the reaction of the people that day. She did what the lady had asked her to do and that was all that mattered to her. It was only later that Bernadette understood the reason for the lady's request. The lady asked her to drink of the spring and eat of the grass as an act of penance, both for herself and for others.

Later that afternoon, long after Bernadette had returned to her home, a few people remained at the grotto. Someone noticed that a trickle of water was issuing from the small hole that Bernadette had dug in the ground that day. The trickle of muddy water was beginning to grow clearer and clearer. In addition, the thin stream of water was becoming wider. As the days passed, the water grew clearer and the stream continued to increase in size. It was considered a miracle, a divine prodigy. Some of the people collected the water into bottles and the sick began drinking it.

It is interesting to contemplate the origin of the spring at Massabielle. Water had never flowed at the grotto until Bernadette dug in the muddy ground and uncovered it. Did the water spring up in a miraculous way at the moment when the lady asked Bernadette to drink of the water? Or, was the spring already there, an underground body of water that no one knew existed until the lady revealed it to Bernadette? It remains a mystery.

On February 25, the evening of the ninth apparition, a policeman came to the Soubirous home informing Louise that the Imperial Prosecutor of Lourdes, Mr. Jacques-Vital Dutour wanted Bernadette to come to the office in his home at six o'clock that evening. Louise was alarmed by the policeman's words. She knew that being summoned for questioning by the Imperial Prosecutor was very serious. It was much more serious than being summoned by the Commissioner of Police as had happened when Mr. Jacomet interrogated Bernadette.

Since François was not home, Louise hurried over to the quarry looking for her cousin, André Sajous. André put on his best suit and accompanied Louise and Bernadette to Mr. Dutour's home at the appointed time.

At Mr. Dutour's home, when the housekeeper opened the door and saw Bernadette and Louise, she refused to let them come inside. She could tell by their worn-out peasant style clothing that they were poor people – country people.

Mr. Dutour then came to the door. He told Uncle Sajous to remain outside and invited Bernadette and Louise to come in. He did not offer them a seat but made them both stand. Mr. Dutour noticed that Louise was already trembling in fear. He hoped that Bernadette would soon feel the same fear and his plan was to convince her to never go to the grotto again.

Mr. Dutour asked Bernadette if she was accepting money, food, or gifts from the people of Lourdes and she said that she was not. He told her that if she was lying about the apparitions and if she and her family were profiting because of it, then serious charges could be brought against her. "I am not counting on any profit in this life," Bernadette replied.

Mr. Dutour reminded her that she had already profited by accepting the hospitality of Mrs. Milhet who had invited her to stay with her. "You deceived Mrs. Milhet in order to live like a princess in her beautiful home," he said. "It was Mrs. Milhet's idea and not mine," Bernadette explained. "However, I no longer stay at Mrs. Milhet's house. My parents told me to come home," she added. "Nevertheless, your life was better when you were staying with Mrs. Milhet rather than living in the dungeon," Mr. Dutour replied. "I only accepted her invitation in order to make her happy," Bernadette said.

Mr. Dutour asked Bernadette numerous questions and took detailed notes on her replies. He asked her what the apparition looked like and she said it looked most like the small gold statue of Our Lady of the Miraculous Medal that was in the parish church. However, the apparition was not a statue but was alive and was surrounded by a beautiful light. Many more questions followed. When Mr. Dutour read her statements back to her, he had distorted and changed her words.

Mr. Dutour had Police Commissioner Jacomet's report on his desk from the time when he too had interrogated Bernadette. "You told Commissioner Jacomet one thing and you told me another. I have proof that you have made false statements," he said. "If Mr. Jacomet made a mistake in recording my words, that is his problem, not mine," Bernadette said boldly. She spoke with great self-confidence and did not show the slightest fear of Mr. Dutour. "I want you to stop the people from going to the grotto!" Mr. Dutour said. "I don't ask them to go. They go on their own accord," Bernadette replied.

Mr. Dutour realized that he had underestimated this young girl who looked no more than twelve years old. He began to feel more and more ill-at-ease. Bernadette was staring at him intently and he had the impression that she was seeing right through him. Her eyes seemed to be saying to him, "You cannot fool me, Mr. Dutour. You are a liar and a fraud!" It was terribly unnerving.

The interrogation was going badly and Mr. Dutour could not seem to turn it around. Later, as the tide of public opinion turned against him, he would destroy all of his notes regarding his meeting with Bernadette.

Mr. Dutour wanted to strike back at Bernadette. "You ate grass like an animal!" he said to her sarcastically. She simply ignored the comment. "You must promise me you will never return to the grotto," he exclaimed. "I will be going again because I am drawn there by an irresistible force," she answered. "Besides, I promised the lady I would return," she added.

Mr. Dutour sent word to the Commissioner of Police, Mr. Jacomet, to come and arrest Bernadette. "You are going to jail now," he said to Bernadette even though he knew that she had done nothing illegal and that he had no grounds to arrest her. At his words, Louise began to sob. Bernadette remained calm and said to her mother, "We have not done anything wrong. Do not be upset."

Louise had been standing for the full two hours of the questioning. She began to feel faint and started to stagger. When Mr. Dutour realized that she was about to fall he said to her coldly, "You may sit down in the chair." Bernadette became angry at the way her mother was being treated. "They think we will get their chairs dirty!" she said to her mother. Bernadette refused to sit down.

Meanwhile, Uncle Sajous, who had been standing outside, went to a nearby cafe and complained to the other quarrymen who were there that Bernadette was being interrogated unjustly by the Imperial Prosecutor. The quarrymen then walked over to Mr. Dutour's office and began to shout angrily and to bang on the door forcefully. "Let Bernadette come out immediately!" they shouted in a threatening way. The noise became almost deafening. They began kicking the door with all their might, trying to kick it in.

Mr. Dutour, who was fearful of the angry mob outside, began trembling uncontrollably. He left the room momentarily to gather his thoughts. He could not understand why the Commissioner of Police had not arrived. Above all, he did not want to lose face. When he came back into his office he said to Bernadette, "You will not be arrested tonight. For now, I am postponing it," and with that he showed her and her mother to the door.

A short time later, Mr. Dutour wrote an official report regarding his interrogation of Bernadette and in a vindictive way, he did his utmost to degrade the entire family. He wrote that François Soubirous had once been arrested for aggravated theft but failed to mention that all the charges had been dropped.

Mr. Dutour learned that after Louise and Bernadette had left his office, the quarrymen who had been standing outside, invited them as well as Uncle Sajous to the nearby café and ordered them a glass of white wine, while asking them about the interrogation. Mr. Dutour included in his report that Louise was a drunkard. He wanted the citizens of Lourdes to believe that Bernadette as well as the entire Soubirous family were immoral and disgusting people. If their reputation had suffered in the past, Mr. Dutour hoped that it would now be ruined forever.

After the contentious interview Bernadette had with Mr. Dutour and considering the threats he had made against her, her parents wanted to protect her from further interrogations and investigations. In Lourdes, according to the city laws, any person claiming to be a visionary could be arrested and committed to a mental institution indefinitely. Bernadette did not claim to be a visionary and she was unconcerned about the danger that surrounded her. She said, "I fear nothing because I have always told the truth."

On February 28, the crowd that gathered at Massabielle had grown to 1,150. Bernadette knelt at the grotto and at the lady's command, kissed the ground. One again, it was a message of penance and reparation. Later that day, Inspector Latapie, who was in charge of all the fountains and springs in Lourdes, threatened Bernadette. "You must stop going to the grotto," he said to her. "I will not stop," she replied. "We are going to put you in prison," he said. "I am ready to go," she answered in a flippant way. "But you better make sure the door is locked tight or I will escape!" she added with no fear at all.

Louise and François Soubirous keenly felt the danger that surrounded their family but were helpless to do anything about it. The police and public officials were always nearby and watching their every move. Late at night, strangers came to their home and peeked into their windows. Others pressed their ears to the door, trying to listen in on their conversations.

The twelfth apparition occurred on March 1st. That morning, Bernadette brought a Rosary with her belonging to a devout woman of Lourdes, Pauline Sans, a dressmaker. Pauline was very ill and was not able to go to Massabielle on that day. She begged Bernadette to take her Rosary and pray with it during the apparition and Bernadette agreed to do so. During the apparition, the lady noticed that Bernadette was not praying with her Rosary but with one that belonged to someone else. "Where is your Rosary?" the lady asked. Bernadette took it out of her pocket and held it up for her to see. "I want you to pray with your own Rosary," the lady said.

There were 1650 people present for the thirteenth apparition which took place on Tuesday, March 2nd. People started arriving at the grotto at midnight. On that day, the lady told Bernadette to let the priests know that she wanted people to come to the grotto in procession. She also asked that a chapel be built. Later that day, Bernadette, along with Aunt Basile and Aunt Bernarde went to the parish rectory together so that Bernadette could deliver the message to Father Peyramale regarding the lady's request.

Father Peyramale had a strong personality. He possessed a deep spirituality as well as a generous and compassionate heart but he also had a temper. Bernadette had seen his temper flare up in the past and it could be frightening. Like many others in Lourdes, she had a reverence and a respect for Father Peyramale but she also feared his outbursts. Nevertheless, his good qualities far outweighed his bad qualities.

When Bernadette introduced herself to Father Peyramale, he said to her, "Are you the girl who has been seeing someone at the grotto of Massabielle?" She replied that she was that girl. She told Father Peyramale that she had a message to deliver to him. She then told him that the beautiful lady of Massabielle stated that she wanted people to go to the grotto in procession.

Hearing Bernadette's words, Father Peyramale became furious. He was not about to let a fourteen-year-old girl dictate to him the wishes of a mysterious lady who would not even reveal her name. He lost complete control of himself and went into a tirade. His voice grew louder and rose to a screaming pitch. "How dare you tell me to order a procession!" he said. "Only a bishop can order a procession!" he added.

Father Peyramale then looked over at Bernadette's two aunts – Aunt Basile and Aunt Bernarde. He knew that they had both been expelled from the Children of Mary Sodality in Lourdes for having a child before they were legally married. Even though they later married, Father Peyramale did not hold them in high esteem.

Aunt Basile and Aunt Bernarde were trembling in fear and Bernadette too felt the deepest distress. Her mind went completely blank and she could not think of a single thing to say. She and Aunt Basile quickly left the rectory together. Her Aunt Bernarde had already left.

As Bernadette and Aunt Basile walked home together, Bernadette suddenly realized that she had forgotten to tell Father Peyramale that the lady had also asked for a chapel to be built. She needed to go back and tell him but Aunt Basile refused to go with her.

Aunt Basile was very angry at the harsh way she and Bernadette had been treated by Father Peyramale. With tears in her eyes, she told Bernadette that she never intended to visit Father Peyramale again. Neither Bernadette's other aunts nor her mother would agree to go to the rectory with her so that she could deliver the rest of the message. They were all well-aware of his temper.

That evening, Bernadette's friend Dominiquette Cazenave, agreed to go back to the rectory with her. Bernadette could not conceal her anxiety when she knocked once again on Father Peyramale's door. "The lady also said to tell the priests that she wants a chapel to be built," Bernadette blurted out as quickly as she could. "Even if it is just a little one," she added. Father Peyramale determined to remain calm on this occasion and he succeeded in doing so.

The fourteenth apparition occurred on March 3rd. There were three thousand people assembled at the grotto on that day. The crush of people was so intense that several people accidentally took a fall into the Gave River. Bernadette was at the grotto early in the morning but the lady did not appear.

Later that afternoon, Bernadette felt the strong, magnetic pull to the grotto and left school in order to return there. The lady appeared at that time and told Bernadette once again that she would like a chapel to be built. That evening Bernadette went to see Father Peyramale wearing a disguise in order to avoid the crowds. She gave him the lady's message. Father Peyramale wanted to know if she asked the lady for her name. Bernadette replied that the lady smiled when asked for her name but did not reply.

Father Peyramale told Bernadette that he did not have the money to build a chapel. It was true. Father Peyramale had very little money of his own and the funds at his disposal from the parish were also quite meager. "Tell the lady to give you the money if she wants a chapel built," Father Peyramale said to Bernadette. "Also, tell her to perform a miracle and make the rosebush bloom at the grotto. If she does that, I will build the chapel," Father Peyramale added. Perhaps it had slipped his mind that the lady had already performed a miracle by showing Bernadette how to uncover the spring of water that was now flowing continuosly at the grotto. People were now referring to it as the "miraculous spring."

On March 3rd, the roads were packed with people in carriages, on horseback and on foot, all headed to Lourdes. Many camped out that night at the grotto in anticipation of the apparition on the following day.

On March 4th, Sergeant Adolphe d'Angla surveyed the crowd at the grotto and estimated that 20,000 people were there. Both sides of the Gave River were overflowing with people. There were a number of people hanging over the top of the rocky cliff of the grotto. If anyone had fallen, they would surely have been killed but fortunately no one took a fall. The entire Lourdes police force was there to maintain order if need be. The crowd was prayerful and peaceful and there were no disturbances.

The lady had requested that Bernadette go to the grotto for fifteen days. March 4th was the fifteenth day. Many of the thousands of people who had come to Lourdes were there because they believed that a miracle would occur on the final day of the apparitions. However, the fifteenth apparition was much like the others. The lady would appear three more times.

Bernadette had attended Mass on March 4th at 6 o'clock in the morning and afterward walked in silence with her father, her cousin Jeanne, and a few others to the grotto. Knowing how difficult it might be for Bernadette to maneuver through the crowd, the police force made a kind of isle for her so that she could get to her usual place at the grotto. Bernadette got separated from her cousin and told the policemen that her cousin wanted to be beside her on that day. Jeanne was quickly found and was then escorted to Bernadette's side.

During the apparition, Bernadette went to the interior of the grotto to speak to the lady and Jeanne followed right behind her. Later when the apparition was over and the two girls were going home, Bernadette said, "Jeanne, the lady was so close to you that if you had reached out your hand, you could have touched her.

Jeanne noticed that Bernadette's expression changed a number of times during the apparition. Sometimes she looked happy and sometimes she looked sad. She asked Bernadette about it. "I am happy when the lady is happy and I feel sad when the lady is sad," Bernadette explained. Jeanne also noticed that Bernadette tried to make the sign of the cross but was not able to do so until she had tried three times. She asked Bernadette for an explanation. "I was not able to do so until the lady finished her Rosary and raised her hand to make the sign of the cross. Then I was able to do so as well."

Bernadette said that the lady made the sign of the cross with perfection. "I learned to make the sign of the cross properly by watching the lady," Bernadette explained. People were awed by watching Bernadette make the sign of the cross. It was made slowly and reverently, her hand touching the farthest tip of each shoulder as she had seen the lady do. It was perfectly gestured and made with a kind of majesty. "If the sign of the cross is made in heaven, it can only be made in this manner," someone observed. Others said that they received the gift of faith by watching Bernadette make the sign of the cross.

That afternoon, more visitors than ever before knocked on the door of the Soubirous home, demanding to see Bernadette. Even the wealthiest citizens of Lourdes were there, dressed in fancy clothing and wearing jewels and stylish hats while their chambermaids stood beside them. Uncle Sajous estimated that ten thousand people visited Bernadette that afternoon.

One man, seeing the extreme poverty of the Soubirous family, wanted to offer them a gift. Since he had no money with him, he offered the family a bag of oranges but Bernadette refused to accept it. Other well-to-do families brought baskets full of a variety of delicious foods. The baskets were all given back untouched. One lady shook Bernadette's hand and placed in it a twenty-franc coin. At once, Bernadette gave the coin to the person next to her saying, "Take this coin. It's burning me." Some offered large cash donations but none were accepted. She would not permit her sister or brothers to accept even the smallest gift, nor would she accept anything for herself. Louise Soubirous later said that if Bernadette had only been willing to accept the money that was offered to her, it would have been a great help to the family.

The visitors wanted to give Bernadette a hug and to kiss her cheeks and hands. Trying to be inconspicuous, they cut small pieces of material from the hem of her dress to keep as relics. People pressed their rosaries into her hands so that she would touch them. She strongly disapproved of the fanatical behavior. Father Pomian, the assistant pastor at the parish of St. Peter's, also took a stand and said that Bernadette was forbidden to touch the rosaries of her visitors.

Later that day, Bernadette put on a disguise and left her house to visit Father Peyramale and tell him about the apparition. She was completely exhausted from the many visitors who had come to her home that day and her cheeks felt sore from receiving so many kisses.

When she arrived at the rectory, Father Peyramale was waiting anxiously to hear the news. She told him that the lady still asked for the chapel to be built. "Did she tell you her name?" Father Peyramale asked. Bernadette replied that she did not. "Did she say she would return again?" he asked. "She did not say," Bernadette replied. "She must give her name and supply the money for the chapel. If she does that, I promise you I will build it," Father Peyramale said. He was disappointed that the lady had not revealed her name.

Meanwhile, Bernadette began to study in earnest as she prepared for her first Holy Communion. She no longer felt the call to visit the grotto. It was a struggle for her to learn the catechism because she had a poor memory and academics were difficult for her. Father Peyramale was impressed by how serious Bernadette was about doing well in the preparatory classes for her first Holy Communion.

The nuns at the Hospice School tried their best to help Bernadette and finally enlisted Julie Garros to tutor her. Julie was a good friend of Bernadette's. She was a good student, had an excellent memory and was happy to help her friend. With great joy in her heart, Bernadette completed her preparatory instructions and made her first Holy Communion on June 3rd. The ceremony took place in the chapel of the Hospice School.

As time passed, many sick people came to see Bernadette and to ask for her prayers. She told them all to go to the grotto and to drink at the spring. She explained that she herself had no power to help them. Many took her advice and were healed.

People continued to visit the spring at Massabielle and to drink the water. They also put the water in bottles and took it home. Many healings were reported. One of the healings concerned Louis Bouriette, a quarryman who lived in Lourdes. Louis had been without sight in his right eye for more than twenty years due to a mine explosion. Louis bathed his bad eye with water that his daughter had brought him from the spring and upon doing so, the sight in his eye was completely restored.

Jean-Marie Tambourré, a four-and-a-half-year-old boy, had coxalgia, a hip disease caused by tuberculosis. His mother brought him to the grotto and placed him in the icy water of the spring. Jean-Marie, who had not been able to walk in months, immediately stood up and walked without any difficulty at all.

Father Peyramale was astonished to learn of the healings that had taken place at the spring of Massabielle. He reported the information to Bishop Bertrand Laurence. He also told Bishop Laurence that a revival had taken place in his parish which was unprecedented. There had been a sharp rise in attendance at Mass. People were now coming to confession in large numbers.

Suddenly there was great enthusiasm for the special devotions that were held in the church each week. Truly, a movement of grace had come over his parish.

Bernadette had not been to the grotto since March 4, nor had she felt drawn to go there. In the very early hours of the morning on March 25, the Solemnity of the Annunciation, Bernadette felt the strong pull to visit the grotto once again. All through the night she had awakened, feeling the irresistible urge to go to the grotto. Before four o'clock in the morning, she got up and got dressed and waited in the darkness for her parents to get up. When her parents awoke, she explained that she felt an urgency to get to the grotto. They dressed quickly and the three left the house in the darkness, before five o'clock in the morning.

When Bernadette and her parents arrived at the grotto, the heavenly light was already shining inside the niche. Bernadette would try once again to discover the lady's name. Father Peyramale had stressed to her the importance of it and she did not want to disappoint him again. But how could she convince the lady to reveal her name? For several weeks Bernadette had been thinking of different ways to frame the question to the lady so as to discover who she was. Seeking to be as respectful and as polite as possible, she practiced different ways to ask the question.

During the 16th apparition, the lady came down to the interior hollow of the grotto. She always came there when she had something she wanted to say to Bernadette. "Will you be so kind as to tell me who you are?" Bernadette asked. The words did not come out exactly as Bernadette had practiced but they were sufficient. The lady bowed and smiled at her but said nothing. Bernadette asked her three more times. With her eyes raised to heaven and her hands folded in prayer the lady finally replied, "I am the Immaculate Conception." With that, she disappeared. Those were the last words the beautiful lady spoke to Bernadette.

Bernadette had finally learned the lady's name. She kept repeating it over and over to herself so she would not forget it as she and her Aunt Basile hurried as fast as they could to the rectory to tell Father Peyramale the news. When Bernadette told him, he asked her if she knew what the words meant and she said that she did not.

The next day, Father Peyramale admitted that he was so shocked to learn the lady's name that he felt himself stagger and feared that he might fall down. He immediately wrote to the bishop of Tarbes and reported to him the details of the 16th apparition and the lady's name.

Shortly after Bernadette had visited Father Peyramale and told him the lady's name, someone explained to her the meaning of the words, "Immaculate Conception." Bernadette then understood that the beautiful lady who had appeared to her was the Blessed Virgin Mary.

The dogma of the Immaculate Conception of the Blessed Virgin Mary had been defined by Pope Pius IX on December 8, 1854. The doctrine was defined in the pope's public decree, *Ineffablis Deus,* where he stated that the Virgin Mary was preserved from original sin from the moment of her conception. Many of the citizens of Lourdes could neither read nor write and very few were familiar with the decree or the words, "Immaculate Conception."

The civil authorities in Lourdes continued to dialogue about Bernadette and the events at the grotto. Some thought it would be to everyone's best interest to have Bernadette committed to the mental hospital in the city of Tarbes. Pressure was put on Mayor Lacadé to have Bernadette examined by a physician in order to determine whether she was mentally ill.

Dr. Balencie, Dr. Lacrampe and Dr. Peyrus were approached and agreed to conduct the tests. They visited Bernadette at the Hospice School in order to give her a physical as well as a psychological examination.

The doctors noted that Bernadette's breathing was irregular and that she was wheezing from asthma. They felt her skull according to the recommendations of Dr. Joseph Gall whose theories were popular at the time. Dr. Gall proposed that certain bumps on the skull which he termed "insanity bumps" were an indication of mental illness. The doctors checked but found no abnormal bumps on Bernadette's skull.

The doctors then talked to Bernadette at length in order to determine if she was of sound mind. None of the doctors believed in the authenticity of the apparitions. They wrote in their report to the magistrate of Lourdes that the apparitions that Bernadette saw were possibly a figment of her imagination or perhaps a hallucination.

The three doctors also concluded that Bernadette was suffering from exhaustion due to the constant questioning and visits that she had to endure on a daily basis. The doctors believed that if she could somehow be freed from the endless inquiries and visits by the local people, her overall condition would improve. They did not recommend hospitalization in Tarbes. The Public Prosecutor, Mr. Dutour and Bishop Laurence, the Bishop of Tarbes both received a copy of the report. Mr. Dutour then informed the Attorney General, Mr. Falconett of the content of the report as well.

The seventeenth apparition came to be known as the "Miracle of the Candle." During the apparition, Bernadette was holding a large blessed candle. It gradually slipped down, causing the flame to directly touch the inside of her hand for several minutes. When the apparition was over, she felt the intense pain of the flame. She immediately dropped the candle to the great relief of a number of people who had been watching.

Dr. Pierre Romain Dozous, a Lourdes physician, was standing near Bernadette and witnessed the incident. Afterward, he took her hand in his own and examined it closely. To his great surprise, there was not a single burn. Dr. Dozous was completely overwhelmed by the incident. It was the cause of his conversion and it changed him at once from a skeptic into a believer. He spread the news of the miraculous event to everyone he met.

After the seventeenth apparition, the mayor of Lourdes drew up a decree ordering the closing of the grotto as well as access to the spring. Calling Massabielle an "illegal place of worship" the grotto was fenced off on all sides and a large sign was put up which said, "It is forbidden to enter this property."

The citizens of Lourdes were very angry and quickly tore down the fences. Criminal charges were then brought against the trespassers. Bernadette advised people to stay away from the grotto in order to avoid arrest. She remained calm and made a prophetic statement to her cousin Jeanne Védère saying, "We must be patient. Those who have put up the barricades will soon take them down."

Charges were brought against Bernadette's friend, Cyprine Gesta, who was found guilty by the Lourdes Tribunal of visiting the grotto. Cyprine was afraid of having to appear in court and asked Bernadette for her advice. "Do not worry. It will not amount to anything," she said. Shortly after, Cyprine received the good news that the charges had been dropped.

At the time, Bernadette was unwell. She had been in bed for several weeks, suffering from severe asthma attacks and continual coughing spells. Father Peyramale, who had been informed of Bernadette's condition, contacted Bishop Laurence who advised that it would be a good idea to send her to the town of Cauterets for a while. She would be away from the public officials who were harassing her at every turn and she would also benefit from going in the thermal springs and breathing the fresh mountain air. A cousin took her to Cauterets and paid for all of the expenses.

When the Lourdes authorities learned that Bernadette was in Cauterets, they immediately notified the police there. All during her stay, she was kept under constant police surveillance. Her every action as well as her conversations were spied upon and scrutinized. The police reported back to the authorities in Lourdes that Bernadette refused all money and gifts that were offered to her during her stay in Cauterets. In addition, when sick people approached her, she told them to have faith in God and to pray for healing. She did not lay hands on the sick or hint in any way that she could heal them.

On July 16, the feast of Our Lady of Mount Carmel, more than three months after the seventeenth apparition, Bernadette once again felt the call in her heart to go to the grotto. She put on an oversized cloak and a hat that hid most of her face so that she would not be recognized. Her Aunt Lucile accompanied her. Due to the barricades that made the grotto inaccessible, Bernadette and her aunt stood in the meadow, across from the Gave River and a good distance away from the grotto. When the Virgin appeared, Bernadette said that she looked enchantingly beautiful, more beautiful than ever before.

Later, when asked how she was able to see the Virgin from such a long distance, Bernadette said, "It seemed to me that I was at the grotto, just as I had been on all the previous occasions. All I could see was the Virgin." It was the eighteenth and final apparition. In the middle of September, the Minister of the Interior of Lourdes ordered the barricades to be removed and the public was once again allowed to visit the grotto.

Bishop Charles Thibault of Montpellier made a special visit to Lourdes for the sole purpose of meeting Bernadette. He was accompanied by his private secretary, Father Euzet, as well as Canon Baudassé, the Vicar General. They arrived at the parish rectory in a carriage. Father Peyramale was awed that such distinguished and high-ranking members of the clergy had come to pay their respects. It would be the first time that Bernadette had ever met a bishop.

The bishop asked Bernadette many questions about the apparitions at Massabielle and was impressed by her simple yet profound answers. The maid at the rectory brought in refreshments to serve the bishop. He invited Bernadette to partake of the food with him but she said that she did not care to.

Bishop Thibault was deeply moved by his visit with Bernadette. He was almost overwhelmed by it. He took her hands in his own with the intention of having her touch his Rosary. "You are so blessed," he said to her. "I would feel so honored if you would accept this gift from me," he said as he handed her his Rosary. It was a beautiful and costly Rosary with a golden chain, but she would not take it. She did not care for fancy or costly rosaries. Her own Rosary was very plain and very simple. "Well then, let's exchange rosaries. I will give you mine in exchange for yours," he said. He was hoping for a relic.

Bernadette was aware of Bishop Thibault's motives but would not comply. She had always tried to discourage relic-seekers from acquiring her possessions. "No, bishop," she answered. "I prefer to keep my own Rosary." "But the Rosary I am offering you has been given indulgences by Pius IX," the bishop said. Not wanting to hurt his feelings in any way she added, "Your Rosary is good for you and mine is good for me."

The doctors told Louise and François that if they wanted their children to live, they would need to move as soon as possible from the unhealthy conditions of their home. Father Peyramale along with the bishop of Tarbes wanted to assist the Soubirous family in finding new living quarters. They helped François get a job as a miller at the Gras mill in Lourdes. Just months after the last apparition, which took place July 16, 1858, the family was finally able to move.

Father Peyramale eventually came to believe in all that had been revealed to Bernadette at the grotto of Massabielle. However, from time to time doubts would creep into his mind and he would wonder if perhaps what she had experienced was nothing more than an illusion. He hoped and prayed that the doubts would go away, but they persisted. He prayed to God to give him a sign, letting him know beyond a doubt whether the apparitions were authentic. The answer to his prayers came one Sunday during Mass.

On that day, Father Peyramale was amazed to see a girl standing at the altar rail at the church with a halo of golden light around her head. The sight of it dazzled his eyes. Because he was not able to tell who the girl was, he followed her closely with his eyes until she returned to her seat. When she turned, he saw that it was Bernadette. From that moment on, he never had another doubt about her or about the truth of the apparitions. Father Pomian, assistant to Father Peyramale, had faith in Bernadette from the beginning and used to say, "The best proof of the apparitions is Bernadette herself."

Bernadette had to travel frequently since people from other parts of France made repeated requests for a visit from her. The citizens in Lourdes were proud of their "celebrity" and were more than happy to show her off. She traveled to Cauterets, Pau, Bagnères and more. She did not enjoy the trips and she especially did not like missing her classes at the Hospice School.

Father Peyramale was worried about Bernadette's poor health and wanted to protect her at all costs. It was taxing for her to be at the mercy of continual visitors and curiosity seekers who sought her out day and night. Finally, Father Peyramale insisted that she move from her home and become a boarder at the Hospice School where the nuns would be able to shield her from the crowds and monitor the visits. She would continue to receive her schooling there and would also receive free room and board.

Father Peyramale made all of the arrangements for the move. He spoke to Mother Ursule Fardes, the Superior of the Hospice, and said that Bernadette would not be allowed to receive any visitors there unless he gave his permission. In addition, one of the nuns would always need to be present when she was speaking to a visitor. Bernadette moved to the Hospice School in July, 1860. She was sixteen years old.

At the Hospice School, Bernadette had always been in the class with the "charity cases," girls who attended school free of charge because their parents could not afford to pay for their education. Now she would be with the privileged group of girls who were both boarders and day students and whose parents could afford to pay their expenses. Bernadette was not happy to find herself in the category of the privileged. She preferred being with the charity cases. That was where she had been her entire

life and that was where she felt the most comfortable. She had
never felt ashamed of her poverty. The girls who were boarders
at the school were thrilled when they learned that Bernadette
would be joining them.

At the Hospice School, Bernadette's friends noticed that
items did not pile up in the small locker she had been assigned.
She had the habit of giving practically everything that she
received away and she had a distaste for accumulating material
possessions.

At the Hospice School, Bernadette was making real progress
in her reading and writing skills. She especially enjoyed being on
the playground with her many friends. On the school yard, she
often sought out the youngest children to play with. She was
not physically strong enough to jump rope but she liked to hold
the rope for the others. She also enjoyed playing blind man's
bluff and hide and seek.

On far too many occasions, Bernadette's school day was
interrupted by visitors. There were often people waiting in line
at the school gate long before the nuns got up in the morning,
hoping to get permission to speak to Bernadette.

If the superior approved the request, a special bell would be
rung and Bernadette would immediately leave her classroom or
the playground and go to the sitting room where the visitors
were waiting for her. The encounters were something that she
dreaded and, on some occasions, she was unable to hold back
her tears. She had no choice but to answer the same questions
over and over again. Visitors to the Hospice School would often
ask her to bless their rosaries. "I cannot do so," she would reply.
"Only a priest can bless your rosaries," she added. One day, 900
people went to the Hospice School in order to see Bernadette.

While Bernadette was living as a boarder at the Hospice
School, she got the very sad news that her little brother Justin
had died. Bernadette had been very close to Justin and as his
older sister, she had cared for him lovingly during his young
years. The doctor had warned Louise and François that the

unsanitary living conditions of their home would have a harmful consequence for the health of their children. Justin was only ten years old when he passed away.

As a boarder at the Hospice School, Bernadette continued to have numerous health problems. She suffered from a chronic cough, heart palpitations and severe asthma attacks. At times, she coughed up blood. On occasion, her parents were called to come to the school immediately as it was feared that Bernadette was dying. She once said that she preferred the asthma attacks to the time spent in the sitting room answering the questions of the visitors.

During the time that Bernadette was attending the school, some of her exceptional spiritual gifts became known to the superiors. On one occasion, a man and woman visited the Hospice School with their daughter who was an invalid. They wanted to ask Bernadette for her prayers. The superior sent for Bernadette and introduced her to the family. She then asked her to straighten the little girl's pillow. When she did so, the child immediately felt a great improvement in her health. The following day, all of the symptoms of her illness had vanished.

It was the responsibility of Bishop Laurence to make a formal judgment regarding the eighteen apparitions that had occurred at Massabielle. He organized an episcopal commission which made a two-year investigation into the matter. On January 18, 1862, Bishop Laurence signed a decree which declared that the Virgin Mary had truly appeared to Bernadette Soubirous and he authorized veneration to Our Lady of Lourdes in his diocese.

Also, in 1862, Bishop Laurence initiated the plans to build a chapel in response to the Virgin Mary's request for one. It would be called the Crypt Chapel. Sixty workmen were hired to begin the construction. Included in the number was François Soubirous, who felt immensely honored to be a part of the project.

Bishop Laurence did not have all of the necessary funds for the building of the Crypt Chapel and he was not sure how he would pay for it. He was hopeful that the money would somehow be provided. The clergy in Lourdes made arrangements for a professional photographer to take a series of photographs of Bernadette. The photos would be sold to the pilgrims who came to Lourdes and all of the proceeds would be used for the expenses of building the chapel.

Joseph Fabisch was chosen to create a statue of the Virgin Mary which would be placed permanently in the niche at Massabielle in the exact spot where she had appeared to Bernadette. The statue would be made of the finest Carrara marble.

Joseph Fabisch was a professor of sculpture at the School of Fine Arts in Lyons, France. He was an extraordinarily gifted artist as well as an expert in religious sculpture. He was the creator of the beautiful statue of Our Lady of La Salette as well as other outstanding statues displayed in churches and basilicas in France.

Wanting to capture a true likeness of the heavenly vision, Joseph Fabisch traveled from Lyons to Lourdes and spent five days interviewing Bernadette at length about what she had seen at the grotto. He was surprised at how young Bernadette looked. She was twenty years old but she looked much younger. Joseph observed that Bernadette was frail, poorly dressed, and looked ill. He suspected tuberculosis. He wanted to know the Virgin's physical features, the expression on her face, her age, her demeanor. Bernadette was able to supply every detail.

At least half of Joseph Fabisch's questions to Bernadette concerned the clothing that the Virgin wore. Bernadette told him that she wore a white dress with a blue sash around her waist. The sash was five to six inches wide and was pleated. She wore a white veil which extended down almost to the bottom of the dress. The dress was gathered high at the neck and had long sleeves.

Joseph wanted to know what type of material the dress was made of. Bernadette said that it was impossible to describe because she had never before seen any material that was even remotely similar. The veil was of the same material as the dress. Bernadette emphasized to Joseph Fabisch that the Virgin was a real and living person, not a ghost or a spirit. "She moved, smiled, and spoke just like we do," Bernadette explained. When Joseph asked Bernadette about the yellow roses on the Virgin's slippers, she corrected him. The Virgin was not wearing slippers but was barefooted. Joseph wanted to know if the roses looked as though they had been embroidered on a piece of cloth and how they were positioned on her feet. Bernadette explained that they did not look at all like embroidered roses. They were the same shade of yellow as the chain on the lady's Rosary. They gently rested on the Virgin's feet and they were glowing.

Joseph Fabisch set to work and first made a clay model of the Virgin of the Immaculate Conception and asked Bernadette for her impressions. She said that the expression on the face of the clay model seemed distant and cold. She also said that the clay model failed to capture the youthfulness and joyfulness of the Virgin and instead depicted her as somber and grave. Joseph Fabisch appreciated Bernadette's critique and was anxious to make the corrections.

On April 4, 1864, 20,000 people attended the dedication of Joseph Fabisch's statue of the Immaculate Conception. For the auspicious occasion, the streets in Lourdes were decorated with beautiful garlands, colorful flags and displays of great pageantry. The huge gathering went in procession from the church to the grotto of Massabielle where all would see the statue for the first time. Bishop Laurence removed the curtain that covered the statue, blessed it, and incensed it. Among the many magnificent statues that Joseph Fabisch had created, this would be considered his finest work of all – his masterpiece.

Bernadette, for the most part, was silent regarding the finished statue. She admired Joseph Fabisch and did not want to hurt his feelings in any way by making any criticism of his work. When several people asked her later about her feelings regarding the statue, she said that she was disappointed. "The statue is beautiful but it does not look like the Blessed Virgin," Bernadette said. "The Blessed Virgin cannot be depicted here on earth," she added.

Later, someone asked Bernadette, "When one gazes at the statue in the niche at Massabielle, is it possible to imagine the beauty of the Virgin Mary?" "No, it is not possible," she replied. "It is as different as heaven is from earth."

Perhaps one of Bernadette's most beautiful descriptions of the heavenly vision of the Virgin Mary is as follows:

> I saw a dazzling light. . .But a light like nothing here on earth, even the sun. In the midst of that light, I saw a wonderful form, but not like any earthly form. It was physical and it wasn't. I heard a melodious voice and I looked, without noticing anything else around me. There I was, and when it was over, my vision was blurred, like someone coming into a room after looking at the sun for a long time. The woman's form I saw there looked nothing at all like what has been reproduced.

On one occasion, a young girl was introduced to Bernadette and asked her, "Is it true that the Virgin Mary was lovely?" "Oh yes, it is true," Bernadette replied. "She was so lovely that when you have seen her once, you would be willing to die to see her again." On another occasion she said, "I have never seen anything as beautiful as the Virgin Mary in my life."

Bishop Forcade, the Bishop of Nevers made a visit to the Hospice School in order to talk to Bernadette about her plans for the future. He asked her what line of work she wanted to pursue. He wondered if she might like to have a small business but she said she was not interested. She told Bishop Forcade that she had no plans for the future but she would do whatever her parents wanted her to do.

Mr. Raoul de Choisne de Tricqueville had contacted Bishop Laurence stating with all sincerity that he wanted Bernadette to take his hand in marriage. Bernadette however, had no interest in getting married.

Bernadette explained to Bishop Forcade that she loved living at the Hospice School with the Sisters of Charity and would be happy to live there forever. "But you cannot live at the Hospice School forever because you are not a nun," the bishop explained. "If you would like to be a nun, you must apply to a congregation that you are interested in," he added.

Bernadette felt certain that not a single religious order would accept her, not only because of her poor health but also because of her poverty. She would not be able to provide the dowry that was required for admittance. "We would be able to take care of the financial requirements for your entrance," the bishop said. Meanwhile, he wanted her to think about the different religious congregations that she might be interesting in joining.

Bernadette was more attracted to the active religious orders than to the contemplative orders. The hands-on service of the active orders to the poor and the sick was very attractive to her. She was interested in learning more about the Sisters of St. Vincent de Paul congregation and they were hoping that she would join their order. They had even invited her to come to their convent for lunch so that they could tell her about their work. The Sisters of the Cross and the Sisters of the Immaculate Conception as well as other congregations held out the same hope that Bernadette would join their order.

Bernadette had been deeply inspired by the nuns who ran the Hospice School. Their official name was the Sisters of Charity and Christian Instruction of Nevers. She especially loved the way they cared for the poor and the sick. She used to say, "The vocation of the Sisters of Charity is precious, because it makes one love the poor." It was for that reason that she decided to apply for admittance to the Sisters of Charity of Nevers.

Father Pomian remembered that while living at the Hospice School, Bernadette nursed some very sick elderly women who had repulsive illnesses. He observed that she had a real talent for assisting the sick and seemed to have a special calling to it.

After much prayer and reflection, Bernadette wrote to the Novice Mistress in Nevers, Mother Marie-Thérèse Vauzou, and requested admittance to the Sisters of Charity of Nevers. Mother Vauzou read Bernadette's letter to the novices at the St. Gildard convent in Nevers and said to them, "You realize what a grace and what a favor it is for us to receive Mary's privileged child and how grateful we should be for this. As for myself, it will be one of the greatest blessings of my life to behold the eyes that have seen the Blessed Virgin."

In 1866, Bernadette was making her preparations to leave Lourdes. Before she left, the superior of the Hospice School took her to Pau to introduce her to the other Sisters of Charity of Nevers who were living at the convent there. After they arrived, someone recognized Bernadette and soon a huge crowd of people descended on the convent. The superior had no recourse but to call the police.

The police did their best to keep order in the courtyard where everyone had gathered. It was exhausting for Bernadette to greet so many people and she began to feel sick. She had a severe asthma attack and asked the Sisters to take her back to Lourdes and they did so.

That same year, to the great delight of Bishop Laurence, the Crypt Chapel was finally completed. The Crypt Chapel was built in order to fulfill the wishes of the Virgin Mary who made her request for a chapel numerous times to Bernadette. Hewn out of the rock at Massabielle, the Crypt Chapel was both beautiful and solemn.

Bishop Laurence insisted that Bernadette be present for the dedication of the Crypt Chapel before leaving Lourdes for the convent in Nevers. Bernadette felt great joy that the Virgin Mary's request for a chapel had finally been granted. Thousands of people were expected to attend the dedication and concerns were voiced for Bernadette's safety.

For security purposes, the Sisters of Charity had Bernadette attend the dedication ceremony with the Children of Mary Sodality that she was a member of. All members of the Sodality wore their customary white dresses and white veils. Bernadette was placed in the middle of the group and looked just like all the other girls. The Sisters of Charity surrounded the girls for further protection. Very few people in the crowd were able to recognize Bernadette but some of those who did cut pieces of her white veil off to keep for relics.

That evening, when the Sisters took Bernadette back to the Hospice School, they made sure to secure all the gates. However, some people managed to climb over the walls hoping to see Bernadette. Matters soon got out of hand. The military had to be called in but they had a great deal of trouble maintaining order.

On the evening of July 3, 1866, Bernadette's entire family was gathered for a farewell dinner at the mill. The family gathering did not conclude until around 11 p.m. A very large crowd had gathered outside, hoping to say a final goodbye to Bernadette.

The next morning Bernadette departed for the trip to Nevers. A well-wisher had given her a light blue dress with dark blue stripes to wear on the journey. It was only with the greatest difficulty that she was convinced to accept the dress and to wear it. She took very little with her as was her habit and had all of her possessions in a canvas bag. She was twenty-two years old.

Traveling with Bernadette to Nevers was Mother Alexandrine Roques, the Lourdes superior, Mother Ursule Court, the Bagnères superior, and two postulants, Léontine Mouret and Marie Larrotis. Their train arrived in Bordeaux in the evening. The second stop was to the town of Perigueux, where Bernadette and her companions visited the Mercy Home for Orphan Girls. They also made a stop at Sainte Ursuele's School where Bernadette was asked to give a talk to the faculty and the students. In Perigueux, they boarded another train which took them to the convent of St. Gildard in Nevers.

For the many nuns at the convent of St. Gildard, the arrival of Bernadette was a great moment, an "event." By now she was a celebrity whose renown had extended far beyond her native France. She had become famous throughout the world. Books as well as newspaper and magazine articles were constantly being published recounting the story of Bernadette and the apparitions at Massabielle.

In Nevers, the students at the nearby boarding school of Our Lady of the Angels were very happy that they were allowed to attend Vespers at St. Gildard convent chapel. Hoping to get a glimpse of Bernadette, during Vespers they looked for her, but she was now wearing the postulant habit and they were unable to discover her among so many other nuns, all dressed alike.

The superiors at St. Gildard's wanted Bernadette to be treated just like all the other nuns and not to be singled out in any way. In addition, they wanted to provide her with as normal a religious life as possible. They knew that would be a challenge considering how famous she was.

The superiors decided that Bernadette was to tell the story of the apparitions at Massabielle one time only and to all of the nuns. After that, the subject was never to be mentioned again. None of the nuns would be permitted to ask her about it and she, likewise, would not be allowed to talk about the subject. In addition, when the nuns wrote letters to their family and friends, they would not be allowed to mention Bernadette.

Members from two other religious communities were invited to attend Bernadette's talk at the convent. A total of three hundred nuns assembled that afternoon and listened as Bernadette spoke listlessly about all that had taken place at the grotto of Massabielle. It was estimated that she had already told the story to perhaps 30,000 people. A number of questions were put forward and she answered them all.

Mother Vauzou, the Mistress of Novices and Bernadette's direct superior seemed most interested in the three secrets that had been given to Bernadette during the seventh apparition. She asked Bernadette a number of questions about the secrets but Bernadette explained that she could not give any of the details.

At the Nevers convent, there were many times when Bernadette wept because of the homesickness she felt for her family as well as for the grotto. She tried to hide her sadness but she was not always able to do so. One of the nuns once saw her in tears and asked her if she was crying because she was no longer able to go to the grotto. "Yes, I miss going to the grotto. If only you knew what a beautiful thing I saw there, but I cannot say any more about it as it is against the rules," Bernadette replied.

Bernadette wrote a letter to the Sisters of the Hospice at Lourdes and said, "I beg you, my very dear Sisters, to be good enough to offer a few prayers for me, especially when you go to the grotto. That is where you will find me in spirit, clinging to the foot of that ledge I love so much."

Bernadette wrote to her family about once a year. They loved hearing from her and they asked her to write more often. However, she learned that her letters were copied and distributed to the public and this was distressing to her. Her letters were personal and private and were meant to be read only by the closest members of her family. She loved her family dearly but she said that if her letters continued to be copied and circulated, she would be forced to stop writing to her family altogether.

Mother Vauzou appointed Bernadette to be in charge of "blessing the hour," which consisted of leading a special prayer when the hour struck. It was considered an honor as well as a serious responsibility and Mother Vauzou chose Bernadette because she was confident in her abilities. She also chose her to lead the recitation of the Rosary in the novitiate. That too was considered a privilege.

While Mother Vauzou appreciated Bernadette's abilities and singled her out for certain responsible posts in the convent, she was often harsh with her and reprimanded her severely. She never gave her a word of encouragement but rather, plenty of criticism. Bernadette was hurt by her superior's coldness and shed many tears because of it. She would sometimes turn pale on being scolded severely but she never answered back. "I would not have wanted to be in Bernadette's place," said Sister Stéphanie Vareillaud, who witnessed Mother Vauzou's treatment of her.

Mother Vauzou seemed to have an unreasonable fear that if Bernadette was not treated severely, she would not be able to acquire a spirit of humility, considering the adulation and praise she received on so many occasions. The truth was that Bernadette was a very humble person. She took no pride in the spiritual favors that she had received and always said that she was undeserving of them.

Mother Vauzou wanted the nuns to confide in her and to share their most intimate thoughts and feelings with her. She encouraged them to come to her for spiritual direction. Bernadette would not confide in Mother Vauzou but instead, she kept her distance. This caused a tension in their relationship because Mother Vauzou considered it a personal slight and resented Bernadette for it.

Mother Vauzou once told her secretary, Mother Bordenave, that she did not understand why the Blessed Virgin appeared to Bernadette when there were so many other girls who were more refined and well-bred. She used to say, "Bernadette is just a peasant and nothing more."

Like Mother Vauzou, Mother Joséphine Imbert, the Mother General, was also unkind to Bernadette. Bernadette confided to another nun that she had a great fear of Mother Joséphine. She referred to Bernadette as, "a useless person," and humiliated her publicly. Once, when Mother Joséphine returned to the convent after being away, she greeted every nun with a kind word except Bernadette. To her, she said nothing.

Right after Bernadette entered the convent in Nevers, the doorbell began to ring incessantly with people requesting to speak to her. She assumed that the constant visits which had become unbearable to her in Lourdes would be over for good in Nevers. However, that was not the case. The tidal wave of attention seemed to follow her wherever she went.

The superiors made every effort to protect Bernadette from the curiosity seekers and the visitors. In addition, they tried to safeguard the peace and quiet of the convent for the benefit of all the nuns who lived there. Her superiors said "no" to most of the requests. However, there were exceptions.

High-ranking members of the clergy often entreated the Sisters to allow them a short visit with Bernadette and the Sisters did not feel they could deny them. As time passed, an increasing number of bishops put in their request to see Bernadette. Often, the bishops were allowed a short visit with her on condition that they not ask her any questions.

In addition, mothers of desperately ill children sometimes came and pleaded with the superiors to permit them a brief time with Bernadette. Such requests were usually granted. In addition, those who were considered to be "exceptionally important people" were generally allowed a short visit.

On July 29, 1866, Bernadette along with forty-three other postulants received the novices' habit, a profession crucifix and Rule, and a Rosary. Bishop Forcade presided at the ceremony. At that time, all of the novices were given a new name. Bernadette would be known as Sister Marie Bernard. On that day, Mother Joséphine Imbert, the Mother General, told Bishop Forcade, "Bernadette is ill almost all the time. She is good for nothing!" Despite the various trials and challenges of religious life, Bernadette described her life at the St. Gildard convent as "heaven on earth."

The schedule at St. Gildard convent allowed for ample private prayer as well as community prayer in the chapel. Bernadette remembered each one of her family members every day in her prayers. She prayed not so much for their material prosperity or even for their health, but that they would remain faithful to God and would lead good Christian lives. Her family had recently been beset by many trials and tribulations. Bernadette thought that there was a direct connection between some of their actions and the troubles that were befalling them.

After Bernadette entered the St. Gildard convent, it became apparent that she had the gift of prophecy. On one occasion, a postulant, Annette Basset became so ill that the doctor recommended that she be sent home. Bernadette said to Annette, "Don't cry. The Lord wants you to be a nun and you will be, but in another congregation." Annette left the St. Gildard convent a year later and entered the Sisters of St. Joseph of Cluny where she stayed for sixty years.

Another instance of Bernadette's gift of prophecy concerned the novice, Jeanne Lannessans. Jeanne became ill in the novitiate and had to stay in the infirmary. At the time, Bernadette was also ill and the two were together in the infirmary for several months. Jeanne asked Bernadette to pray for her recovery. Bernadette made a novena for Jeanne and when she completed the novena, she said to her, "You will not recover from your sickness but you won't die either. But you will suffer." Jeanne continued to suffer but after talking with Bernadette, she felt she received the grace to accept her illness with complete resignation.

While in the novitiate, Bernadette received a letter from the Mother Superior at the Hospice School in Lourdes telling her the sad news of her dear mother's death. Louise Soubirous was forty-one years old. Doctors felt that she died prematurely due to the extreme poverty and hard work that she had been subjected to throughout her life. Louise passed away on December 8, 1866, on the Feast of the Immaculate Conception. Her death had occurred between two and three o'clock in the afternoon, when the first procession in honor of the Immaculate Conception was making its way toward the Crypt Church just above the grotto of Massabielle. Bernadette felt a great sorrow on learning the news but she said she believed that her mother was in Heaven.

As a professed Sister of Charity of Nevers, Bernadette was assigned the job of assistant infirmarian. Later she was promoted to head infirmarian and head pharmacist. She loved caring for the sick nuns in the infirmary and worked with a certain authority that inspired confidence in those around her. She learned how to prepare the different medicines and how to calculate and measure out the complex doses. Dr. Robert Saint-Cyr, the convent doctor, said that as head infirmarian, Bernadette did her work with perfection.

One of Bernadette's patients in the infirmary was Sister Anne Marie Lescure, who had terminal cancer. Julie Garros (later Sister Vincent Garros) a novice, was asked to help Bernadette take care of Sister Anne Marie. Bernadette and Julie were friends and had known each other when they both lived in Lourdes. Sister Anne Marie had seeping and festering sores covering her body and Julie helped Bernadette change the dressings. Julie found the work very repulsive and could barely force herself to do it. Not long after, Sister Anne Marie died.

A short time later, Julie was passing by the infirmary when she saw Bernadette preparing Sister Anne Marie's body for burial. Bernadette asked Julie to come and help her but Julie was very much afraid and said that she could not touch a dead body. Bernadette reminded her that she was a Sister of Charity and needed to overcome her feelings of dread and fear so that she could do the work that was required of her.

On one occasion, a fire broke out in the convent pharmacy and the novice who was in charge that day was badly burned. Suffering unbearable pain, she screamed continuously. Bernadette could find no suitable medicine in the infirmary to ease her pain. She gave her some Lourdes water to drink and prayed to the Blessed Virgin Mary. In just a matter of minutes, all of the novice's pain subsided.

Bernadette also helped Jeanne Jardet, a domestic worker in the convent kitchen who had become very ill. When the domestic workers became sick, they were cared for in a large attic room on the third floor of the convent.

Bernadette visited Jeanne's bedside in the attic of the convent, fluffed her pillow, wiped the perspiration from her brow and held her hand. Jeanne responded to Bernadette's loving kindness and appreciated the prayers she offered up for her. One is reminded of the words of St. Vincent de Paul, "Every sickroom is a chapel where Jesus resides."

Jeanne was so weak that she could barely speak. She told Bernadette how sorry she was to be so far away from her mother and how much she missed her. Bernadette pointed to a statue of the Virgin that was nearby and said, "That is your mother, my dear. She is the mother of us all."

On one occasion, one of the nuns at St. Gildard convent, Sister Carteron, spoke to Bernadette in confidence. She was disappointed because she had not been given the work assignment that she had longed for and she was complaining about it. It would have been a promotion and a job with more responsibility. "Can you believe it?" she said to Bernadette. "Sister Veronique was chosen for the position instead of me. At least you are in charge of the infirmary." Bernadette replied to Sister Carteron in a serious tone, "Know this, that I do not seek to be in charge of anybody or anything. I seek only to be in charge of myself, and I can't seem to manage that."

Bishop Pierre Dreux-Brézé, the bishop of Moulins, had a great desire to see Bernadette. He was aware that her health was poor and that the many visitors who came to the convent were a burden to her. He did not want to add to that burden. He spoke to Mother Vauzou and said that he would be completely satisfied if he could simply see Bernadette from a distance. He did not need to have a face-to-face conversation with her. Mother Vauzou agreed and they came up with a cleaver plan.

Sister Julienne was instructed to take Bernadette outside and walk with her by the flower garden. At the moment when they came close to the window of the bishop's parlor in the convent, Sister Julienne was to stop and engage Bernadette in a short conversation. That way, the bishop would be able to see

Bernadette clearly without being seen himself. Mother Vauzou waited with Bishop Dreux-Brézé in the parlor. Through the window, he was able to see Bernadette clearly and he left Nevers very thankful and very satisfied.

On one occasion, Bishop Leopold Léséleuc de Kérouara, the bishop of Autun, asked to see Bernadette who was ill and in the infirmary. He received permission to do so. While he was talking to Bernadette, his bishop's hat dropped onto her bed. The Sister who was assisting in the infirmary that day saw the incident and had the impression that the bishop purposely dropped his hat on her bed. He wanted her to pick it up and hand it back to him so that he could possess something that Bernadette had touched. There was an awkward silence because she did not pick up his hat nor did he reach for it.

Bernadette knew exactly what the bishop had in mind. She had seen such things many times in the past and she disapproved of it. "Please give me my hat back," the bishop said. "You can pick it up yourself," she replied. The Sister working in the infirmary that day spoke up and said, "Bernadette, please give the bishop his hat" and she immediately picked it up and handed it to him.

A priest, Father Alix, a professor at the Sorbonne University in Paris, visited Bernadette in Nevers. The encounter resulted in a deep and lasting conversion experience for Father Alix. He was so overwhelmed by the visit that he cancelled his trip to Spain, made a general confession, and not long after, became one of Bernadette's spiritual directors.

Once a woman brought her two-and-a-half-year-old son, Ferdinand Paquet, to the convent. He was seriously ill and his mother was terribly worried. Mrs. Paquet hoped to see Bernadette so that she could ask her to pray for her son. The Mother General told Bernadette to take little Ferdinand to the garden while she talked to his mother privately. Later, when Bernadette brought the child back to his mother, all of the symptoms of his illness had vanished. Little Ferdinand enjoyed good health from that time forward and lived to be eighty years old.

Bernadette enjoyed immense prestige in the convent of St. Gildard among the postulants and other nuns and many of them counted themselves fortunate to be able to talk with her and ask for her advice. Sister Eugénie Calmès was one of them.

Sister Eugénie was considering leaving the convent because of the intense loneliness she was experiencing. She spoke to Bernadette who encouraged her not to give up or to leave. "You are going to persevere in your vocation. I am certain of it," Bernadette said to Eugénie. Bernadette repeated the words several times to her. Bernadette seemed so confident and so sure of what she was saying that Sister Eugénie was deeply affected by her words. "Come and talk to me anytime you feel discouraged," Bernadette said. "I will be praying for you," she added.

After her conversation with Bernadette, the feelings of loneliness that Sister Eugénie had been experiencing subsided and they never returned. Sister Eugénie was almost disappointed by the turn of events. Bernadette had invited Sister Eugénie to talk with her whenever she felt discouraged. She would have loved to do so again but her discouragement and loneliness had vanished.

Bernadette's father became seriously ill while working at the Lacadé mill. He lived a faith-filled and holy life and he died a holy death on March 4, 1871. It was the anniversary of the fifteenth apparition of Our Lady of Lourdes. He was sixty-four years old. A month later, Bernadette's dear aunt Lucile Castérot passed away. Also, in 1871, Toinette's little daughter Bernadette passed away. Six months later, she lost her little boy, Bernard. Tragically, Toinette lost all five of her children during the time Bernadette was in the convent of St. Gildard.

In January 1873, Bernadette suffered from a very severe asthma attach and had to spend three months as a patient in the infirmary. She offered up all of her sufferings to the Lord and prayed to St. Joseph for a happy death. Later in the year when Bernadette had recovered her strength a little, she and Mother Joséphine Imbert traveled by carriage to visit the convents of the Sisters of Charity in the towns of Varennes and Fourchambault.

They visited the Varennes orphanage where everyone gathered outside in the grove around a statue of the Virgin Mary. In the beautiful outdoor setting, Bernadette and Mother Joséphine sat in two armchairs that were placed by the statue of the Virgin. Since it was the month of Mary, they all sang hymns together and offered prayers to Our Lady of Lourdes.

Afterwards, Bernadette was asked to say a few words to the orphans. She talked to them about devotion to the Virgin Mary. "All of you have a mother," she said to the orphans. "Your mother is the Blessed Virgin Mary and she loves you all very much." Bernadette was suffering from exhaustion and she began to feel very weak. When it appeared that she was about to faint, four of the older orphans carried her back to the carriage and helped her inside.

At the beginning of 1874, the superiors at St. Gildard determined that working in the infirmary was too strenuous for Bernadette's fragile health. She was assigned instead to work as sacristan in the convent chapel where her duties would be much lighter. She had loved working in the infirmary and it was difficult for her to give it up, but she found that she was happy working as sacristan.

In Bernadette's new position, it was her responsibility to make sure that the furnishings, vestments, and decorative objects in the church were kept clean and in good repair. She set out the liturgical books for Mass, took care of the sacred vessels and altar linens, and arranged bouquets of fresh flowers for the altar. She made all the preparations in the church for solemnities and special feast day celebrations such as Ash Wednesday, Palm Sunday and Easter Sunday. As sacristan, she now had more free time for prayer and spiritual reading. She enjoyed reading the lives of the saints - her favorites being St. Bernard of Clairvaux, St. Aloysius Gonzaga and St. Francis of Assisi. She had become a member of the Third Order of St. Francis before entering the convent.

At the end of 1874, Bernadette's health was in such decline that she was no longer able to have regular duties at the convent. Mother Vauzou was aware of her wisdom and her gift of counsel and sent many of the troubled novices and postulants to the infirmary to talk to her. She was able to encourage them in a remarkable way. She reminded them of the power of the Rosary and encouraged them to pray it daily.

Even though Bernadette was no longer able to have a work assignment, she still had the desire to be useful to her community. She painted Easter Eggs for the orphans at Nevers and decorated them with the greatest care. With a small penknife she etched designs on the brightly colored eggs. She also used her artistic talent to embroider beautiful vestments for members of the clergy.

Bernadette received the sad news that Father Peyramale had passed away on September 8, 1876. He died on the feast day of the Blessed Virgin Mary's birthday. Although he had been skeptical initially, he became Bernadette's greatest friend, supporter and advocate. He had served at the parish in Lourdes for twenty-two years.

In 1876, Bishop de Ladoue of Nevers was going to visit Pope Pius IX in Rome and he was certain that the pope would ask him about Bernadette. Bishop de Ladoue went to Bernadette's bedside in the infirmary where she had been a patient for many months. He told her that he would like her to write a note to the pope and he would deliver it personally to him. She was very ill but she agreed to do so.

Because Bernadette was so weak, Sister de Vigouroux held the writing pad for her while she slowly penned her message. She wrote:

> Most Holy Father, I should never have dared to take up my pen to write to Your Holiness – a poor little Sister like me – if our worthy bishop had not encouraged me by telling me that the sure way to receive a blessing from the Holy Father was to write to You and that he would have the kindness to take charge of my letter. I am torn between fear and confidence.

Never could a poor ignorant little Sister like me dare to write to the most Holy Father. Never! . . . I pray every day to the Sacred Heart of Jesus and the Immaculate Heart of Mary to keep you among us for a long time to come, since you make them so well-known and loved. Every time I pray for your intentions, it seems to me that the Blessed Virgin must often look down from heaven upon you, most Holy Father, because you proclaimed her "Immaculate" and four years later this good Mother came on earth to say: "I am the Immaculate." I did not know what that meant; I had never heard that word, but since then, whenever I ponder the matter, I say to myself: How good the Blessed Virgin is. One would think she came to confirm the words of our Holy Father.

Pope Pius IX, in acknowledgment of the letter he received from Bernadette, gave her a beautiful silver crucifix as a gift. Bernadette was very surprised and very humbled to receive such a gift from the pope.

The harsh treatment of Bernadette by Mother Vauzou and Mother Joséphine Imbert lasted for years but finally ended for good when Mother Adélaïde Dons became the new Mother General. Mother Dons was aware of the unkindness of her predecessors toward Bernadette and was appalled by it. Mother Dons was affectionate and motherly and created an environment of love and understanding that the nuns thrived in.

During her final illness, Bernadette suffered from a very large tumor on her right knee caused by tuberculosis of the bone. Her leg atrophied and withered and the pain became unbearable. Due to the tumor, her right leg remained outside the bed, resting on a chair.

Bernadette's beloved brother Jean-Marie came to visit her during the last year of her life. He had seen her last when he was fifteen years old and now he was a grown man who was twenty-seven years old. The reunion was emotional for both Jean Marie and Bernadette and the bond of love was as strong as ever. Due to her weakness, she did not talk very much yet she was interested in any news he had about the family. She did not complain to Jean-Marie about her failing health. Jean-Marie later said that she gave him some good advice during their visit.

Bernadette knew that her brother earned his living by working at Massabielle and she was under the impression that he was well paid. He told her that he did manual labor at the grotto and earned a pitiful wage, hardly enough to survive on. Bernadette promised Jean-Marie that she would write to the priest who was in charge of the grotto in Lourdes. Hopefully, Jean-Marie's work situation would then improve.

On December 11, 1878, Bernadette became permanently bedridden. The slightest movement of her leg caused her to scream in pain. Her screams woke the other nuns in the infirmary and kept them awake through the night. With the agony she was enduring, it sometimes took the nuns one hour to find a position that felt comfortable to her. Her face became cadaverous. During her last months, she suffered from bedsores that spread over her body. In addition, abscesses formed in her ears causing partial deafness. She also experienced a terrible pressure in her chest and felt like she was suffocating.

A few days before her death, Bernadette asked that all the holy cards and holy pictures that were pinned to the curtain by her bed be removed. She was detaching herself from everything. She kept only her crucifix.

Bernadette Soubirous (Sister Marie Bernard) died on April 16, 1879 at the age of thirty-five. She had spent twelve years at St. Gildard convent in Nevers. Her body was taken to the chapel where it lay in state while four nuns kept vigil. People handed their rosaries, medals and religious articles to the nuns to touch to Bernadette's body. In addition, soldiers gave the nuns their swords, carpenters gave their tools, and seamstresses gave their thimbles, all to be touched to Bernadette's body.

The funeral was held on April 19 with Bishop Etienne Lelong of Nevers presiding. Eighty priests and religious were in attendance. The Sisters of Charity, the Sisters of the Holy Family, the Sisters of Hope and the Little Sisters of the Poor occupied the main body of the church. None of Bernadette's relatives were able to travel the 435-mile distance to Nevers to attend her funeral.

Bernadette was declared a saint by Pope Pius XI on December 8, 1933 on the Feast of the Immaculate Conception. To this day, Lourdes remains one of the greatest healing centers in the world.

When for one reason or another, we contemplate the reality of death, it is not uncommon that we begin to think about the sin and failure in our past. And for many, this thought can be a cause of great unhappiness and even despair. After all, the past is past, we are told; it can never be recovered; the chance of grace is gone. But when we pray the Hail Mary, there is contained in one small word an entirely different message, and one which can, in itself, completely transform our thinking and transform our lives. It is the word "now." "Pray for us now." What Mary discovered, deep in her being at the Annunciation, was that nothing was impossible to God. In a single moment, in an instant of grace, everything can be changed. And this of course is true, or can be true, for each one of us. . .In our lives, we can say that there are only two moments that are of supreme importance: the moment of our death and this moment now, the present moment. Part of the greatness of the Hail Mary is that it contains, and contains together in one breath, as it were, both of these moments: Mother of God, pray for us now and at the hour of our death.
*   - Father Paul Murray, O.P.*

Chapter 2

Saint John Marie Vianney

We have heard the saying before - "The saints did not all start out well, but they all ended well." Looking at the life of St. John Marie Baptiste Vianney, we see that he started out well, he continued well through the various seasons of his life, and as his life came to a close, he ended well.

John Marie Vianney was born May 8, 1786 in the small village of Dardilly in France. His parents, Matthieu and Marie Vianney, were poor farmers as well as devout Catholics. They had six children, of whom John Marie was the fourth.

The Vianney family farmed several acres of wheat fields and hayfields and also had a vineyard. When John Marie was seven years old, one of his duties was to watch the donkey, cows and sheep while they grazed in the fields. It was the custom for the children in Dardilly to knit socks while watching their animals in order to make constructive use of their time. During harvest season, the whole family worked together in the fields. At midday, they stretched out and took a siesta in the orchard before continuing their work.

The one and only elementary school in Dardilly was forced to close due to the political upheaval of the French Revolution. Because of that, Christine, John Marie's sister, took it upon herself to teach him how to read. When John Marie was nine years old, the school reopened and he was finally able to attend public school where he studied history, arithmetic, geography, reading and writing.

As John Marie grew older, his farm duties increased. He ploughed the ground, raked and pitched hay, picked chestnuts, acorns and fruit from the various trees on their land and helped with the reaping and binding of corn. In addition, he cleared ditches, cut wood, cared for the cows in the stable, and worked in the vineyard.

Pierre Vianney, John Marie's grandfather, was known for his exceptional kindness to the poor, a quality carried on by Matthieu and Marie, John Marie's parents. One time several destitute men called at Pierre's farmhouse. Pierre gave them a meal and allowed them to sleep in the bakehouse that night. Several weeks later, Pierre was surprised to receive a beautiful hand-written letter of thanks from Benedict Joseph Labre, one of the men he had given shelter to. Benedict Joseph Labre was revered as a saint and later canonized. He was known for his penitential lifestyle, his love for solitude and his long hours given to prayer.

John Marie's father Matthieu remembered the incident well. He was seventeen years old when Benedict Joseph Labre paid a visit to their farmhouse. His father Pierre treasured the letter he received from Benedict Joseph, considering it a second-class relic. Later, when Pierre became elderly, he gave the letter to Matthieu who felt blessed to receive it. Many years later, Matthieu gave the letter to John Marie.

On December 8,1793, during the time of the French Revolution, attendance at Sunday Mass was abolished by law. The Vianney family faced the choice of supporting the priests who were part of the revolt against the Catholic Church or remaining faithful to those who refused to sign up in the new Order.

Matthieu and Marie Vianney sided with the priests who remained faithful to Rome. As a result, they had to practice their religion secretly as part of the underground church. Even though it was illegal, the Vianneys travelled at midnight to distant farms, barns and wooded areas to attend Masses celebrated by priests who had been forced to go undercover. Realizing that these priests risked their lives on a daily basis, John Marie began to look upon them as heroes and role models.

When John Marie was a youth, his mother gave him a small wooden statue of the Virgin Mary. He loved it so much that he kept it with him day and night. During the Reign of Terror, when crucifixes and religious articles were confiscated and destroyed, he kept the statue in his pocket. While taking the sheep to pasture, he put it in the hollow of a tree or on the grass beside him.

Although they were well-aware of the danger, the Vianneys sheltered hunted priests in their home. One was Father Groboz who sometimes went about the village disguised as a cook. Once when Father Groboz was staying at the Vianney farmhouse, he asked eleven-year-old John Marie how long it had been since his last confession. "I have never made my confession," John Marie replied. Father Groboz heard his confession that very day. Later John Marie said, "I shall always remember my first confession. It took place in our farmhouse at the foot of our big clock."

Father Groboz made arrangements for John Marie to join a catechism class in the town of Ecully in preparation for his first Holy Communion. The classes, which lasted for a period of two years, were held at night by candlelight and were taught by two Sisters of St. Charles whose religious community had been dissolved during the Revolution.

Thirteen-year-old John Marie made his first Holy Communion in 1799 along with fifteen other youth. The shutters were closed and hay carts were placed in front of the windows of the room where the ceremony took place. Everything had to be done in secret. When the Reign of Terror ended in 1802, the Catholic Church was re-established in France, resulting in religious peace and freedom throughout the country.

When John Marie was seventeen years old, he decided that he wanted to become a priest. However, his father Matthieu was against it and would not give his permission. John Marie's sister Christine had just married and Matthieu had incurred expenses with the wedding. Also, Matthieu was getting older and depended on John Marie's excellent help on the farm. He could not afford to pay a new farm worker to work in his son's place.

Two years later, John Marie leaned that Father Charles Balley had opened a school in the town of Ecully for young men who were considering a vocation to the priesthood. The curriculum included math, history, Latin and other subjects, and was like a Junior Seminary for Junior High and High School aged young men. Matthieu now gave his consent for John Marie to enter the preparatory school for priestly studies.

John Marie's mother, Marie Vianney, went to Ecully and introduced herself to Father Balley. Marie told Father Balley that her son John Marie wanted with all his heart to become a priest and would like to attend his school. Father Balley said that unfortunately he was not able to take even one more student.

John Marie's sister Christine and her husband Melin wondered if anything could be done to help John Marie enter the school. Melin decided to talk to Father Balley in person. He asked Father Balley to reconsider his decision regarding John Marie's admittance to his school. However, Father Balley would not change his mind. "I would at least like you to interview John Marie," Melin said. "I feel sure you will be impressed by his excellent character," he added. Father Balley agreed to the interview.

Nineteen-year-old John Marie, the lowly field laborer with very little formal education, accompanied by his mother, visited Father Balley at his parish in Ecully. Father Balley asked John Marie a number of questions and found that he was well-informed and knowledgeable regarding his faith. John Marie made a very favorable impression on Father Balley. Sensing the young man's goodness and piety, Father Balley offered him admittance to his school. Wanting to help him in every way, he said to John Marie, "Do not worry about anything. If need be, I will make sacrifices for your sake."

John Marie moved to Ecully and lived with his Aunt Marguerite Humbert on her farm. He attended Father Balley's school each day and was the oldest student in the class. Some of the other students were thirteen-years-old. The school furnishings were sized for students in Junior High School and John Marie had to sit cramped behind a small desk. From the beginning, he had trouble with the academics. The other pupils made fun of him when he could not get through the lessons that they learned with ease. He was considered the dunce of the class. For John Marie, it was a terrible beginning. Although they made fun of him, all of the students in the class liked John Marie and admired him for his piety.

At Father Balley's school, Latin was the subject that proved to be the hardest for John Marie. In the summer of 1806, to obtain the grace of learning Latin, John Marie decided to walk to the tomb of St. Francis Regis in the town of La Louvesc in order to pray for his intercession. It was a sixty-mile journey. On the way back home to Ecully, John Marie was convinced that St. Francis Regis was interceding for him. He had a deep sense of peace and was filled with renewed hope about his ability to succeed at his studies.

For three years, John Marie continued to study under Father Balley. He worked hard but the results were disappointing. His memory was poor, his understanding was slow, and his grades continued to be unsatisfactory. He told Father Balley that he was discouraged and wanted to go back to his home in Dardilly. He felt like a failure and did not believe he could succeed in his studies. Father Balley would not hear of it and said to John Marie, "If you go back to your home, your parents will want you to stay there and you will have no chance of ever becoming a priest." With Father Balley's constant support, John Marie was able to persevere.

In the autumn of 1809, when Jean Marie was twenty-three years old, his studies were interrupted when he received his calling up papers for military service in the French army. It was the same year that Napoleon had seized the papal states and arrested the pope.

For an unknown reason, John Marie's name was not on the list submitted by the diocese of the seminarians who were to be exempted from the draft. Father Balley rushed to Lyons to set the matter straight. He explained to the recruiting officers that there had been a terrible mistake. John Marie's name was supposed to be on the list of seminarians who were exempt from military service. He did not know why his name had been omitted. Father Balley gave them a letter from the Vicar General, Bishop Corbon, formally stating that John Marie was a seminarian and therefore should be considered exempt from military service.

The recruiting officers would not accept the letter from the Vicar General. They told Father Balley that John Marie's name was not on the original list and therefore he would not be considered exempt. They added that John Marie had no recourse but to report to the military station in Lyons at once. He was assigned to the infantry and would soon be leaving with his regiment for Spain.

John Marie travelled to Lyons to report for duty but two days later he became ill with a high fever. After an examination, the army doctor sent him to the General Hospital in Lyons where he spent two weeks. When he was discharged from the hospital, he joined the other recruits in the town of Roanne.

While in Roanne, John Marie suffered a relapse and was hospitalized for six weeks. When he recuperated, he was ordered to join a detachment that was to set out on the following day for Spain. He left the hospital in ample time and as he walked, he passed a church and went inside to pray. He became absorbed in prayer and lost track of the time. When he finally reached the military office, it was closed. The next day, John Marie returned to the office where he was told that his detachment had set out without him. He was advised to leave at once to join his regiment. Still weak from his prolonged illness, he walked alone to Renaison.

On the road to Renaison, John Marie met a young man who offered to carry his heavy pack. John Marie was once again suffering from a fever and he was so weak that he could hardly walk. After conversing with John Marie for a while, the young man said, "You do not seem to be the type of man cut out to be a soldier." He invited John Marie to come with him to his village, Les Robins, where he could hide from the military authorities. He explained that his village was completely surrounded by forests and he assured John Marie that he would be safe. In a protest against the government of Napoleon and his unjust wars, many men at the time refused to serve in the French army and instead went into hiding. John Marie had never considered such an action, but when the young man presented the idea to him and invited him to come to his village, he accepted the invitation.

At Les Robins, John Marie was introduced to the mayor of the town, Paul Fayot, who greeted him kindly. The mayor agreed to allow John Marie to hide in Les Robins. He was hiding two other deserters as well. Mayor Fayot was aware of the risk he was taking, for at the time, whoever was caught harboring a deserter was imprisoned for a year and fined between one thousand and three thousand francs. The mayor was willing to take the chance.

Arrangements were made for John Marie to help on the farm that belonged to the mayor's cousin, Claudine Fayot. John Marie slept in the stable which was located between the Mayor's house and Claudine's farm. Claudine, a widow with four children, became almost like a mother to John Marie. He was advised to change his name as a safety measure, so he became known to all as Jerome Vincent.

John Marie was happy to find ample work in the small village. Since most of the inhabitants of Les Robins were illiterate, he invited them to come to the farmhouse where he taught them to read and write. He also taught them the catechism. People of all ages came to his classes and enjoyed them very much. He had his theology books sent to him from Ecully so that he could continue his studies for the priesthood while in Les Robins.

On Sundays, John Marie took care of Claudine's three-year-old daughter while the family went to Mass. He would have loved to attend Mass with them but it was too risky. If anyone from the outside suspected that he was a deserter and reported him, he would be arrested on the spot. Police occasionally came to the small hamlet of Les Robins searching for deserters. On those occasions, a signal would be given and John Marie would rush to the barn and hide beneath the hay.

In January 1811, approximately one year after coming to Les Robins, John Marie received word that amnesty had been declared and all military deserters were free to return to their homes. The people of Les Robins had grown to love John Marie and felt very sad that he was leaving their village to return to Ecully. A collection was taken up and the proceeds were used to pay a tailor to make a priest's habit for the future Father John Marie Vianney. They asked him to put it on briefly so that they could see what he would look like in priestly attire. Claudine Fayot gave him a gift of a dozen linen table napkins which she had received years before as a wedding present. "Priests will one day visit you at your parish. You must have a nice table setting when you entertain them," Claudine said. Some pressed money into his hand and forced him to accept it. There were many tears. "When you are ordained, we would like you to return to Les Robins and be our parish priest," the villagers said to him.

Father Balley was overjoyed at John Marie's return. He had not seen him for sixteen months and had continually prayed for his safety. John Marie would now live at the presbytery (priest's residence) at the parish rather than at his Aunt Marguerite's house. That way Father Balley could supervise his studies more closely. John Marie worked in the presbytery garden and assisted as Father Balley's sacristan and altar server. John Marie was now twenty-four years old. The following year, Father Balley sent him to the Verrières Seminary.

In the Minor Seminary in Verrières, John Marie applied himself to his courses in philosophy but had difficulty with the subject. Once again, he was older than the other students, older even than his professor. The very first time the teacher asked him a question, he felt so intimidated that he was not able to say a word. All of the students burst into laughter. Even so, he was popular with his classmates who looked up to him as a spiritual role model. One of his classmates said many years later, "There was nothing extraordinary about John Marie Vianney. He was just perfectly simple."

John Marie had received good grades in zeal, conduct, and character, but his general knowledge grade was very weak. The questions on the tests were put to him in Latin, his weakest subject. He came out at the bottom of a class of two hundred students. By this time, his mother, Marie Vianney had passed away. When he received failing grades in the Minor Seminary, he went to his mother's grave and wept. During the following summer, Father Balley encouraged John Marie and told him not to worry about anything. He was to continue on with his studies and then transfer to the Major Seminary. Father Balley assured him that he would help him in any way he could.

There were two hundred and fifty students at the Major Seminary of Saint Irenée in Lyons. Almost from the start, John Marie began to feel that familiar feeling of despair. A fellow classmate said that his problems occurred because he did not understand Latin. The superior of the seminary assigned Jean Duplay to tutor him. Jean was one of the best students at the seminary. In addition, one of the professors gave John Marie private lessons. During the examinations, John Marie became confused and his mind went totally blank.

After five months at St. Irenée, John Marie was dismissed in the middle of the term and given the lowest grade possible. He submitted to the decision without a complaint. Nevertheless, he said that it was one of the saddest experiences of his life. "I was overcome with grief," he said.

Later, when John Marie reflected on his life, he said, "God has shown me this great mercy in that he has given me nothing on which I could rely - neither talent, nor wisdom, nor knowledge, nor strength. When tempted to despair, I have only one resource - to throw myself at the foot of the tabernacle like a little dog at the feet of his master."

John Marie let go of his dream of becoming a priest and determined instead to apply to be a lay brother. He went to Lyons to visit a childhood friend, Jean Dumond, who had taken vows as a lay brother and was now known as Brother Gerard. He told Brother Gerard that he wanted to join the same Order.

When John Marie returned to Ecully, he could not hold back his tears when he told Father Balley about his dismissal from Saint Irenée. He explained that he had visited his friend, Brother Gerard in Lyons, and had decided to be a Brother. Father Balley would not hear of it. "Write to Brother Gerard and tell him not to breathe a word to anyone about your conversation with him. Tell him that you have decided to continue your studies for the priesthood."

Father Balley told John Marie that even though he had been dismissed from Saint Irenée, he would still be allowed to take the final examination for ordination. "The examination will take place in three months and I will tutor you privately, preparing you for the test," Father Balley said. He was convinced that God had called John Marie Vianney to the priesthood and that he would do great things for the Church.

When the important day arrived, Father Balley was confident that John Marie would do well on the examination. Canon Bochard, the Vicar General, and a number of the most well-educated priests of the diocese of Lyons conducted the test. John Marie was awed to be in the presence of such distinguished members of the clergy and his nerves got the better of him. He was unable to answer the questions that were put to him in Latin. He was notified that he did not pass the test and he would not be among those preparing for ordination.

The next morning, Father Balley hurried to Lyons to talk to Canon Bochard. He wanted Canon Bochard to know that even though John Marie's Latin was weak, he was the most pious of all the seminarians. Father Balley asked Canon Bochard if he would reconsider the decision regarding John Marie's ordination. He was certain that John Marie would make an excellent priest. Canon Bochard as well as the other priests in the diocese had great respect for Father Balley and trusted his opinions. Many considered him a saint. "Yes, if you want me to reconsider my decision, I will do so," Canon Bochard said. Father Balley then asked Canon Bochard if he would come to the parish presbytery in Ecully the next day and retest John Marie. Father Balley believed that he would do better on the test if he was in familiar surroundings. Canon Bochard agreed to do so and brought the superior of Saint Irenée with him.

On the day of the examination, the parishioners in Ecully were in the church lighting candles and praying that John Marie would pass the test. He scored much better on his examination and the score was so good that Canon Bochard allowed him to be ordained. Years later, as he looked back on his long struggle to the priesthood, John Marie felt that God had been opening doors and assisting him each step of the way, making the impossible, possible.

When twenty-nine-year-old John Marie walked from the town of Ecully to the Cathedral of Grenoble for his priestly ordination on August 13, 1815, he was alone. There was no one there to support him - not a fellow student, not a relative or a friend to make the sixty-mile journey with him. His ordination, which was presided over by Bishop Claude Simon of Grenoble, was very simple. There was no pomp, no festivities, no reception, no celebratory dinner. The bishop said to him kindly, "It is not too much trouble to ordain a good priest." The bishop had no idea that John Marie Vianney was on his way to becoming one of the most famous and most loved priests in the history of the Catholic Church.

When Father John Marie Vianney returned home, he served as assistant priest to Father Balley at the parish in Ecully. He proved to be an outstanding and exemplary priest at his first assignment and the parishioners loved him. They admired him most for his tremendous enthusiasm and zeal for the faith.

Father Balley was happy to observe the long lines of people waiting to make their confession to Father John Marie. Remembering the numerous obstacles John Marie had faced in the seminary, Father Balley though it ironic to witness his almost instant success as a parish priest. However, he had always believed in John Marie and was not the least bit surprised. Father Balley thought so highly of him that he chose him as his confessor.

Living in the parish presbytery together, Father Balley and Father John Marie became the best of friends. They seemed to be of the same mind and spirit. They recited common prayers together every morning, made a day of recollection together every month, and attended a spiritual retreat together every year. When time allowed, they enjoyed making short pilgrimages together to nearby shrines. Together, the two composed the beautiful prayer - *The Chaplet of the Immaculate Conception* which became popular in many of the parishes in France.

Two and a half years after Father John Marie was assigned to the parish at Ecully, his beloved friend and mentor, Father Balley, died. Some of the parishioners at Ecully spoke to the bishop and said that they would like Father John Marie to be assigned as the new pastor, but it was not to be. Father Tripier succeeded Father Balley as pastor and Father John Marie remained the associate pastor.

After a short time of serving at the parish in Ecully, Father Tripier came to the conclusion that Father John Marie was an extremist. He did not approve of Father John Marie's austere and penitential lifestyle and complained that he was far too rigid. Father Tripier said that he had no intention of turning the priest's house into a Trappist monastery. Father John Marie would not accompany Father Tripier on his social visits to the homes of well-to-do parishioners nor would he go out to dinner with Father Tripier and his friends. It was not an ideal situation for either of the priests.

When the parish in Ars became vacant, the bishop of Lyons decided to send Father John Marie to serve there as pastor. The parish in Ars was the poorest and most remote parish in the diocese. Because it was so small, there was a question as to whether it would be worth it to send a priest there. Before John Marie left for his new assignment, the bishop said to him, "There is hardly any love in that parish. It will be up to you to bring love there."

Father Vianney was thirty-one years old when he left Ecully to serve as the parish priest of Ars. In Ars, he would be alone. He would not have the consolation of having a fellow priest to work and live with as he had in Ecully with Father Balley. John Marie walked to his new assignment with a cart full of books and a few simple belongings. Although he had always been very strict about not accumulating personal possessions, he kept Father Balley's looking glass and took it with him to his new assignment. He regarded it as a relic since he considered Father Balley to be a saint. "I treasure this looking glass because it used to reflect Father Balley's dear face," he would say. Likewise, he took Father Balley's worn black umbrella and he cherished it. On rainy days in times past, the two priests had walked together under one umbrella, because they could not afford two.

It took Father John Marie four days to walk the eighteen miles from Ecully to Ars. When he was close to his destination, he got lost due to very thick fog. He finally saw a young man on the road and asked him for directions. The young man, Antoine Givre, told him the right road to follow. Father Vianney said to Antoine, "You have shown me the way to Ars. I will show you the way to heaven."

To Father John Marie, the village of Ars seemed lost in an inaccessible wilderness. No matter which way he turned, the surroundings looked depressing. The town consisted of two streets lined with about forty dreary houses that were scattered among the orchards. The ponds were stagnant and the landscape was bleak. A peculiar air of melancholy seemed to hang over the village which was home to about two hundred and thirty people. To the priests of the diocese of Lyons, Ars was considered a distant and forsaken place. None of the priests wanted to be assigned there. Even the air was considered unhealthy.

The church in Ars, which was dedicated to St. Sixtus, was very small and very poor. It looked more like a chapel than a church. Not only was it small, it was also dilapidated. Father John Marie noticed that the sanctuary lamp was extinguished and the tabernacle was empty. Everywhere he looked he saw cobwebs and thick layers of dust. There were numerous cracks in the ceiling and the paneling was discolored. The interior of the church had only twenty rows of seats. Father John Marie would soon learn that was more than sufficient for the small number of parishioners that attended Mass. Behind the church was a grove of twenty walnut trees.

Father John Marie was to live in the priest's house, which was called the presbytery. It was just a few steps from the church. When he moved in, he asked that the beautiful furnishings in the house be removed. A quilted coverlet of white and gold taffeta, six velvet covered chairs, and other fine pieces of furniture were taken out of the residence at his request. He kept only the bare necessities which included one frying pan, one saucepan, one bowl, one spoon, two old tables, a bookcase, and a small bed. The presbytery was gradually stripped of almost all of its furniture and much of it was given to the poor.

Shortly after Father John Marie moved into the presbytery, he was given three pretty china cups. Soon, they were nowhere to be found. It was discovered that he had already disposed of them. He seemed to always be on guard against any form of materialism. About people who accumulated wealth, he used to say, "They are like people filling a sack with mist or like those who store pumpkins. When winter comes, you discover that they are all rotten."

The curtains in the presbytery were threadbare but Father John Marie said they would suffice. There were loose tiles on the floor which he refused to have repaired. Some of the panes of glass had fallen from the casements and were laying on the ground outside. The small yard in front of his house was overgrown with grass and a tree shoot had taken root and was growing up the chimney.

The house was greatly in need of a paint job but Father John Marie refused to have it painted. Everything was dilapidated and appeared to be in ruins. Oddly enough, he liked it that way. Later, the mayor of Ars, Antoine Mandy tried to send repair men in to the presbytery when Father John Marie was out of town. He advised them to do their work quickly and to finish before Father John Marie returned.

On February 13, 1818, Father John Marie Vianney was officially installed as parish priest of Ars. The people of Ars who attended his installation noticed that his priestly vestments looked quite worn and his shoes were in bad condition. They were the kind of shoes that peasants wore. One person observed, "His body was frail, his height below average, less than five foot two inches, and his manner timid and awkward. His face was pallid and angular. His whole appearance was rather common and lacking distinction. Apart from his ascetical air and piercing eyes, there was nothing about him to attract attention or to draw people to him. He looked like someone without any natural endowments whatsoever." In addition, his extreme thinness and his long hair, which was much longer than was the custom, made him seem peculiar. The residents of the village addressed him simply as Curé, which means pastor or minister.

When the Curé offered Mass, he seemed different from other priests and this was noticed by the citizens of Ars from the very beginning. He celebrated Mass with great reverence and devotion which set him apart from all the other members of the clergy. The mayor summed it up in simple words, "We have a poor church but a holy priest."

Upon arriving in Ars, the Curé's first priority was to get in touch with everyone in the village. He visited all the residents individually in their homes. For the most part, the people were indifferent regarding matters of faith and were rough in manner. Most had very little education. Upon meeting the Curé, they found him friendly and likeable. He asked them the names and ages of their children and inquired about their crops and their day to day lives. He showed a genuine interest in each person he visited. He wore an old hat and a threadbare cassock. They could relate to him because he was poor just like they were. Before concluding the visit, he invited them to attend Mass on Sunday. The overall impression that he made on the people of Ars was very positive. He continued to visit all of his parishioners regularly.

Almost all of the men in Ars refused to go to church. Some had not been to church for ten, fifteen, or even twenty years. In the beginning, so few men went to Communion at Easter that the Curé was filled with sadness. After coming from a devout parish at Ecully, he was shocked by his parishioners' apathy toward their faith. Considering the poor attendance at Mass, the Curé did not think he would have enough to do as parish priest to justify his being in Ars.

Beautifying, repairing and restoring the broken-down little church was uppermost in the Curé's mind. He repainted the faded woodwork himself. The large bell atop the church was far too heavy for the wooden structure that housed it and the entire edifice was in danger of collapsing. With the mayor's permission, a proper bell tower was constructed and a second bell was purchased which the Curé named, the "bell of the Holy Rosary." In addition, he bought a new high altar for the church with his own meager funds.

The church of Ars was very plain both inside and out. The Curé contacted a statue maker and told him that the church in Ars had only a little plaster statue of the Virgin Mary that needed to be replaced. He ordered a beautiful gilded wood statue of Mary with rays of light coming from her hands. It was the image of Our Lady of the Miraculous Medal. He purchased two carved angels which he placed on either side of the tabernacle as well as a new set of candlesticks. The tabernacle was gilded in glittering gold. He bought altar linens of the highest quality and ordered three banners – one of the Blessed Sacrament, one of the Virgin Mary and one of St. Sixtus. The banners were made by the most skillful embroiderers in Paris.

The priestly vestments at the parish in Ars were completely worn out. The Curé walked the eight miles to Lyons, the silk capital of the world, so that he could purchase vestments of the richest fabric as well as altar linens of the highest quality. In Lyons, he also planned to visit the goldsmith shops. Walking was his preferred mode of transportation and he usually refused to take a carriage. The people who worked in Lyons said, "In this district there lives a little priest, thin, badly dressed, looking as if he had not a penny in his pocket, yet only the very best is good enough for his church."

In 1823, the Curé commissioned a side chapel to be built dedicated to St. John the Baptist. At the time of his Confirmation when he was twenty-one years old, he had chosen St. John the Baptist as his patron saint. After that, he always signed his name John Marie Baptiste Vianney.

The Curé had paid the mason for his work on the side chapel but did not know how he was going to pay the carpenter who was pressing for the wages that were due him. The Curé was solely responsible for the cost of the chapel and began to feel great anxiety about the money that he owed.

One day, as the Curé was walking down a stretch of road near Ars, he was almost overcome with worry about the debt. A woman he had never seen before approached him on the road. "Are you the Curé of Ars?" she asked. "Yes, I am," he replied. "I would like to give you this offering for your charitable works," she said as she handed him an envelope. It contained 600 francs, more than enough to pay the carpenter for his work. The Curé said that he learned an important lesson from that experience and would never again hire anyone to do work on the church unless he had the money to pay for it in advance.

At a later date, the Curé added a side chapel dedicated to St. Philomena, one dedicated to the Suffering Christ, and another dedicated to the Holy Angels. In addition, he had an artist from Villefranche construct a beautiful gilded side chapel dedicated to the Virgin Mary. The Curé loved the quiet and secluded chapel dedicated to the Virgin and every Saturday morning for forty years he said his Mass there. During the last year of his life, plans were in his mind for major improvements throughout the church but he did not live to see it happen.

The Curé believed that beautiful statues, religious art and religious artifacts on display in a church had the power to inspire and to change people's lives. "Sometimes the mere sight of a beautiful religious painting or statue is enough to convert a person," he said. At times he would gaze at the chapel of the Suffering Christ and was so moved that his eyes would fill with tears.

The entrance to the church was a winding staircase that was on the verge of collapse. The Curé wanted to replace it with proper stairs supported by graceful columns and a railing. The mayor was informed of the design that the Curé thought to be most attractive and he approved it. The citizens of Ars were asked to help by carrying the building materials to the church and many of them did so. In 1826, the new entrance to the church was completed.

Not long after the Curé moved to Ars, his sister Marguerite and her friend Mrs. Bibost came to visit him. He was very happy to see his sister and wanted to offer her and Mrs. Bibost something to eat. He looked quickly about but all he could find was a basket of potatoes that were just beginning to get moldy. "These potatoes do not look good but they are actually just fine. I cooked them a few days ago," the Curé said to Marguerite. Marguerite had suspected that there would be little food in the house so on the way to Ars she bought a loaf of bread. She and Mrs. Bibost would not dare eat the potatoes.

Marguerite looked through the house and found a few eggs, a bit of flour and some butter. She used the ingredients to make pancakes which she knew her brother liked very much. During her stay in Ars, her brother ate very little. She knew that he liked milk but he would only drink a small amount. He spent most of the hours of the day in the church and only returned to the presbytery at nightfall.

When François, the Curé's oldest brother visited him in Ars, he also observed that there was very little food in the house. One day he got so hungry that he went out into the garden and dug up some potatoes. The Curé only possessed one saucepan, so François used that to boil the potatoes.

One morning, when Marguerite went to make the Curé's bed, she looked under the sheets and blankets and noticed that instead of a mattress, there were vine shoots laid out on the wooden bed frame. She found some straw wrapped in a sheet and that was what her brother slept on.

The Curé had many challenges to face in Ars, more than he would have ever imagined. Sundays found the people in the village dressed in their working clothes with hayforks and scythes in hand, getting ready for a full day's work in the fields. From the church, the Curé could hear the sound of the blacksmith's hammer and anvil and the wagon wheels rolling by.

On Sundays before Mass, the Curé asked the sacristan to walk around the outside of the church and tell anyone who was milling about that the Mass was about to begin. Each Mass on Sunday began with a procession.

Those few who attended Mass, maybe five families in all, often spent the better part of the time talking to their neighbor next to them rather than listening to the sermon. Some appeared to feel sick when the time came for the Word of God to be proclaimed and before the reading was finished, they would hurry outside to get a bit of fresh air. Some showed their rudeness with noisy yawning. Others who came in late would bang the front door loudly and when Mass was over would rush for the exit as though they had just been let out of prison.

The Curé would frequently say to his congregation, "Other priests may grant permission to their parishioners to work on Sundays rather than attending Mass. I, however, cannot do so. Do you think that God does not see you? He sees you my children, as I see you. Do you think that your Curé will allow you to go down the road to perdition? No, he won't. Are you going to cause this suffering to your Curé?" He gave the impression of a man calling out for help for himself.

Feeling a great sadness, the Curé's eyes would often fill with tears during his Sunday sermons when he spoke about the non-attendance at Mass. He was never embarrassed by such a display of emotion. Fifty years later, a number of the parishioners of Ars, now elderly, remembered the experience and said that they would never forget the sight of the Curé's tears.

In an effort to encourage his parishioners, the Curé would say, "Oh my dear friends, let us endeavor to get to heaven. There we shall see God. How happy we shall be. If our parish is converted, we shall go there in procession together and I will be with you." At other times he would say, "We must get to heaven. What a pity it would be if some of you were not to do so."

The Curé taught an instructional class for adults on the teachings of the Catholic church every Sunday afternoon after Mass but there were not many who were interested in attending. He could just here them saying, "Attend a religion class after Mass? No, it is out of the question. Our pastor has already bored us enough for one day!" He often thought nostalgically about his parishioners in Ecully and remembered with longing how devout and pious they were.

The Curé spent many hours preparing his sermons for the Sunday homily. He spoke loudly from the pulpit and was very animated. Someone once asked him why he talked so loudly and gestured so frequently while preaching. "I am speaking to people who are either deaf or asleep and that is why I preach the way I do," the Curé answered. He liked to take his spiritual reflections from ordinary, everyday life and from nature. He wanted to make his message easy to understand.

In one of his sermons, he said to his parishioners, "You must do like the shepherds when they stay in the fields during winter. Life is a very long winter. The shepherds make a fire, but from time to time they hurry off to pick up some more wood to keep it going. If only we knew, like the shepherds, how to keep up the fire of the love of God in our hearts, by prayers and by good works." He also liked to say, "The earth is a bridge for crossing the water. It is only useful to bear us upward."

The Curé went to great lengths to impress upon his parishioners the importance of cultivating a spiritual life. He wanted with all of his heart to reach at least some of the people. He said:

> Nothing is more essential than the love of God. It is the first of all virtues, a virtue so necessary, that without it we shall never get to heaven; and it is in order to love God that we are on the earth . . . But the misfortune is that we lavish our love upon objects unworthy of it, and refuse it to him alone who deserves to be infinitely loved. Thus, my children, one person will love riches, another will love pleasures; and both will offer to the good God nothing but the languishing remains of a heart worn out in the service of the world . . . God alone . . . deserves that we should love him above all things; more than our possessions, because they are earthly; more than our friends, because they are mortal; more than our life, because it is perishable; more than ourselves, because we belong to him. Our love, my children, if it is true, must be without limit, and it must influence our conduct.

Even though the village was small, Ars had four taverns and the taverns were usually full. Two of the taverns were in the center of the village and the other two were on the outskirts. At the end of the day, many of the men in Ars would visit the taverns and drink late into the night until they became completely intoxicated. They spent most of their money on alcohol, money that was needed for food and clothing for their families. This was one of the main causes of poverty for many of the households in Ars. Also, many marriages were broken up because of it. To the Curé, it was a desperate situation that demanded an immediate response and he tackled the problem head on.

The Curé spoke about the problem of drunkenness very clearly and very directly from the pulpit. He said, "If the pastor sees that there is scandal in the parish, he must overcome motives of respect and the fear of being hated by his parishioners. He must address the problem." He let his parishioners know that drunkenness was a vice that caused the ruin of many lives. He repeated it over and over.

The Curé also spoke out about the problems that arose as a result of the dances that were held in Ars. The dances were a meeting place where vulgar songs, dirty jokes and immorality of every kind was celebrated. The Curé did not see any good coming from the dances.

A number of the citizens of Ars became very angry that the Curé was confronting them about their drinking habits and calling for the removal of the taverns. The tavern owners too were furious and considered the Curé their enemy. A petition was circulated calling for his dismissal as parish priest of Ars. Hateful letters of complaint were sent to the bishop stating that the Curé was too strict, too uncompromising, and should be removed at once. The Curé was haunted by the fear that he would have to leave his parish in disgrace.

The citizens of Ars spattered the Curé's door with mud and lewd pictures. He was the target of blackmail, slander and persecution. He was given the nickname, "the old sorcerer" and "the old hypocrite." A woman of the town who wanted to make trouble for him, stood in front of his residence every day for eighteen months and screamed vicious lies about him in a shrill voice. She claimed that he was the father of her child.

The Curé became more and more depressed about the people's actions against him. His nerves were always on edge and he felt he was at the end of his rope. He feared that the bishop would suspend him and ban him from all of his priestly functions. His life in such a hostile environment became difficult to endure and he began to feel that it would be better for him to leave Ars.

Bishop Devie read the letters of complaint and said that he would conduct an investigation into the matter. At the time, he did not know the Curé personally. He asked the parish priest of Trevoux, who was the dean of the region, to conduct the investigation.

When the dean concluded his thorough investigation, he submitted his report to Bishop Devie. The dean found no wrongdoing whatsoever in the Curé's actions as parish priest of Ars. Bishop Devie then assured the Curé of his full support. He was happy to allow the Curé to transfer to another parish if that was what he wanted or he was free to stay in Ars if he chose to do so. The bishop would leave it up to him.

Several of the Curé's friends convinced him to stay in Ars. They told him that if he left, it would look as though he was guilty of the accusations and they knew he had done nothing wrong. He said later, "If I had known when I went to Ars, all that I would suffer there, I would have died on the spot."

The Curé said:

> To suffer - what does it signify? It is only for a moment. If we could go and pass a week in heaven, we should understand the value of this moment of suffering . . . The cross is the gift that God makes to his friends. How beautiful it is to offer ourselves

every morning in sacrifice to the good God, and
to accept everything in expiation for our sins. We
must ask for the love of crosses. Then they become
sweet. I did this for four or five years. I was greatly
calumniated, greatly contradicted, greatly knocked
about. Oh, I had crosses indeed! I had almost more
than I could carry. Then I took to asking for the love
of crosses, and I was happy . . . We must not wonder
where our crosses come from. They come from God.
It is always God who gives us this way of proving our
love to him.

The Curé began to diligently pray for the people who were
tormenting him and he also began to fast and to offer sacrifices
for their conversion. He continued to speak out against the
drunkenness and other vices that were all too prevalent in Ars.
He refused to compromise and would not yield an inch on his
position. He used to say, "A pastor must speak the truth even if
the people do not want to hear it. Even if a pastor knew that
someone had a gun and was going to kill him when he stepped
down from the pulpit after speaking out against certain vices in
the parish, he would still need to do so."

Many years later, the Curé spoke to several of his friends
about that dark time in his priesthood when people were calling
for his dismissal. He imagined that the citizens of Ars might rise
up and run him out of town with sticks. If charges were brought
against him, he could be imprisoned. "I see that I was not worthy
of such a grace," he said.

A number of the teenagers and young adults in Ars were
wild and rebellious and they were getting into trouble. Knowing
this, the Curé began to offer activities in the church suited to
their age group. He organized special celebrations for important
feast days of the saints as well as festivities and processions that
the teenagers could participate in. He wanted to show them that
spiritual activities could be very enjoyable.

The Curé wanted his parishioners, from the youngest to the oldest, even though few in number, to know and to understand the doctrines and teachings of their Catholic faith. The children, even the very young ones, worked in the fields and tended the sheep and cattle. The Curé asked the children to come to church for a catechism class every morning during the week at six a.m. before beginning their work in the fields. For many months, he helped them to prepare to receive their first Holy Communion. In order to encourage the children to attend the classes, he would say, "The one who arrives first will receive a holy card." Some of the children began to arrive before five o'clock in the morning in order to get the prized holy card.

The Curé also taught a catechism class to the children of the parish on Sunday afternoons. He rang the bell summoning the children to the class, led the opening prayers and presented the spiritual reflections. He did not have an aide so he did the job himself for twenty-seven years. In 1845, he received an assistant to help with the task. During the six weeks of Lent, he gave three catechism instruction a day – one in the morning for the children of the parish, one at midday for the orphans at *La Providence* and one in the evening for the adults. He also meticulously trained the altar boys for their duties at the Mass.

As time went by, the children of Ars knew there catechism better than any of the other children in the surrounding parishes. Bishop Devie became aware of this on Confirmation day and declared that the children of Ars were the best instructed in the whole diocese.

In addition to the children, the adults of the parish, who were for the most part simple and uneducated people, had an amazing knowledge and understanding of their faith due to the continuous efforts of the Curé to instruct them. Paradoxically, the parish of Ars, so small and so poor, became superior to every other parish in the diocese. During a clergy retreat, Monsignor de Langalerie said to his fellow priests, "Do you want to see a parish where all the ceremonies of the church are carried out with perfection? Go to Ars!" Eventually, the parish of Ars became the focal center of spirituality for all of France.

The Curé tried to speak of the spiritual life in such a way as to make it desirable and attractive to his parishioners. He used to say, "Worldly people have not the Holy Spirit, or if they have, it is only for a moment . . . The noise of the world drives Him away. A Christian who is led by the Holy Spirit has no difficulty in leaving the goods of this world, to run after those of heaven; he knows the difference between them. The eyes of the world see no further than this life . . . The eyes of the Christian see deep into eternity . . . We must therefore find out by whom we are led. If it is not by the Holy Spirit, we labor in vain."

The Curé dedicated his parish to the Virgin Mary under the title of the Immaculate Conception. On special feast day Masses in honor of the Virgin Mary, the Curé wore magnificent vestments of deep blue velvet detailed in gold embroidery. On the evening of the feast day, he would lead a torchlight procession through the streets of Ars. He ordered a heart to be made in sterling silver. He wrote the names of all of his parishioners on a white silk ribbon and placed it inside the heart. The heart was then placed like a necklace on the statue of the Virgin Mary that was in the church.

From the statues, to the priestly vestments, to the smallest details in the church, the Curé would have only the best. Later, when the bishop made his official visitation to the parish of Ars, he was very impressed by the improvements that had been made and by the beauty in the church. The bishop wrote in the church register, "Everything is so beautiful and so rich here in the parish of Ars that all one can do is admire it."

It was the Curé's habit to carry in his pocket a silver reliquary with relics inside. He loved his prayer book so much that he carried it with him wherever he went. When asked why he always had his prayer book with him, he said simply that he could not bear to be without it. The Sorrowful Mysteries of the Rosary were hand-written in the margin. Those were the Mysteries that he loved the most. He also loved religious articles and sacramentals such as holy cards, Rosaries, scapulars, crucifixes, and holy water. He belonged to the Third Order of St. Francis and to many sodalities and confraternities. He had a special devotion to St. Peter, St. Joseph, St. Blaise, St. John the Baptist, St. Michael the Archangel, St. Benedict Joseph Labre, St. Sixtus, the patron saint of Ars, and St. Philomena. He had a great devotion to the Stations of the Cross. He used to repeat, "The only happiness we have on earth is in loving God and in knowing that God loves us."

On one occasion, a woman in the village of Fareins who had a terminal illness asked to see the Curé before her death. The Curé walked to Fareins but lost his way enroute. When he finally reached the woman's home, he was completely exhausted and his habit was splattered with mud. Even so, he would not take anything that was offered to him, not even a glass of water. People thought so highly of him that the whole village of Fareins turned out to greet him when he arrived. After the Curé blessed the sick woman and prayed for her, arrangements were made for a carriage to take him back to Ars but he said that he preferred to walk. It was only on very rare occasions and under very special circumstances that he would consent to ride in a carriage.

The Curé never tired of assisting those who asked him for his help. Mrs. Scipiot, a woman who lived in Ars, once went to the presbytery very late at night, seeking the help of the Curé. Knowing that he was sound asleep, she stood below his bedroom window and called his name out very loud until he woke up. Mrs. Scipiot's mother was gravely ill and she wanted the Curé to visit her and give her his priestly blessing. He got out of bed immediately and went on the sick call. Later, Mrs. Scipiot apologized to the Curé for bothering him in the middle of the night. "Oh no, my child, it is nothing. I have not yet sacrificed my all for you," he said.

As time went by, the Curé began to identify more and more with his parishioners. All of his thoughts were fixed on them. Their adversities were his adversities, their joys were his joys, their holiness, became the great desire of his heart. He prayed to God, "If you will only grant the conversion of my parish, I will be willing to suffer whatever You wish for the rest of my life." He used to say:

> Nothing is so beautiful as a pure soul . . . Purity comes from heaven; we must ask for it from God. If we ask for it, we shall obtain it. We must take great care not to lose it. We must shut our heart against pride, against sensuality, and all the other passions, as one shuts the doors and windows so that nobody may be able to get in. What joy it is to the Guardian Angel to conduct a pure soul. . .The purer we have been on earth, the nearer we shall be to Him in heaven . . . My children, we cannot comprehend the power that a pure soul has over the good God.

The Curé was asked to travel to neighboring villages from time to time in order to help with parish missions by preaching and hearing confessions. He assisted at parishes in Savineux, Montmerle, Saint Trivier, Chaneins, Saint Bernard and more. The priests at the various parishes marveled at the Curé's success at the missions. His presence generated great enthusiasm from those who participated. People of the upper class began to seek him out – judges, magistrates, public officials and professionals were now among his penitents. His influence continued to grow and his name became well-known in many parts of France.

In 1826, the Curé assisted at the Jubilee in Montmerle. Mrs. Mondesert, who was the sacristan of the parish in Montmerle, provided the meals for the priests who attended. During the Jubilee, the Curé asked someone to boil a saucepan of potatoes for him and put it in his room. At the conclusion of the Jubilee, one of the priests who attended thanked Mrs. Mondesert and wanted to pay the expenses for the Curé's board and room. "There are no expenses," Mrs. Mondesert told the priest. She explained that during the six days of the Jubilee, the Curé never came to the presbytery at mealtime, not even once. He stopped by the presbytery for about five minutes each day at noon. Other than that, he spent all of his time in the church and ate only the potatoes that he kept in his room.

The Curé also assisted at a mission in the village of Trévoux and it proved to be a big success. During the mission, the Curé stayed with one of his former classmates from the seminary. His classmate was mystified because the Curé never appeared for meals. One evening, he decided to go and look for him. He found the Curé in the church hearing confessions and he noted that the Curé did not leave the confessional until midnight.

On the night before the conclusion of the mission, there was a huge crowd of people in the church. They began to push and shove as they tried to get closer to the Curé who was hearing confessions at the time. In the confusion, the confessional almost tipped over with the Curé inside. Fortunately, he was not hurt. The Curé told the story of his near mishap on a number of occasions and always had a good laugh about it.

Before leaving the mission at Trévoux, the Curé was presented with a gift from his fellow priests – a pair of winter pants made of velvet to wear under his priestly robe. The material was chosen because it was warm as well as durable. On Saturday night, when the Curé was walking back to Ars, he met a beggar on the road who was shivering from the cold. The Curé went behind a hedge and took off his new pants and gave them to the poor man.

When the destitute knocked on the presbytery door in Ars, the Curé often invited them inside. He addressed them simply as "my friends" and he truly considered them to be so. Because he knew they were ashamed of their poverty, he took them to the privacy of his room where no one would see them. He let them try on his clothes and take what they needed. When Catherine

Lassagne learned what he was doing, she decided to put just a few shirts in his closet at a time in order to discourage him from giving so much away. However, he continued to give his clothing away to the needy. He helped pay the rent for thirty families, both in Ars and in the surrounding villages. He used to say, "I do not lend, I give." He gladly helped those who would never be able to pay him back.

In the winter time, the Curé frequently invited the poor to sit with him by the fireplace in his residence in order to warm themselves. When he was away, the destitute would sometimes knock on the presbytery door. Other priests or brothers would answer the door and try to assist them, but they would invariably say, "We wanted to speak to the Curé. We will come back another time."

Father Borjon, who lived in the village of Ambérieux, thought so highly of the Curé that every year he took the children of his parish who had made their first Holy Communion to Ars in order to receive a blessing from the saintly priest. Toward the end of the Curé's life, more than twenty founders of religious orders came to Ars to ask him for advice. Everybody and everything seemed to feel the power of his influence. A vine-grower from the Mâconnais region of Burgundy travelled to Ars to meet the Curé and said, "I have seen God in a man."

The Curé was also visited by his parishioners from Ecully as well as his childhood friends from Dardilly. In addition, friends from Les Robins who had known the Curé from the days when he was a defector from Napoleon's army, visited him in Ars. Some of the Curé's friends moved to Ars permanently in order to be close to him. During the years that the Curé spent in Ars, the population more than doubled.

From 1825 onward, the Curé of Ars no longer had the luxury of having any free time. He was not able to prepare his Sunday sermons like he had painstakingly done in the past. He made a novena to the Holy Spirit, asking that he might receive the grace to be able to preach his Sunday sermons and daily catechism classes without study or preparation. The number of people making their way to Ars was continually increasing.

The Curé established the Confraternity of the Blessed Sacrament for the men of the parish and provided other spiritual activities for the women as well as the youth of the parish. He counseled people to remain small, to remain humble. He said, "Those who are led by the Holy Spirit have true ideas. That is why there are so many ignorant people who know far more than the learned."

A number of the people of Ars had the bad habit of swearing and cursing. The Curé talked about it from the pulpit regularly and conducted a real campaign against the blasphemies. His efforts were so successful that the curse words eventually vanished from the vocabulary of the people of Ars.

When the Curé arrived in Ars, the custom of family prayer had all but died out. The Curé did everything in his power to bring it back. He encouraged families to pray together every day and to say grace together before meals. Those who worked in the fields could not be expected to be at Mass on the weekdays but the Curé wanted them to say their morning prayers and to stop by the church for a visit before beginning their work day. He used to say to his parishioners, "Never do anything before saying your morning prayers."

On their way to the fields to work, the Curé encouraged the people of Ars to reflect on the life of Christ or on one of the stories from the Gospel. He would give many examples to them of reflections to ponder. Sometimes the people complained that they were not able to make such meditations. "If you feel unable to meditate, say the Rosary or recite a few prayers on your way to the fields," the Curé said.

The Curé asked his parishioners to carry a Rosary with them at all times and to use it regularly. He used to say, "My friends, always be armed with the Rosary. Mine never leaves me." It was not uncommon to see men praying their Rosaries while leading their horses in the fields. Once they arrived at their place of work, the Curé wanted them to make the Sign of the Cross even if others were present and to say a silent prayer, offering their day's work to God. He used to say, "Our prayer is an incense which God receives with extreme pleasure. My children, your heart is poor and narrow; but prayer enlarges it, and renders it capable of loving God. Prayer is a foretaste of heaven, an overflow of paradise. It never leaves us without sweetness . . . Troubles melt away before a fervent prayer like snow before the sun."

One Sunday, the Curé was taking a walk in the countryside after the Mass. One of his parishioners had decided to skip Mass that day and tend to his farm work instead. He was surprised that afternoon when he saw the Curé walking near his property. Embarrassed and ashamed, he hid behind his horse cart hoping he would not be seen. "O my friend, you seem very surprised to see me here today," the Curé said as he approached the man. "But God sees you all the time!"

The Curé had a great belief in the value of regular confession. He would encourage his parishioners to go to confession by saying, "Our faults are like a grain of sand beside the great mountain of the mercies of God." He used to tell his penitents, "I am much guiltier than you are. Do not be afraid to confess your sins." One of the girls who lived in Ars said, "Though the Curé showed great firmness in rooting out abuses, he never hurt anyone's feelings." He was tactful and discreet when conversing with people.

While hearing confessions, the Curé often gave light penances to his parishioners and did the rest of the penance himself. The people took notice of his dedication as a priest, his long hours of prayer in front of the tabernacle, and his deep concern for the spiritual well-being of his parishioners. The people of Ars used to say, "Whatever our parish priest recommends, he first does himself. He practices what he teaches. We must follow his advice for he seeks only our good."

Father Paul of Moll said, "To be a child of love is to sacrifice oneself to the love of God for the conversion of sinners . . . If we had to pray hundreds of years in order to have a man brought back to the love of God, we would have reason enough to rejoice on account of it . . . Ask God that all your actions, from the beginning of your existence, be actions of love for God, performed in union with the sorrowful passion of Jesus."

The Curé asked his parishioners to join him every evening for the eight o'clock night prayers and recitation of the Rosary that was held in the church. Slowly, more and more people began to attend. The time would come when every evening throughout the year the church bell would ring and the entire village would be seen walking down the path toward the church for night prayers. He also encouraged his parishioners to make an examination of conscience and to do spiritual reading before going to bed at night.

The resentment and anger that the residents of Ars initially felt toward the Curé, gradually diminished and finally disappeared altogether. The people came to realize that their Curé cared deeply about them and that he had their best interests at heart. Gradually they began to frequent the taverns less and less. The four taverns were finally forced to close down for good due to lack of customers. Public drunkenness had ceased altogether.

Mass attendance in Ars steadily increased with the passage of time. The children of Ars were amazed during the consecration of the Mass, when they saw the Curé raise his eyes and hands to heaven and remain completely still for four or five minutes. His face became transfigured. The children used to say, "He is seeing God." He told them not to look at him during Mass but instead to concentrate on their prayers.

At the pulpit, the Curé's preaching style was both direct and personal and the people began to listen to his Sunday sermons with attention. After Mass, the parishioners used to say, "No priest ever spoke of God as the Curé of Ars does." Even those who characteristically never showed emotion in public sometimes wept when they heard him preach. He continued to urge everyone to come to Mass regularly. He used to say to his parishioners, "Without the Holy Eucharist, life would be unendurable."

It took the Curé more than ten years of constant effort and sacrifice to bring about a spiritual renewal in Ars. In one of his sermons he spoke about the transformation and said, "My brethren, Ars is no longer Ars. I have heard confessions and preached at jubilees and missions but never have I found anything to compare with what I witness here at Ars."

Even in seemingly small ways, the Curé was able to bring about great spiritual benefits to the people of Ars. Once, several girls stayed after the evening prayer service in the church to make their confession. The Curé saw the two girls in the church and suggested that they pray the Rosary with him before they went to confession. The girls did not attend Mass regularly and didn't even know how to pray the Rosary. One of the girls was very resistant to the idea of praying the Rosary with the Curé but she did so anyway. That girl testified many years later and said, "The Curé of Ars changed my life." Shortly after that, he formed the Rosary Guild for all the girls of the parish.

Many people came to the Curé and asked him to pray for their healing. He often asked them why they wanted to be healed. He used to say that one should not be in too great a hurry to be relieved of the cross. He believed in the redemptive value of suffering when offered as a sacrifice to God. The Curé once said to a woman who was ill, "I see that your illness is a ladder that will carry you to Heaven."

In 1832, Jean Picard established his business in Ars as a farrier, specializing in the care of horses. Jean was surprised to find that a great change had come over Ars. He was well aware that in the early days, Ars was much like all the other villages. Due to the efforts of the Curé, Jean Picard said that "Ars was unrecognizable." Every home in Ars had a picture of the Virgin Mary on display - a gift from the Curé. Most had a small statue of the Virgin in their front yard. Visitors often commented that they could feel a great sense of peace upon arriving in Ars. One priest who visited Ars was equally impressed with the spiritual fervor of the townspeople and described the village as an "island of holiness."

The Curé set a very high standard of behavior for his parishioners. In Ars, Jean Baptiste Mandy and Claudine Trève had become engaged and were making plans for their wedding. One night, some of the men from the village snuck in to the hen houses of the Mandy family and the Trève family and took the very best chickens. Those chickens were served at a banquet in honor of the engaged couple.

By Sunday morning, the men who were involved were already feeling guilty about their actions. The Curé had been informed about what had happened and he was upset. He spoke about it from the pulpit that Sunday morning and said to the men who were involved, "There is another wedding that will soon be held in our parish. If you ever do anything like that again, I will leave Ars and I will never return!" The men never did it again.

In 1835, the Curé travelled to the seminary of Brou to attend the annual retreat for priests. He had been looking forward to the retreat as it would be a much-needed break from his heavy work schedule. When Bishop Devie saw him at the retreat, he sent him back to his parish saying, "You have no need of a retreat. At your parish in Ars there are so many people who need your help. You must go home at once!"

As the feast of Corpus Christi approached each year, the Curé put all his energies into the preparations, desiring that it be carried out with great reverence and solemnity. He had the choir boys from the parish participate in large numbers, as many as were able. He trained the children himself. Four young men were specially chosen to carry the silken canopy while others carrying lighted candles, processed behind. All of the girls, including the orphans at *La Providence,* came in white dresses and the boys were dressed in white as well. The Curé used his own funds to buy the special clothing for the children. Bouquets of flowers hung from the trees and rose petals were scattered all along the processional path. The houses were decorated with garlands and flags were flying everywhere. Antique tapestries and banners were on display throughout the village. Beautiful and solemn Latin hymns were sung by everyone who attended. Musicians were brought in to accompany the choir of voices. The Curé carried the Blessed Sacrament in a shining Monstrance that glittered with precious gems. By all standards, the feast day celebration of Corpus Christi was magnificent in Ars.

The Curé wanted the girls as well as the women of Ars to dress modestly and to maintain their dignity at all times. He would never approve of low cut or tight-fitting dresses. He disapproved of high fashion and extreme styles. He felt that the popular "crinoline" petticoats and huge hoop skirts looked ridiculous and he was not afraid to say so. On occasion, the hoopskirts were so large that the doorways were not wide enough for women to pass through. Once, one of the girls of Ars was showing off her new and stylish collar. "I would like to buy that collar from you," said the Curé. "Why is that?" the girl replied. "So that I can put it on my cat!" he answered.

Although he would never admit it, the Curé of Ars possessed many charismatic gifts, including the gift of reading hearts. His abilities can only be explained as a special favor granted to him by God. His gift of reading hearts was apparent on one occasion when a man whom he did not know came into the confessional. "How long has it been since your last confession?" the Curé asked. "It has been ten years," he replied. "It has been longer than that," the Curé said. The man thought for a moment and then said that it has been twelve years since his last confession. "A little longer than that," the Curé exclaimed. "It has been thirteen years," the man finally said. "That is right," the Curé answered.

Visitors to Ars soon realized that little could be hidden or concealed from the Curé. One day a woman from Lyons and her ten-year-old daughter travelled to Ars to see the Curé. They handed him some religious articles and asked him to bless them. He was happy to do so. He blessed all but one which was a medal. "I cannot bless that medal because your daughter stole it from a store," the Curé said to the woman.

The Curé's gift of reading hearts was also evidenced on one occasion in his encounter with a woman named Mrs. de

Lacomble. Mrs. de Lacomble had a son who was eighteen years old. He had fallen in love and was going to marry a girl even younger. Mrs. de Lacomble was very much against it. She became depressed, often saying that she felt "more dead than alive." It was a three-day journey to Ars but Mrs. de Lacomble decided it would be well worth it to travel there in order to speak to the Curé about the situation. She would only be able to spend a few hours in Ars before returning to her home.

The church was packed on the day that Mrs. de Lacomble arrived in Ars. At the time, the Curé was hearing confessions in the St. John the Baptist chapel. Mrs. de Lacomble managed to find a seat in the very back of the church. She realized that she would not be able to stay for the length of time it would require to speak to the Curé privately. There were just too many people waiting for the same opportunity. She was very disappointed.

Before leaving to return home, Mrs. de Lacomble sat quietly in the church for several hours praying. As she was getting up to exit the church, she suddenly saw the Curé leave the confessional. He was staring intently at her as he walked toward her. He whispered in her ear, "Let them marry. They will be very happy!" No one knew of Mrs. de Lacomble's trip to Ars and the Curé had never seen her before. He had no way of knowing about her family situation. After speaking to her briefly, he went straight back to the confessional. As it turned out, the young couple married and had a long and happy life together.

Jean Claude Viret, a farmer who lived in Ars, attended the Curé's eleven o'clock catechism class one morning and was shocked by the Curé's ability to read his heart. Jean Claude listened listlessly to the Curé for a while and then pulled out his Rosary and began to recite it mechanically. Suddenly the Curé spoke from the pulpit and said, "Oh, my children. People come to church and appear to be praying but they do not realize that our Heavenly Father sees them. For instance, that man who is sitting near the sacristy appears to be praying his Rosary, but he is actually using the beads to add up his income." When he pointed at Jean Claude, everyone who was assembled turned and stared at him. "It makes me tremble to see so little reverence before our Lord," the Curé added. Jean Claude was stunned by the Curé's words and he was deeply embarrassed.

In addition to his gift of reading of hearts, the Curé also possessed the gift of prophecy. One day, a nineteen-year-old girl visited Ars and attended the Curé's catechism class. She was on her way to the city of Lyons for a job opportunity. The Curé picked the girl out from the crowd and told her he wished to speak to her privately. She was a complete stranger to him. "You are on your way to Lyons," he said to her. "Know that a great misfortune awaits you there. When you are in the midst of it, think of me and pray to God."

On her journey to Lyons, she passed by a ridge where a number of workmen were nearby. As she rounded a bend, she found herself in an isolated spot. The only person in sight was a man who was staring at her intently. She sensed danger and was seized with terror as she suddenly remembered the words the Curé had spoken to her earlier that day. She said a heartfelt prayer and ran as fast as she could. The man ran after her and tried to throw a lasso around her neck. She finally reached safety where there were other people nearby. She learned that the man who almost accosted her was Mr. Dumollard, a notorious criminal. When he was brought to justice, she testified against him in court.

There were many abandoned and homeless children roaming the streets and country roads during the time that the Curé served as parish priest of Ars. Often, when he was on his way to a sick call, a child would approach him on the road, begging for a piece of bread. Some of the homeless children were placed at an early age as domestic servants with adults who took advantage of them. No one was looking out for their welfare or their well-being. It was a heartbreaking situation that the Curé felt he had to do something about.

The Curé asked his brother François, who was still maintaining the farm in Dardilly, to come to Ars and bring him his portion of the inheritance from his father. With the money, the Curé bought a simple building which he turned into an orphanage. He sacrificed everything he possessed in order to purchase the property which was located very close to the church. He also reached out to his brother-in-law Melin for financial help. After careful consideration, he gave his orphanage the name, *La Providence*, a suitable name because the orphanage was destined to depend solely on the providence of God for all of its many needs.

The Curé asked two devout women, seventeen-year-old Catherine Lassagne and twenty-year-old Benoite Lardet, to supervise the daily operations of the orphanage. When they agreed to do so, he sent them to the convent of the Sisters of Saint Joseph in the village of Fereins to study practical teaching methods. Catherine and Benoite assisted in one of the classrooms at the school owned and operated by the Sisters of St. Joseph, receiving on-the-job training. The Curé paid for Catherine and Benoite's board and room and all of their expenses while they were at the convent. *La Providence* orphanage opened the following year.

Twenty-six-year-old Jeanne Marie Chanay was hired by the Curé to cook the meals, bake the bread, do the laundry, and assist Catherine and Benoite in caring for the children at *La Providence*. The three women did not receive a salary. They gave up long years of their lives in order to participate in the Curé's great work of mercy and they dedicated themselves wholeheartedly to the task.

The orphans ranged in age from eight years old to twenty years old and were very happy at *La Providence*. They looked upon the Curé as their father and their friend. The Curé had a great love for children. He especially admired the qualities of innocence and purity in children. The welfare of the orphans at *La Providence* was always one of the Curé's greatest concerns.

The Curé wanted the orphans to have the same opportunity for religious education that the children in the parish had. Every day he went to *La Providence* at eleven o'clock in the morning, sat on the edge of the table, and taught a one-hour catechism class to the orphans. The classes eventually became famous. As time went by, lay people, priests, even bishops attended the simple instructions. A number of people were forced to stand outside and listen through the open windows because all the seats inside were taken. Later, the eleven o'clock classes had to be moved from the orphanage to the church because of the crowds who attended.

On one occasion, the Curé rushed to the orphanage in his stocking feet to teach the morning catechism class. He tried to pull his priestly robe down, hoping that no one would notice that he was not wearing shoes. "But where are your shoes?" someone asked him. "There was a poor man on the road whose shoes were ruined and I had no choice but to give him mine," he replied.

The Curé was responsible for paying the expenses of *La Providence*, including all of the food and clothing for the many orphans who were housed there. As time went by, the Curé had great and growing financial worries regarding the orphanage. It was running on a shoestring budget and the cash box was often empty. People sometimes overheard the Curé praying quietly in the church, petitioning God to help *La Providence*.

Three years after *La Providence* opened its doors, it needed to be enlarged. Without having the financial resources to do so, the Curé made a novena to the Blessed Virgin Mary, praying that the funds would be supplied. He then felt inspired to make some bricks and asked for volunteers to help him. One thing led to another and soon there were carpenters and masons pitching in, building an expansion for the orphanage. He worked alongside of them, carrying the lumber and mixing the mortar until the work was complete.

The orphans not only learned how to read and write at *La Providence*, they were also taught practical skills like how to wash, iron, knit, and sew. From time to time, the Curé walked to Lyons in order to ask people of means for donations to the orphanage. One priest promised to supply all of the wood for heating *La Providence*. The Curé also regularly wrote letters to wealthy people, asking for donations to *La Providence*.

The Curé tried to find the orphans suitable work when they were old enough to leave *La Providence*. Most left by the time they reached nineteen or twenty years of age, but the Curé continued to keep in touch with them, making sure that they were well and that their needs were being met. For the girls who married, the Curé helped them financially if they needed his assistance.

On one occasion, a newborn baby was left at the doorstep of the orphanage. The Curé told Catherine and Benoite to take the baby in. As the youngest orphan at *La Providence*, the baby thrived and remained there many years until she was of age to depart. On another occasion, the Curé travelled to a village some distance away, to make a sick call to a woman who was dying. When she passed away, there was no one who was able to care for her infant. The Curé sent Jeanne Marie Chanay to get the woman's baby. That baby too was cared for tenderly at *La Providence*.

By working at *La Providence* orphanage, Jeanne-Marie Chanay got to know the Curé well. On one occasion, she gave him a brand-new pair of fur-lined shoes because his shoes were in such bad condition. That very evening, she saw him wearing his old shoes once again. She realized then that she should have taken the old ones away when she gave him the new pair. Jeanne Marie was very annoyed and said to the Curé sharply, "I am under the impression that you gave away the new shoes I bought for you." "It is quite possible I did so," the Curé replied, but he would say no more.

In 1829, the country was suffering from economic hardship and money was scarce. The funds for the orphanage ran so low that the store of grain was almost gone and there was not enough money to replenish the supply. The orphans at *La Providence* were about to go without food. When the Curé was told about the critical situation, he went up to the grain loft in the attic of the presbytery and put a relic of St. Francis Regis in a small amount of grain that he had scraped together. He prayed for the saint's intercession and asked the orphans to pray as well. St. Francis Regis had come to the Curé's aid during his seminary days when he faced dismissal due to failing grades.

Later on, when Jeanne Marie Chanay went up to the loft and looked inside, she found that it was overflowing with grain. There was so much grain inside that it was very difficult for Jeanne Marie to open the loft door. She also noticed that the grain was a slightly different color than the usual. She was amazed that the floor did not give way due to the weight of the grain. She immediately went to find the Curé so that she could show him the miraculous occurrence.

La Providence was in critical need on another occasion when the supply of flour was almost exhausted. The orphanage had just enough flour left to make three loaves of bread. That would not be sufficient to feed even a quarter of the orphans. Jeanne Marie Chanay, who was responsible for baking the bread, told the Curé about the problem and asked his advice. He told her to use what flour she had and make the bread just like she always did. While she was kneading the dough, it kept thickening in a very unusual way. She continued to add water and the dough continued to thicken. She was amazed to see that the small amount of flour made ten huge loaves of bread over twenty pounds each. Everyone was astonished. When she told the Curé what had happened, his response was, "God is very good!"

The multiplication of the grain and the multiplication of the flour were the first two documented miracles that occurred in Ars. Many more would follow. News of the two miracles hit the village like a thunderbolt. The Curé's fame increased and so too did the number of visitors who began arriving in Ars.

The excitement caused by the two events worried the Curé. He found it deeply troubling to think that people were attributing the miracles to him and he wanted them to know that he had nothing to do with it. He attributed all of the good things that were happening in Ars to the intercession of St. Philomena. St. Philomena was born in Greece in 291 A.D. but her tomb was not discovered until 1802 in the ancient catacombs of St. Priscilla in Rome. She was martyred at the age of thirteen. The transfer of her bones to Naples had been accompanied by astonishing miracles. The Curé had a great devotion to St. Philomena and encouraged people to pray to her. He called St. Philomena his "deputy before God."

After the founding of *La Providence* orphanage, the Curé began to experience something very frightening in the presbytery where he lived. Late at night, he heard shouting in the front yard as well as banging on the door at the foot of the staircase leading to his bedroom. It sounded like someone was trying to break down the door with a mallet. He then heard three more knocks on the door that were even louder than the previous ones. He wondered if it was robbers who were intending to enter the house in search of valuables. When he investigated, there was no one there.

One night when he heard a deafening commotion outside, he got up and looked out the window. The snow on the ground was untouched. There was not a single footprint of an intruder anywhere. The Curé was terrified and could not understand the cause of the strange occurrences. He began to dread being alone in the presbytery. For protection, he placed a pitchfork near the head of his bed and asked one of the parishioners, twenty-eight-year-old André Verchère, the village wheelwright, to come and spend the night with him in the presbytery.

André was happy to help his pastor and he agreed to spend the night. He wanted to be prepared so he took a loaded gun with him. He and the Curé sat by the fireplace and talked together until around ten o'clock in the evening. The Curé had André sleep in his bedroom and he slept in an adjoining room.

Around one o'clock in the morning, André heard the latch of the hall door being shaken violently. It also sounded like a club was striking the door, making a thunderous noise. André grabbed his gun and rushed to the window and opened it but there was no one there. Nevertheless, the presbytery was shaking as if there had been an earthquake. The Curé lit his lantern and came to André's side. The house continued to shake for about fifteen minutes.

The next evening the Curé asked André if he would be willing to spend the night once again. André said that he could not do so because the experience had been too frightening for him. It took two weeks before André was able to regain his composure.

Very much afraid, the Curé had no choice but to spend the nights alone. Before long, it began to dawn on him what was happening. It was the devil who was revealing himself to the Curé in terrifying manifestations. At times, the devil hurled him out of bed with great force. It seemed obvious that the devil was trying to kill him. Due to these incidents, the Curé felt it was the right time to introduce Perpetual Adoration in his parish. He also asked the orphans at *La Providence* to sign up for adoration and they were enthusiastic about it. They began to feel that they had a share in the Curé's important work.

Dr. J.B. Saunier and Dr. Aimé Michel were informed of the strange occurrences that had been taking place in the presbytery. They both knew the Curé well. Dr. Saunier was his personal physician. The two doctors agreed that the Curé had a sound mind as well as mental and emotional stability. Dr. Saunier and Dr. Michel concurred that the Curé was not hallucinating or suffering from psychosis when he spoke about the frightening events. When the Curé stated that it was the devil who was tormenting him, Dr. Saunier and Dr. Michel believed him.

The frightening manifestations continued to plague the Curé. Accepting an invitation to preach a mission at Saint Trivier, he set out toward the parish. Strangely, as he walked, the atmosphere all about him took on a sinister quality. The roadside bushes and shrubs glowed in an eerie way as though they were on fire. He believed that it was the devil who was trying to terrify him so that he would turn back, but he continued to walk on. During the mission, the Curé spent the nights in the presbytery. Four witnesses watched his bed get flung around and deposited in the middle of the room accompanied by high-pitched screams. As it happened, the Curé helped many souls during the mission. In Ars on one occasion, the devil set fire to the Curé's bed in broad daylight. Speaking about the incident the Curé said, "The devil is very angry. He could not catch the bird so he has burned the cage."

Denis Chaland once asked the Curé to hear his confession. The Curé agreed to do so in the presbytery. In the middle of his confession, the room began to shake and the kneeler began to tremble. Terrified, Denis tried to stand up. The Curé quickly held his arm so that he would remain seated. "Don't worry, it is nothing," the Curé said. "It is just the devil." Denis never had the courage to go to confession to the Curé again.

Once, as the Curé was going upstairs to his bedroom, he heard the distinct sound of boots going up the stairs, one stair at a time, just ahead of him. From experience, he knew it was the devil. In addition, a beautiful painting of the Annunciation in the Curé's presbytery had filth flung at it to such a degree that the Virgin was no longer recognizable. The painting could not be repaired and had to be removed.

Marguerite, the Curé's sister, looked forward to visiting her brother in Ars when she could. On one occasion, she heard the Curé leave the presbytery late at night to go to the church to hear confessions. A few minutes after he left, Marguerite heard a deafening noise close to her bed. It sounded like someone was striking heavy blows to the furniture in her bedroom. When she lit the lamp, she discovered that everything was in perfect order. Terrified, Marguerite rushed to the church and told the Curé what had happened. "Do not be frightened. It was the devil, but he cannot hurt you," he said to her.

After a time, the Curé came to realize that the diabolical manifestations were usually a signal that a person who had been away from the church for many years would soon be arriving in Ars. The Curé used to say that he owed his protection from the devil to the statue of St. Michael the Archangel that stood at the entrance of the church. The frightening incidents in and around the Curé's presbytery eventually came to an end, to the relief of everyone.

In times past, the parishioners at Ars had made a yearly pilgrimage to Lyons. Gradually, as enthusiasm waned, the pilgrimages were discontinued. So much time had elapsed that it was but a distant memory in the minds of the people of Ars. The Curé had a great desire to revive the yearly custom and he began making plans. In 1836, he invited his parish to accompany him on pilgrimage to the shrine of Our Lady of Fourvière in Lyons. When he announced it, the people showed great interest and enthusiasm. Two-thirds of his parishioners signed up to make the pilgrimage with him. Two priests from neighboring villages came as well. One of the priests was eighty years old but felt that he had the stamina to make the journey.

Those making the pilgrimage set out around midnight, walking in procession. Three banner bearers led the procession, holding the beautiful banners that the Curé had purchased for the parish. Singing hymns and praying the Rosary, they arrived in the village of Trévoux at daybreak. They then set out in a boat for Lyons. At the shrine of Our Lady of Fourvière, the Curé said Mass. There was also time for quiet prayer at the shrine. At the end of the day, when the group prepared to return to Ars, the three banner bearers led the way while all the others walked in procession behind them. Many of the citizens of Lyons stood on the roadside and watched in awe as the procession left town.

The Curé was one of the first to get on the boat going back to Ars. Some of the people in the group were a little slow in making their way back to the boat which caused the boatmen to become very angry. When they began to swear and use all manner of profanities, the Curé refused to continue on with them. He immediately got off the boat and all of his parishioners followed after him. They walked back to Ars together, thankful for the blessings of their pilgrimage.

As the Curé grew older, he began to suffer from numerous physical ailments. A visiting priest from Montpellier, thirty-nine-year-old Father Alexis Tailhades, spent the winter of 1839 in Ars in order to assist the Curé at the parish. The Curé was delighted to welcome Father Alexis to the presbytery and he enjoyed his company immensely. On one occasion, the Curé had a terrible stomachache and was having a very difficult time walking up the stairs to his bedroom. Father Alexis hurried to help him. "Let me try to walk up the stairs without assistance," the Curé exclaimed. "Otherwise, how will I be able to manage when you are no longer here?"

The Curé received a great deal of mail which only increased with the passage of time. Many sick people wrote to him, asking for his prayers. Others wrote to him regarding their family problems, financial problems, and every other sort of difficulty. With the long hours in the confessional as well as his other obligations, the Curé no longer had the time to answer the letters personally. Father Alexis helped him with the task. If Father Alexis had any question as to the appropriate reply, the Curé would advise him. Brother Athanase and Catherine Lassagne helped with the mail as well.

Father Alexis had numerous heart to heart talks with the Curé while assisting him at the parish. On one occasion, he asked the Curé what he did in order to protect himself from sensual temptations. The Curé told him that twenty-three years earlier when he was serving as assistant priest in Ecully, he made a vow to daily say the prayer - *Hail, Holy Queen* and six times a day to repeat the prayer - *Blessed be forever the most Holy and Immaculate Conception of the Blessed Virgin Mary, Mother of God, Amen.* He felt that the prayers purified his heart and his mind.

Father Alexis went over to *La Providence* orphanage and told the teachers to make sure to write down any miracles they witnessed at the hands of the Curé. He was certain it would be valuable information to have in the future because he believed that the Curé might one day be canonized. He was well-aware of the Curé's many spiritual gifts. "It would take up a lot of our time to write down all of the miracles because we see so many of them," said Jeanne Marie Chanay. "We are very busy taking care of the orphans and do not have a free minute," she added.

From time to time, the Curé sent Father Alexis to the diocese to take care of various church matters with Bishop Devie. "You have been with the Curé for some time now. What do you think of him?" Bishop Devie once asked Father Alexis. "I think he is a saint," Father Alexis replied. "That is my opinion too," Bishop Devie said. On another occasion Bishop Devie exclaimed, "The Curé of Ars may not be learned, but he is enlightened." Bishop Devie thought so highly of his abilities that he added his name to the list of priests who were authorized to hear confessions at important clerical functions.

In the early years of the Curé's ministry, as his reputation of holiness was growing, visitors to the church of Ars numbered about twenty a day. They wanted attend the Curé's Mass and make their confession to him. Some came simply out of curiosity. As the years passed, the number of pilgrims to Ars steadily increased. From 1830 to 1859, three to four hundred people arrived daily in Ars. Many people reached Ars by walking and some came by boat while others came by horseback. It was a common sight to see horses and donkeys tied to the chestnut trees in the main square by the church.

By 1855, there was a daily service of two horse carriages between Lyons and Ars. In that same year, the number of visitors to Ars had reached 20,000 a year. Hotels could not be built fast enough for the crowds who were coming to Ars. At the principal train station of Perrache in Lyons, a special booking office was opened in order to issue round-trip tickets to Ars. The round-trip tickets were good for eight days. In addition, special coaches met the trains from Paris and transported people to Ars.

Because of the crowds, confessions were short, lasting five minutes or less as a general rule. People were willing to wait for many days in order to see the Curé. When night came, they would lie down and sleep on the grass until morning. Others would wait all night in the little cemetery beside the church. Many of the citizens of Ars opened their homes to the pilgrims to offer them food and lodging. The visitors came from all parts of Europe and beyond. The last year of the Curé's life, 100,000 people travelled to Ars to see him.

All who knew the Curé of Ars were aware that he led a penitential life and practiced extreme self-mortification. He literally stripped himself of everything. As one person observed, "His penance was constant, extreme, universal. It embraced his whole existence." He usually ate one meal a day and he ate it standing up. He survived mainly on boiled potatoes, pancakes, and milk. He was so thin that someone described his body as more like a shadow than a human form. His thinness was considered alarming. He took no wine and he never ate at night. His daily intake of food was so small that it seemed as though he only ate enough to keep himself from dying. He declined the fresh homemade bread that a resident of Ars offered to supply him with. As an act of penance, he gave up eating desserts and other foods that he enjoyed.

After the clerical conference each year, the priests were served a fine meal. The Curé asked for a dispensation from the meal and was granted one. The clerical conference was the only gathering that the Curé attended at any time, and it was observed by the other priests who attended, that he always appeared poor. He wore an old hat and even older shoes. He never in his life possessed an overcoat but would walk long distances in near freezing temperatures clad only in his priestly robe. "There is holiness in the Curé of Ars," someone once observed. "There is holiness but there is nothing else."

The Curé never indulged in any light reading, not even a newspaper. He never had any interest in seeing the railway station that was being built and that daily brought so many pilgrims to Ars. He left Ars on occasion to assist at parish missions, but he never travelled for pleasure or took a vacation. When people spoke to him of worldly or frivolous matters, he tried to be courteous but he had no desire to prolong the conversation. As a rule, he did not speak about himself either favorably or unfavorably.

The Curé took no part in political events. When friends told him that the political climate was improving and that the French government was becoming more accepting of Catholics, he stated the opposite. He warned a friend, Jules Maubou, "Do not accept any employment in the new government. Napoleon Bonaparte will one day be a great enemy of the Church." The Curé had a great distrust of the future Napoleon III and his statements about the dictator proved to be prophetic.

From 1830 until his death in 1859, the Curé regularly spent sixteen hours or more each day in the confessional. In the early hours of the morning there was already a crowd gathered at the door of the church waiting for the Curé to open it. He could be seen as he walked from the presbytery toward the church wearing his purple stole and holding his small storm lantern in his hand. He heard the women's confessions from one o'clock a.m. to six o'clock a.m. When confessions were over, he celebrated Mass and afterward he blessed images and religious articles. At eight o'clock a.m. he went back to the presbytery to have half a glass of milk. Shortly after that, he started hearing the confessions of the men. At ten o'clock in the morning he recited morning prayers from the Liturgy of the Hours. At eleven o'clock a.m., he taught a catechism class to the orphans at *La Providence*. He had lunch around noon and his meal usually consisted of a boiled potato and a glass of milk. After his lunch, he visited the sick.

As the Curé walked out of the presbytery to make his sick calls each day, he was greeted by a crowd. He could not cross the village square or move along the street except slowly and protected by two or three men who acted as his bodyguards. They walked in front of him with outstretched arms to shield him from the people. Some tried to slash a small piece off his priestly robe to keep as a relic. Sometimes they snatched his prayer book and tore out a few pages to keep as a treasured possession. He had to burn the cuttings of his hair, otherwise people would keep them as relics.

Priests frequently asked the Curé if they could go with him on his sick calls and he allowed them to do so. Many of the pilgrims also walked with him on the sick calls and waited for him outside the sick person's house. Father Toccanier said of him, "One approached the Curé of Ars as one approaches a relic. Never have I seen so much energy and strength of will. Nothing daunted him, neither opposition, nor infirmities, nor temptations."

Back at the church after sick calls, the Curé prayed Vespers and then heard the women's confessions till five o'clock p.m. and men's confessions until eight o'clock p.m. At the conclusion of the confessions, he went to the pulpit to lead the evening Rosary. After the Rosary, he went over to the presbytery and gave interviews to missionaries, priests and brothers who had come from a distance to seek his counsel. The church was closed from nine o'clock in the evening until midnight.

When the Curé's duties were finally over each evening, he was so exhausted he could hardly climb the stairs to his bedroom. Brother Athanase said that he sometimes saw the Curé fall against the wall as he walked upstairs to his room. At last in his room, he read from a book on the lives of the saints before retiring. He usually slept no more than three hours each night.

The Curé often felt crushed under the grueling schedule that kept him busy both night and day. He admitted that the responsibilities of the priesthood frightened him, yet he kept up his timetable year in and year out. "He was visibly helped by God," said Father Faivre.

One man who found his life changed forever by his encounter with the Curé was an artist by the name of Mr. Maissiat. Mr. Maissiat was a non-believer. On one occasion, he set out from Lyons for a one-month vacation. In the coach, Mr. Maissiat met an old friend who invited him to travel with him to Ars to visit the Curé. Mr. Maissiat had heard about the Curé and the miracles that had taken place in Ars, but he was skeptical and had no interest in making a trip there. His friend continued to dialogue with him, and finally he was persuaded to go.

In the church, the Curé noticed Mr. Maissiat and motioned to him, inviting him to come into the confessional. Mr. Maissiat refused to do so. However, quite suddenly he changed his mind and decided to go into the confessional. He wanted to converse with the Curé for a few moments and nothing more. The two had a friendly conversation together and before Mr. Maissiat left, the Curé invited him to come back the following day. He also asked him to go to the side altar of St. Philomena and to pray for the gift of faith.

When Mr. Maissiat visited the St. Philomena altar as the Curé had asked him to do, he burst into tears. The next morning, he spoke to the Curé again. "Father, I do not believe in anything. Help me," he said. The Curé helped him more than he could have ever imagined. Mr. Maissiat stayed nine more days in Ars and went back to Lyons a changed and faith-filled man. Many, many people were amazed to learn of his conversion.

Another man who found his life radically changed by his encounter with the Curé was an architect who lived in Lyons. The architect often got into terrible arguments with his wife. One day after a particularly angry exchange with her, he told her that he was leaving her for good. "You will never see me again!" he said as he slammed the door and left the house.

Outside on the street, the architect saw a large coach with the words written on the side of it: *Connection to Ars*. He asked a passer-by, "What is Ars?" "Ars is a village where an extraordinary priest lives," the man replied. The architect's curiosity was sparked so he boarded the coach that was headed for Ars. During the trip, it was announced that the coach would be arriving in Ars in time for everyone to attend the Curé's eleven o'clock catechism class.

The architect attended the catechism class and afterward spoke to Father Toccanier who assisted at the parish. He said to Father Toccanier, "The Curé of Ars is so steeped in the love of God, if I had stayed much longer in the church, I too would have taken the plunge!" The architect decided to spend the afternoon in Ars and before he made the return trip to Lyons, he went to confession to the Curé. When he returned home, much to his wife's surprise, he asked her to forgive him. Peace was restored in his marriage and in his life.

Once a sailor visited the parish in Ars. At the time, he was employed as a boatman on the Seine River. He had lost his way in life and was subject to dark moods and violent behavior. Some of his friends were going to Ars to see the Curé and invited him to join them. He had a strong dislike for priests but he accepted the invitation just so that he could spend the time with his friends.

When they arrived in Ars, the Curé was hearing the men's confessions. The sailor was walking around nonchalantly in the church, not the least bit impressed by any of it, when he suddenly felt like he was going to faint. He quickly went outside to get a little air. After a short time, he went back into the church. Once again, he felt weak and began shivering and shaking. One of the parishioners noticed that he looked sick and led him over to the Curé. Face to face with the famous priest, the sailor decided on the spur of the moment to make his confession. From that time forward, he led a very devout life.

A brief encounter with the Curé also had a radical impact on the life of thirty-two-year-old François Dorel, a plasterer from Villefranche. François, a thoroughly secular man, had been invited by a friend to visit the church in Ars. His friend told him many amazing stories about the Curé and encouraged him to make his confession to the saintly priest. "I will be happy to accompany you to the church but I do not intend to go to confession," François said to his friend. His intent was to go duck hunting that afternoon after he and his friend paid a visit to the church.

With his shotgun slung over his shoulder, François happened to be standing with his dog in the square by the church when the Curé noticed him in passing and admired his handsome dog. "If only your soul was as beautiful as your dog," the Curé said. The full impact of the Curé's words hit François like a thunderbolt and he began to cry. It proved to be a turning point in his life. Later, feeling a call to consecrated life, he sought out the Curé and asked for advice regarding the religious congregation he should apply to. The Curé suggested the Trappists. François joined the Trappist's austere order at Our Lady of Aiguebelle Abbey, persevering as a cloistered monk until his death thirty-six years later.

Catherine Lassagne said, "It will never be known what graces of conversion the Curé obtained through his prayers. A real change has been wrought in the hearts of the people. Grace had proven to be so strong that not many of the people who lived in Ars were able to resist it."

Sylvain Dutheil, who lived in Clermont-Héault, like many others before him, experienced a profound grace when he visited Ars. He had been discharged from the army at sixteen years of age because of his failing health. He was plagued with a serious pulmonary disease. One day when Sylvain was in Montpellier with his sister, they saw a portrait of the Curé of Ars on display in one of the shops. Sylvain immediately began making fun of the image of the Curé. "You might receive a healing if you put your trust in that saintly man," his sister said to him. Sylvain scoffed at her words, considering them ridiculous. That night Sylvain had a vivid dream in which the Curé appeared to him, holding an apple that was half-rotten.

The strange dream made a great impression on Sylvain and even though he was very sick, he asked his mother to take him to Ars so that he could meet the Curé. Once in Ars, because he was too ill to walk, Sylvain was carried into the church. It was winter time and the church was very cold so he was taken into the sacristy and placed near the stove. When Sylvain returned to the hotel, he told his mother that he had made his confession and had received Holy Communion. "I am overflowing with happiness," he said. "I don't want to leave Ars. I never want to leave Ars!" he added. Sylvain remained in Ars and passed away a short time later.

For years, the Curé suffered from painful facial neuralgia, excruciating toothaches, headaches and fainting spells. He fainted on one occasion while on his way to a parish mission in the village of Saint Trivier. He was discovered lying unconscious in a snow bank. On another occasion, a family asked the Curé to come to their village and minister to their loved one who was gravely ill and wanted to make his confession. The Curé left Ars in the midst of a storm and reached the house soaking wet, with chills and a fever. He was so ill that he was compelled to lie down in bed beside the sick man and it was there that he heard his confession.

Sitting in one position throughout the day at the church in Ars, hearing confessions in a tiny space, was a grueling task for the Curé. The church was like an ice box in winter and in the summer, the heat was almost unbearable. One severe winter day when the church was especially cold, one of the parishioners thought of a way to make the Curé more comfortable. When the Curé had left the church, he installed a sliding wood panel on the floor of the confessional. It was impossible to tell that any work had been done. Just before the Curé returned to the church, the man put bottles of boiling water onto the floor of the confessional and covered them over with the panel. "My feet have been so warm," the Curé said later that day but he never guessed what the kind man had done for him.

During the chill of winter while hearing confessions in the sacristy of the church, the Curé sometimes set paper on fire in order to warm his numb hands. Eventually he was convinced to put a stove in the sacristy when it was pointed out to him that his vestments were getting moldy due to the damp air. Jean Pertinand, the village schoolteacher, used to light a fire in the fireplace at the presbytery on winter evenings in hopes that the Curé would be warm through the night. Nevertheless, during the winter, the Curé suffered from the cold whenever he tried to sleep.

On one occasion, a very wealthy and arrogant woman arrived at the church in an expensive carriage. Wanting to make her confession and seeing the many people who were waiting in line, she told the usher who was on duty that she was in a hurry. She insisted that she was not to be kept waiting and demanded to see the Curé immediately. She went on to say that she had visited the King of Bavaria as well as prelates at the Vatican and was never kept waiting. The Curé was told about the woman and went over to her and said, "In Ars, there are no favorites. If you want to make your confession, you will have to wait in line like all the others. Even the empress herself would have to wait."

Once, when a lady was making her confession to the Curé, she decided not to confess a particular sin. She reasoned that she would confess the sin at some later date. When she finished her confession, the Curé named the exact sin that she had withheld and confronted her about trying to keep it a secret from him. The woman was shocked and thought to herself, "How could he possibly know that?" At that very moment he replied, "It was your Guardian Angel who told me about it."

Once in the confessional, a woman of Ars confessed to reading books that had very bad subject matter, books that were pulling her spirit down. "You must agree to throw them all away," the Curé said to her. "Otherwise I will not be able to give you absolution."

One man said that he had never intended to go to confession to the Curé but to his surprise, he was practically pushed into the confessional. Once inside, there was no way to turn back. At the moment his eyes met the Curé's, he experienced what he described as a sensation of "indefinable comfort." He had not been to confession in thirty years. Another man said that going to confession to the Curé was such an overwhelming experience that he could never talk about it without shedding tears.

Both inside and outside the confessional, the Curé had an extraordinary ability to counsel people and to console them. Mrs. Des Garets' oldest son, Eugene, died at the early age of twenty-five. The Curé's counsel helped Eugene to resign himself to an early death. Mrs. Des Garets too was comforted and helped by the Curé and she was able to accept the loss of her son. But five months later, Mrs. Des Garets lost her second son. Despair seized her and she became immobilized by her grief. She sought out the Curé and he said to her, "Be great. Be strong. Do not let yourself be crushed but know how to accept the blow!" Mrs. Des Garets later said, "After the Curé counseled me, I felt myself reborn and capable of accepting and bearing my cross."

As the years passed, the long hours of work and the demands of the people, took a toll on the Curé. In his mid-fifties, he looked like an old man. He had a great longing for solitude as well as a desire to be free from the burden of unceasing work. He said that from the time he was eleven years old, he had an attraction and a desire for solitude. He often spoke longingly about retiring.

The Curé became more and more frail. He had attacks of dizziness in the confessional and sometimes lost consciousness for two or three minutes. He often inhaled vinegar salts or cologne so that he could continue hearing confessions. Father Raymond, who observed the Curé's grueling sixteen-hours-a-day work schedule said, "Even though I am in good health and relatively young, I would not have been able to endure the Curé's schedule for one week. It would have been impossible." Doctors told the Curé that rest was the only remedy for his failing health.

In the autumn of 1843, the Curé wrote to his brother François, telling him that he was planning on visiting him at his farmhouse in Dardilly. He also wrote to the bishop and told him that he wished to retire as parish priest of Ars. He added that he would await his reply at his brother's home in Dardilly.

On the evening of his departure from Ars, the Curé went to *La Providence* and told Catherine Lassagne of his plans and bid her farewell. Catherine knew that he had suffered from extreme exhaustion for a long time and that his pastoral duties had become a burden to him. He told Catherine he was leaving that very night and asked her to keep it a secret. She agreed to do so. The secret somehow leaked out to a few of the parishioners. Several men posted themselves around the presbytery in order to keep watch for any attempt on the Curé's part to flee.

At one o'clock in the morning, several of the men who had been on the lookout for the Curé, spotted him leaving the presbytery. They begged him not to go but he was walking very fast and would talk to no one. Jean Pertinand was summoned and asked to intervene. He walked as fast as he could in order to catch up with the Curé. As it turned out, the Curé had lost his way in the darkness and was wandering about in a field.

Jean Pertinand walked with the Curé through the night and accompanied him all the way to Dardilly. On the way, they recited the Rosary together ten times. It took them seven hours to reach François' home. When they arrived there at daybreak, the Curé felt ill and had to go to bed at once.

The Curé had a wonderful reunion with François and his family. Even though many years had passed since they had seen each other, the bonds of brotherly love were as strong as ever. The two shared beautiful memories of life at the farmhouse in their younger days. The Curé noticed that the old clock was still on the wall under which he had made his first confession.

Several days later, twenty-three young men from Ars walked all night to François' home carrying a signed petition for the Curé's return. Shortly after that, more people arrived from Ars. They had chartered a large horse-drawn carriage to get there. François saw all the strangers outside and would not let them into his house. He became very upset about the situation. The Curé knew that the steady stream of people now arriving at the farmhouse was a terrible inconvenience for François and his family and that it could not continue.

Bishop Devie contacted the Curé and told him that he could serve as parish priest in Beaumont if he wished to leave Ars. Bishop Devie as well as Bishop Chalandon who succeeded him, did not want the Curé to retire from the active ministry. They were aware of the great good he was doing as a parish priest and they wanted him to continue as long as he possibly could. However, they were not at all opposed to transferring him to another parish if that was his wish.

As soon as the Curé received the permission from the bishop, he and François set off for Beaumont. The Curé rode on the farm horse for part of the journey while François held the reins and walked beside him. Beaumont, an isolated village surrounded by ponds and long stretches of flat marshlands, was located thirty miles from Dardilly. When the Curé arrived at the parish in Beaumont, he said Mass and continued to pray to God for guidance. It wasn't long after that, the Curé felt that God was calling him to return to Ars.

When the villagers in Ars got word that the Curé was coming back, they rang the church bells as they did on important solemnities and special feast days. Everyone in the village rejoiced to hear the good news and waited for the Curé in the square. Though he had only been gone a week, it seemed like a month to his parishioners.

The Curé arrived back in Ars just before sundown. He was walking with difficulty and using a cane for support. He was greeted with shouts of joy by his parishioners who could now breathe a sigh of relief as their pastor had come home. He was at peace and he was happy to be back with his spiritual family. He had tried to leave Ars on three separate occasions but had always returned.

Through the years, there were numerous physical healings reported through the Curé's intercession. Sick people from many parts of the world came to him, seeking his prayers. One little boy had a large tumor under his eye. One day in the church, the mother took the Curé's hand in her own and touched it to the tumor on her son's face. At that moment, the tumor disappeared instantly. Many people who were in the church that day witnessed the miracle.

A poor woman, Mrs. Anne Dévoluet, came to Ars from the village of Saint Roman with her eight-year-old son John Marie, in order to ask the Curé for his prayers. John Marie had a hip disease and was unable to walk. When Anne arrived in Ars, she found lodging with a kind family who offered to watch John Marie for her so that she could go to the church. It was late and Anne was exhausted from the journey but her desire to see the Curé was so great that she was willing to make any sacrifice. She waited outside the church on the porch where many others were waiting. When the Curé saw Anne in the crowd, he motioned to her and asked her to step forward. In her excitement at being able to speak to the Curé face to face, she forgot to mention that she wanted him to pray for her son's healing.

The next morning, Anne put John Marie in a small cart and took him to the church. The Curé blessed both of them and prayed for them. He said to Anne, "That child is too big to be carried about in a cart. Let him stand up on his own two feet and walk." "It is impossible because he is not able to walk," Anne replied.

The Curé told Anne to take John Marie to the St. Philomena altar in the church and to pray for healing. Slowly and with great difficulty, John Marie managed to stand up. He and his mother knelt together at the St. Philomena altar and prayed for a long time. When they finished their prayers, John Marie was able to walk. With great excitement, he walked about the church in his stocking feet. Delighted, he went outside where he skipped about and played, to the great joy of everyone who was nearby.

In 1850, a girl had a terrible accident on an icy road and nearly died. She survived the accident but her injuries were such that she was in constant pain. When her condition improved a little, she went to confession at two o'clock in the morning to the Curé. He asked her why she came at such an early hour to confession. "I am in less pain in the early morning hours," she explained. Four months later, the girl went back to the Curé's confessional and told him the details of her accident. She wanted him to pray for her healing but at the same time she felt ashamed to ask because she knew that he too suffered from constant pain.

The girl explained to the Curé that she wanted to be well enough to be able to work during harvest season. "You should consult a doctor in Lyons," the Curé said. "I do not need to go to a doctor in Lyons because the person who can heal me is right here in Ars. It is you," she replied. "I do not ask to be completely cured but only to be well enough so that I can earn my living," she added. "Well, I will think about it," the Curé said. By the end of the week, the girl was healed of all of her maladies and was able to participate fully in the harvest.

The Curé was aware that extraordinary things were happening in his parish but he never took credit for any of them. He blessed the sick but he sometimes did so reluctantly because he did not want people to think he had healing powers. What filled him with the greatest joy was when a person who had been away from the Church for a long time, returned. He believed that the spiritual healings were even more of a grace than the physical healings. "The body is so very little," he used to say. When people claimed that they had received a healing through his hands, he was heard to say, "No, you are wrong. I am an ignorant man who used to tend sheep." His humility was one of his greatest attributes. Jean Pertinand, the village schoolteacher said, "The most arduous, the most extraordinary, and the most prodigious work that the Curé accomplished, was his own life."

Besides the numerous physical healings, there were other miraculous occurrences that took place at Ars. On one occasion, Father Marie Barthelemy was spending his vacation in Ars at the house of Jean Pertinand. Late one night, Father Barthelemy looked out his window and beheld a great light, like a supernatural brilliance hovering over the presbytery where the Curé lived. On another occasion, a young seminarian saw a mysterious brightness in the sky over the church of Ars. Once, a man was making his confession to the Curé, when he suddenly burst into tears. The Curé asked him why he was crying. The man told him that when he looked at him, he saw his head surrounded by a ring of light. "He told me he had seen little candles around my head," the Curé said.

Even in the natural world, Ars appeared to be under special protection from weather disasters. Madeleine Scipiot related that from the year 1825 until the death of the Curé in 1859, there was not one destructive hailstorm in Ars. She ascribed the protection to the holy life of the Curé. Also, Mrs. Marthe Des Garets observed that during the time of the Curé's ministry at Ars, no damage to property or land had occurred due to winter storms.

In 1849, Marie Roche of Paris travelled to Ars to speak to the Curé about a personal matter. She felt that he alone would be able to advise her. At the time she was enduring great spiritual suffering. After waiting a long time, she finally got close to his confessional and was able to look into the dark corner where he was seated. His face projected two fiery rays and his features were hidden by the brilliance of the light. Marie gazed at his dazzling countenance for about ten minutes and finally left the church. The next day after the catechism class, the Curé happened to see Marie. He greeted her and said, "Fear nothing, my child. All will be well."

Numerous people through the years spoke about the intense and piercing gaze of the Curé. People often described his blue eyes as shining with a supernatural brightness. Denis Chaland said, "The Curé of Ars seemed to guess my thoughts. When his glance met mine, it pierced me to the depth of my soul. I knew a person who confessed to being terrified of his gaze."

The Curé never allowed himself to be photographed yet his portraits were on sale throughout the village and all the pilgrims wanted one. The Curé did not approve of the practice and the only reason he tolerated it at all was because it helped the shopkeepers. The portraits that were on display in the shop windows were a poor likeness of the Curé since he refused to pose for a picture. The images came in all shapes and sizes from very small engravings to large and brightly colored portraits. To show his disapproval, he refused to sign or bless them.

Father Toccanier, who knew the Curé well, felt that it was important to have a likeness of him preserved for posterity. Knowing that the Curé would never agree to it, Father Toccanier and his friend Emilien Cabuchet, a gifted sculptor, planned out their strategy. Father Toccanier found a seat in the very back of the catechism class where Emilien Cabuchet could sit every day and study the Curé's face and sculpt it in wax. Nobody would notice what he was doing.

Mr. Cabuchet came into the class with his provision of wax hidden in his large hat. He was able to make a beautiful wax sculpture of the Curé's face. When the Curé found out, he made Mr. Cabuchet promise not to give it to the public until after his death.

By 1850, the Curé had become the most well-known and most admired priest in all of France. Bishops, famous preachers, and people of high positions visited him but he was not overly impressed. He said that he preferred the poor. Worldly honors came to the Curé although he tried to avoid them. He received a great tribute from the emperor of France, the coveted medal of the Legion of Honor. The medal was delivered to him by the mayor, but he refused to wear it. The Curé learned that plans were being made to have a biography written about his life and that distressed him.

Bishop Chalandon elevated the Curé to the title of honorary canon of the Church in recognition of his dedication and accomplishments as a parish priest. He visited the Curé and placed the canon's silk cape bordered with ermine over his shoulders. The cape was worn only by popes, cardinals, bishops and canons. The Curé did not feel worthy of such an honor but he humbly accepted it.

In the winter of 1854, the Curé learned that his brother François was dangerously ill. François had a great desire to see the Curé so he had his son Antoine travel to Ars to pick him up and bring him back to Dardilly. It happened that the Curé was quite ill at the time. Antoine and the Curé left for Dardilly in a carriage. Father Toccanier also travelled with them.

After going about ten miles, the Curé said that the jostling of the carriage was making him feel worse. He said that he felt too sick to continue on the journey. Antoine and Father Toccanier had to continue on to Dardilly without the Curé who walked back to Ars alone. When Antoine and Father Toccanier arrived in Dardilly without the Curé, François was deeply disappointed.

As the Curé was walking back to Ars, he saw a large horse-drawn wagon approaching on the road. It was returning to Lyons from Ars. When the people in the wagon saw the Curé, they all got out and greeted him. They told him that they had come to Ars from Lyons to make their confession and had been disappointed to learn that he was away. They walked back to Ars with him and followed him into the church, forming a line at the confessional. Some in the number had not been to confession in forty years.

François Vianney passed away on Good Friday, April 8, 1855. Like his famous brother, he had been a devout Christian throughout his life. The Curé wanted with all his heart to attend his brother's funeral but it proved to be impossible. The funeral took place on Holy Saturday, the day on which the Curé was obligated to hear confessions for eighteen hours. On the day of François' funeral, the Curé sat in the darkness of his confessional and wept.

Dr. Aimé Michel examined the Curé ten years before his death. Dr. Michel said that given the Curé's poor health, his long hours of work and his lack of sleep and proper nourishment, there was no logical explanation as to how he could remain alive. "His life, his words and his extraordinary powers will always remain beyond human comprehension," said Dr. Michel.

A missionary once summed up the Curé's life by saying, "He was the embodiment of supernatural life." Father Louis Beau, the parish priest of Jassans was the Curé's confessor during the last thirteen years of his life. He said of the Curé, "He was surrounded by a halo of sanctity." Father Alfred Monnin, who knew the Curé personally said, "I cannot think of even one instant when the Curé's conduct did not bear the stamp of perfection."

When the Curé had first come to Ars, almost none of the men in the village attended Mass on Sunday. At the end of his life, the population of the town had risen from 240 to 500 people and out of that number, all but seven or eight men were attending Mass every Sunday. The Curé prophesied for Ars a dark and dismal future. He predicted that in less than a century after his death, the people of Ars would lose their religious fervor and once again become completely indifferent to spirituality.

At the time of his final illness, the Curé had a suffocation attack in the confessional and had to be repeatedly taken out of the church to get some fresh air. That morning he had a burning fever, but he insisted on keeping to his schedule and somehow managed to teach the 11:00 a.m. catechism class. At end of day he almost fainted and had to lean on Father Jerome's arm to steady himself. Father Jerome took him to his room and put him to bed. He said that the Curé looked "like death."

The Curé tried to rise at one o'clock the next morning in order to go to the church to hear the women's confessions, but he was too weak to get up. He was growing weaker by the minute and he knew that his end had come. For his comfort, a mattress was brought in to his bedroom to replace his hard pallet and he did not protest.

Informed about his health crisis, Dr. Saunier, the Curé's physician and Father Louis Beau, the Curé's confessor arrived at daybreak. Dr. Saunier was alarmed at his condition and feared that death was close at hand. The Curé was very well-prepared for death and he was not afraid. He used to like to repeat, "The earth is a bridge for crossing the water. It is only useful for bearing us upward."

Even after the Curé became bedridden, there were those who wanted at all costs to make their confession to him. Along with a number of priests, some of his parishioners were given access to his bedroom. He was so weak that he could hardly speak but he did manage to hear confessions, although it was difficult for him to raise his hand in absolution. Finally, it was decided that his visitors had to leave. Though barred from his bedroom, some of the pilgrims were still able to force their way inside.

As news spread regarding the Curé's grave condition, a huge influx of people descended on Ars. The highways and byways in all directions were crowded with people trying to get there as fast as they could. Everyone wanted to see him one last time and hopefully to speak a word to him. The pilgrims purchased so many medals and religious articles in Ars that the shops were stripped bare. The medals were sent up to the Curé's room in large baskets and he continued to bless them on his death bed. At night, the pilgrims laid down on the grass and slept in the open air.

People began gathering in large numbers outside the Curé's residence. They were told to kneel down on the grass when they heard the bells ringing. It was a signal that the Curé was, at that moment, giving them all his last blessing. The Curé's confessor made arrangements for him to receive the Last Sacraments. A priest brought the Blessed Sacrament from the church to his bedside while twenty priests followed in procession carrying lighted candles.

At the time of the Curé's final illness, Ars was having a heatwave. The Curé's bedroom grew more stifling as more dignitaries arrived. The youth of the parish climbed on ladders to the roof of the presbytery and hung long sheets of canvas from the roof. Throughout the days, they ceaselessly watered the canvas and the tiles of the roof hoping it would cool the bedroom where the Curé was lying.

The Curé told one of the men looking in on him, "I have thirty-six francs left to my name. Ask Catherine Lassagne to give them to Dr. Saunier. Then tell her to ask him not to come back again because I would not be able to pay him for his services." After five days of suffering, Father John Marie Baptiste Vianney, the Curé of Ars, passed away. Brother Jerome held him in his arms as he took his last breath. He passed away peacefully while Father Monnin was reciting the prayers for the dying. It was Thursday August 4, 1859. The Curé was seventy-three years old and had served the parish of Ars for forty-one years.

At five o'clock in the morning the bells of Ars began to toll, announcing the Curé's death. Bells were also tolling in the villages of Savigneux, Mizérieux, Trévoux, and Jassans, declaring the death of Father John Marie Vianney. The news was also transmitted by telegraph.

The body of the Curé was brought down to a room on the ground floor of the presbytery. In preparation for his funeral, he was dressed in the same priestly vestments he had worn when he was installed as parish priest of Ars. His photograph was then taken. It was the one and only photograph that was ever taken of him. During his lifetime he would not permit it. The prestigious medal of the Legion of Honor was seen for the first time when it was pinned on his vestments after his death.

For the next forty-eight hours, an endless stream of people came to the presbytery and filed past the Curé's coffin, touching medals and religious articles to his body. A guard of honor composed of several of the Brothers from the religious congregation as well as a number of the orphans from La Providence stood watch beside the coffin day and night. In addition, the mayor had soldiers brought in to make sure order was maintained.

The night before the funeral there was a huge influx of people into Ars. Most had to sleep in the open air as all provisions quickly ran out and it was impossible to find lodging. At eight o'clock in the morning on August 6, the day of the funeral, the coffin was taken in procession through the streets of Ars.

Wearing their best white dresses, orphans from *La Providence* led the funeral procession followed by members of the clergy. The coffin was carried in turn by priests, Brothers of the Holy Family and the young men of Ars. Antoine Givre had the privilege of walking directly behind the coffin. It was Antoine who guided the Curé to the village of Ars some forty-one years earlier, when the Curé had become lost in the fog and asked him for directions. Thousands of people lined both sides of the streets and knelt down as the coffin passed. Six thousand people and three hundred priests attended the Curé's funeral.

John Marie Vianney, the Curé of Ars, was canonized by Pope Pius XI in Rome in 1925. In 1929, the pope honored him in a profound way by naming him the patron saint of parish priests throughout the world. His feast day is celebrated on August 4.

Never let us put aside the thought of our ultimate aim. And what is this ultimate aim? To know God, principally, is why he conceived our days, our years. Therefore, let us try never to forget this ultimate aim, for everything depends on it. And for what reason? To serve him with faith, with love, and with constancy. Let us try to excel in all of this, then. Since God created us for love, he takes care of us for love, and for love he has promised us the prize.
-St. Pio of Pietrelcina

Chapter 3

Saint Damien of Molokai

Joseph de Veuster (Father Damien) was born on January 3, 1840 in Tremelo, Belgium. His parents, Joannes and Anne Catherine, were devout Catholics who earned their living by farming. They raised and sold grain and were quite successful at it.

Joannes and Anne Catherine de Veuster were the parents of eight children. Joseph, the future Father Damien, was the next to the last child. He and his brother Auguste both became priests. Joseph's sisters, Eugenie and Pauline became nuns in the Ursuline Order while his other three siblings - Leonce, Gerard, and Constance all married. His sister Mary died when she was fourteen years old.

At seven years of age, Joseph started attending elementary school. His teacher found him to be very bright and very capable. At thirteen years of age, Joseph was taken out of school to help on the family farm. He worked with his father in the fields, took care of the animals, planted, harvested, drove the wagon and worked in the orchard. He had great physical strength and endurance and seemed especially suited to the work.

People who lived in Tremelo remembered that as an adolescent, Joseph was always generous and helpful to others. When called upon, he would stay through the night with a neighbor's sick cow and was glad to do it. If one of Joseph's classmates was hungry, he would insist on giving him his lunch. From his youth, he had a natural instinct to be concerned about the needs and the well-being of others.

When Joseph was eighteen years old, his father Joannes sent him to college in Braine le Comte to study French. Joseph would need to be proficient in French in order to help with the grain trading side of their farming business. Joannes wanted to ensure the future of the family business and was counting on his son's help. During the time that Joseph was in college, he began to feel a calling to the priesthood.

With his parents' permission, Joseph entered the novitiate of the Congregation of the Sacred Hearts of Jesus and Mary in Louvain, Belgium. He was in the same religious house as his brother Auguste who had taken the name Pamphile once he entered the Order. The Congregation promoted devotion to the Sacred Heart of Jesus and the Immaculate Heart of Mary. It also promoted adoration of the Blessed Sacrament. Adoration took place twenty-four hours a day in all of the Congregation's religious houses.

At the time of his first vows, Joseph took the name Damien, after the ancient physician St. Damien, who cared for the sick and infirm and was later martyred. Damien was easy going, hard-working and had a winning personality. He was known for his good sense of humor and was well-liked by his fellow students. His brothers in religion called him "big, good natured Damien." He prayed daily to St. Francis Xavier, patron of missionaries, to be sent to the missions.

In 1863, when the Congregation of the Sacred Hearts decided to seek out volunteers for its mission in the Hawaiian Islands, six men stepped forward to offer their services. Pamphile was one of the six who volunteered but he became ill with typhus fever and was unable to make the trip. Damien wrote to the Superior General in Paris and asked permission to take his brother's place and his request was granted. Damien made the voyage with five other religious brothers and ten nuns of the Sacred Hearts Congregation.

The trip by boat from Bremerhaven, Germany took five months. Damien arrived in Hawaii on March 19th, 1864, and was ordained to the priesthood just two months later at the Cathedral of Our Lady of Peace in Honolulu. He was twenty-four years old.

Father Damien's first priestly assignment was to missionary work in the Puna district on the big island of Hawaii. Father Clement Evrard, who had been ordained at the same time as Father Damien was assigned to the much larger Kohala and Hamakua districts on the same island. Bishop Louis Maigret, the Apostolic Vicar of the Honolulu diocese, traveled with the two new priests on an inter-island steamer in order to escort them to their first assignment.

For seven years, no priest had lived among the 350 Catholics in Puna. Father Damien's initial tour through his district took weeks. There were no roads in the primitive area and the villages were separated by great distances. Father Damien traveled on horseback with a pack mule trailing behind as he journeyed from one small Christian community to the next. He carried a collapsible altar for Mass as well as church supplies on the back of the pack mule.

Father Damien found the Hawaiian people to be very gentle and very hospitable. When he visited families in his mission territory, he was usually invited to the evening meal. Inside the thatched hut, Father Damien joined the family and sat cross-legged with them in a circle on the floor. Family members took turns dipping their fingers into a large bowl of poi and enjoying a hearty meal. No plates, forks or spoons were necessary. Father Damien adapted easily to the Hawaiian customs and participated fully in the lives of his parishioners.

Energetic and healthy, Father Damien could easily trek through the rough volcanic terrain, hike through lava fields and maneuver through valleys, mountains, rain forests and deep ravines in order to reach his parishioners. Because he had diligently studied the Hawaiian language, he was able to speak it fluently. He built chapels from the wood of mango and breadfruit trees, taught catechism and called the people together for Mass with a conch shell.

The two districts of Kohala and Hamakua where Father Clement served, were twice the size of Father Damien's district.

While Father Damien was strong and robust, Father Clement had a weak constitution and it wasn't long before he became unable to perform the physically taxing work in his districts. The isolation of his life as a missionary was also taking a toll on him and he felt a deepening sense of loneliness and depression. He asked his superior if it might be possible to switch districts with Father Damien. He had confidence that he would be able to manage the smaller district of Puna. Less than a year after the appointments, Bishop Maigret allowed the two missionaries to exchange mission fields.

In the Kohala and Hamakua districts, Father Damien had approximately 1000 Catholics in his charge. He had a small home-based church with a rectory attached for his living quarters but he was hardly ever there. In his vast district, he was nearly always traveling. When summoned, he would gladly get on his horse and go on a sick call that was twenty or twenty-five miles away.

During the eight years that Father Damien spent in Kohala and Hamakua, he was almost always involved in a building project of one sort or another. He built attractive chapels for the Catholics in both districts. Because he loved carpentry work and enjoyed manual labor, he found great satisfaction in constructing the chapels.

In Puna, Father Damien often saw another priest every ten days, but in his new districts, he went three months at a time without seeing another clergy member. Just like Father Clement, Father Damien experienced the loneliness of his missionary assignment. He asked his superiors to send another priest to the Kohala and Hamakua districts so that he could have a companion and a fellow-worker in the field, but they said they did not have an extra one to send.

On one occasion, Father Damien was making plans to take a canoe to visit one of the Catholic communities in a remote area of his district. For safety's sake, he had to wait for a day when the sea was calm before he could embark on the trip. Knowing that the journey could be hazardous, he made an act of contrition and prayed for protection before leaving. He took two boatmen with him.

On the way, the canoe, which was nothing more than a hollowed-out tree, capsized and the three men had to swim to shore. Fortunately, they were all good swimmers and no one was hurt. Father Damien had tied his small suitcase to the canoe so he was able to recover his possessions. Not wanting to attempt another canoe trip to the village, he decided on an alternative plan. He hiked for part of the way, climbing the rough and steep terrain in a mountainous region. He rode on his pack mule for part of the way and he swam part of the way. Four days later, he finally arrived at his destination to the surprise and delight of the small Christian community who had not been visited by a priest in four years.

On another occasion, when Father Damien was about fifteen miles from home, the mule that was carrying him suddenly broke into a run. Try as he might, Father Damien was not able to slow the mule down or gain control of him. The mule finally came to a complete stop in the middle of a herd of wild cattle.

Night was falling and Father Damien was in a dilemma. He had gotten turned around while trying to regain control of his mule and he could no longer distinguish the direction home. He was hungry, cold and soaking wet as he contemplated what he should do. In the distance he heard a dog barking, so he decided to follow the sound. He finally arrived at the simple hut of a kind Hawaiian couple who offered him food and lodging for the night.

In the 1860's, an epidemic of leprosy swept through the islands of Hawaii. It was a disease that was contagious, incurable and fatal. On January 3, 1865, King Kamehameha V signed into law the "Act to Prevent the Spread of Leprosy." It was decreed that segregation and quarantine of those infected with the disease was the only way to stop the spread.

Individuals who had leprosy were ordered to step forward and make themselves known to the authorities. Those who were suspected of having the disease were transported to Honolulu and examined by a government physician at the Kalihi Hospital, the temporary holding facility for those suspected of having leprosy. Individuals at the Kalihi Hospital who were found to be afflicted with the disease were sent to the leper settlement of Kalawao on the island of Molokai.

There were terrible and tragic scenes at the Honolulu waterfront when those who had been diagnosed with leprosy were forced to say goodbye to their families forever and to board the steamer to Molokai. Families clutched their loved ones in their arms and wept. Once on board the ship, there were heartbreaking and inconsolable cries of despair.

Government officials knew they had instituted very severe measures in dealing with the epidemic but they felt they had no other recourse. Some of the lepers resisted by arming themselves with weapons. One man who feared he would be banished to Molokai, shot and wounded Dr. George Trousseau, the examining physician at the Kalihi Hospital.

Many refused to hand over their relatives and friends who had leprosy to government officials. They did not want their loved ones to die alone in some faraway place but to spend their last days surrounded by their family. On many occasions, the police had to intervene and use force to remove lepers from their homes. In addition, the police hunted down those who were hiding in the cane fields, ravines and underground caves. They set their bloodhounds loose to track down those who were evading them.

Leprosy or Hansen's Disease as it is known today, attacks the peripheral nervous system. The leprosy bacillus is transmitted through breathing, coughing, and sneezing and is absorbed through the respiratory tract or through open wounds on the skin. The disease has been described as a "slow crucifixion" and the skin lesions and deformities that result can be very disfiguring. Historically, individuals who were infected with the disease were considered outcasts to be shunned and feared.

When Father Damien served as a missionary in the Hawaiian Islands, little was known about leprosy. Regarding the origin and transmission of the disease, there were only theories. The first breakthrough did not take place until the 1940's when the drug *dapsone*, an antibiotic, became available to successfully treat the disease.

The leper settlement of Kalawao was situated on the north side of the island of Molokai. Bounded on three sides by rough seas and on the fourth by towering two-thousand-foot cliffs, the settlement was like a natural prison. For those who were sent there, no escape was possible. The rest of the island was sparsely populated. Molokai was considered the most forlorn of the seven inhabited Hawaiian Islands which included Oahu, Maui, Kauai, Hawaii, Lanai and Niihau.

Molokai was called the "land of great cliffs" and was considered a perfect spot on which to assure the isolation and seclusion of the lepers. It was often described as a paradise, complete with graceful tropical trees, white sandy beaches, a majestic ocean and an over-arching blue sky. When compared to the other Hawaiian Islands, Molokai had some of the most beautiful and spectacular scenery of all.

With only a few possessions, the lepers were forced to board the steamer in Honolulu which then sailed to the small peninsula of Kalaupapa on the tip of Molokai. They were then taken ashore in rowboats.

Dr. J.H. Stallard, a member of the College of Physicians in England, made a visit to Molokai and observed that when the steamer dropped the lepers off at the Kalaupapa landing wharf, they were simply "dumped" on the shore and left to fend for themselves. He wrote a highly critical report and condemned the Hawaiian government for gross neglect.

From Kalaupapa, it was a two-and-a-half-mile walk to the remote Kalawao leper settlement. When the lepers reached the settlement, there was no one there to receive them or care for them and no shelters to protect them from the elements. The lepers built themselves primitive huts by making frameworks of branches and tree roots to which they attached wild grass and sugar cane leaves.

Molokai had a humid and tropical climate in the summer but was chilly and rainswept in the winter. Strong trade winds often blew down the grass huts and left the people without shelter. They would then huddle between the large boulders on the island trying to protect themselves from the cold. In general, the lepers had a life expectancy of less than five years after arrival at the Kalawao settlement.

Molokai was known as a graveyard, a place of anarchy, a death camp. There were no police to maintain order. Visits from a doctor were rare and no real efforts were being made to provide medical care for the lepers. Relatives of the lepers were banned from making the trip to Molokai to visit. The lepers frequently wrote letters to their friends and relatives back home but never received any replies. They later learned that the letters were never delivered. They had the impression that the authorities simply threw the letters away.

There was no school for the children to attend and no activities to pass the time. Lepers who were unable` to care for themselves were often abandoned and left to die alone. As one observer said, "There was no doctor, no priest, no work, no comfort, and no hope." The lepers were at the settlement to die and they knew it. Some considered them already legally dead.

Bishop Maigret was wrestling with the problems at the leper settlement in Molokai. There were six hundred lepers confined there and two hundred of them were Catholics. The extreme sadness of the situation continually weighed on his mind.

Bishop Maigret felt a responsibility to the lepers who were pleading with him to send them a priest. He was well-aware of the danger of exposure to the deadly disease for any priest who might serve on Molokai. Working at the isolated settlement would be difficult, dangerous and lonely. It would also be a potential death sentence. Bishop Maigret decided that he could not ask any of his priests to make such a sacrifice.

May 4, 1873 was the date that the beautiful St. Anthony's Church in Wailuku, Maui was going to be consecrated by Bishop Maigret. St. Anthony's had taken six years to build. Bishop Maigret invited the Sacred Hearts missionaries from neighboring islands to join him on May 4 for the consecration of the new church. Father Damien took what he believed to be a short leave of absence from his assignment in the Kohala District and boarded an inter-island steamer for Maui. While on the steamer, he had a very strong feeling, almost like a premonition, that he would never return to Kohala again.

After the dedication, Bishop Maigret gathered the priests together for a general meeting. He talked about the wretched conditions at the leprosy settlement of Kalawao on the island of Molokai. It had been in existence for seven years. He explained that he had received repeated requests from the lepers who lived there to send a priest who would be able to stay with them on a permanent basis. He had recently received a petition signed by two hundred Catholic lepers, begging for a priest. They were living and dying without the sacraments in the most awful physical and spiritual misery imaginable.

There were many devout lepers on the island of Molokai who wanted to attend Mass on Sundays as well as go to confession regularly. They stated that seeing a visiting priest once a year was not sufficient. They wanted a priest who would be with them on a full-time basis. When death approached, they wanted to receive the Last Rites and to have a Catholic funeral and burial. As far as Bishop Maigret was concerned, no one in the Hawaiian Islands needed a pastor more than the poor, sick and dying lepers at Molokai.

As the discussion continued at the meeting, four priests volunteered to go to Molokai. One of the priests proposed that visitations to the leper settlement be made on a rotation basis. Each of the four priests would serve for a period of three months. Bishop Maigret approved of the plan, but on condition that there would be no physical contact with the lepers. They were not to eat food prepared by a leper, shake hands with a leper or sleep in a leper's house. It was decided that Father Damien would be the first to go.

Father Damien and Bishop Maigret set sail for Molokai that very week. The steamer that they were traveling on was carrying a group of fifty lepers as well as cattle to the settlement. Because he had not anticipated a change in his priestly assignment, Father Damien did not have a suitcase or even a change of clothing with him. He had only his breviary and a crucifix.

Bishop Maigret and Father Damien landed on Molokai on May 10, 1873. Two hundred Catholic lepers were assembled on the shore at the Kalaupapa landing wharf waiting to greet them. Many were horribly disfigured and had festering and running sores on their bodies which gave off a terrible stench. It was the suffocating smell of rotting human flesh. Nevertheless, the happiness and excitement of receiving their own resident priest showed on every leper's face. With great joy, they thanked Bishop Maigret again and again for bringing Father Damien to them.

Bishop Maigret spoke comforting words to the lepers and introduced Father Damien to them saying, "I have brought you one who will be a father to you." At the time, no one knew how true the bishop's words would prove to be. Bishop Maigret was overcome with emotion as he looked at the assembly of lepers who stood before him. He felt the tragedy of their situation yet tried to hide his sadness.

Before returning to Honolulu, Bishop Maigret emphasized to Father Damien the importance of taking every precaution to protect himself from the disease. He reminded Father Damien not to join in meals with the lepers or to shake hands with them. "Damien, do not touch any of the lepers, please. Promise me that you will not touch anyone!" Bishop Maigret said emphatically.

Father Damien was thirty-three years old with nine years of experience as a missionary in the Hawaiian Islands to his credit. Father Damien's work at the Kalawao settlement in Molokai began the very day he arrived. He visited with every leper on the island and extended a personal invitation to attend Mass each morning at St. Philomena church as well as to stay for the catechism lesson at the conclusion of Mass. He encouraged everyone to come back at the end of the day for Evening Prayer. St. Philomena church had been built in 1872, one year before Father Damien arrived.

Within ten days of being at the settlement, Father Damien was approached by twenty lepers who asked to receive instructions in the Catholic faith. He would prepare all who had made the request for full communion into the Church. For those who were Chinese, he gave religious instruction through an interpreter. By the third week of his stay at the settlement, he had performed thirty baptisms.

During Mass, the odor from the open wounds and rotting flesh of the poor afflicted people filled the small church of St. Philomena with a terrible stench. It caused Father Damien to feel nauseated and he feared that he would gag if he tried to swallow the Holy Communion wafer and the consecrated wine. On one occasion, the stench became so unbearable that Father Damien had the overwhelming urge to run out of the church in the middle of Mass. He forced himself to stay until the end of Mass.

Just one week after his arrival in Molokai, Father Damien wrote to the provincial, Father Modeste Favens, and asked him to send him some shirts, pants and shoes as well as a bell and altar breads for Mass and some catechism books. He asked Father Modeste to send the items quickly because the lepers were arriving in Molokai "by the boatloads."

Father Damien also told Father Modeste that he wanted to remain permanently at the settlement. He believed that priests serving at the settlement on a three-month rotation basis would be far less effective than a permanent pastor. If he was allowed to stay on a permanent basis, he would be able to develop a strong relationship with those confined to the settlement. Gaining their confidence and trust, he would be in a better position to help them. He wrote, "You know my availability. I would like to sacrifice myself for the poor lepers."

After careful consideration, Father Modeste granted Father Damien the permission to stay. Knowing how important it was to Father Damien to go to confession regularly, Father Modeste assured him that he could take the steamer to Honolulu and stay overnight whenever he wanted to make his confession.

For a number of weeks, Father Damien slept outdoors under a pandanus tree. He had no protection from the wind, rain, tree rats, scorpions, centipedes and other poisonous insects. His only other option was to share a hut with a leper and he would not do that. Bishop Maigret had repeatedly and emphatically warned him to avoid close physical contact with the lepers.

Father Damien was solicitous in the beginning about taking every precaution to protect himself from the disease. He prepared his own food in the open air and used a flat rock as a table. As soon as the steamer brought a supply of lumber, he planned to build himself a small cabin. He also planned to build wooden cottages for the lepers to replace the squalid grass huts they were living in.

Right after Father Damien arrived at the settlement, a Honolulu newspaper published an article about him. The article stated that Father Damien had volunteered to go to "the island of the doomed" and had become Molokai's first resident pastor. The article went on to say that he had gone to the settlement without even a change of clothes and he was sleeping outside in the open air. "We care not what this man's theology may be, he is certainly a Christian hero," the article stated.

The impact the newspaper article made on the people of Hawaii was profound. Almost immediately, a collection was taken up and sent to Father Damien. Although he was not aware of it, in less than one week, he had become famous throughout the Hawaiian Islands. A month later, newspaper reports about Father Damien were published in European and American newspapers.

Father Damien wrote a letter to his brother Pamphile giving him an update on his work in Molokai. He told him that the lepers looked on him as a father, "a father and a friend." Damien also wrote to his mother and said, "I'm very happy with my lepers and wouldn't want to be separated from them for anything in the world." Damien hoped that his brother could someday join him at the settlement.

While in Molokai, Father Damien received a letter from one of his parishioners in Kohala. He thanked Father Damien for the countless ways he had improved the lives of the people in Kohala. He also wrote that since Father Damien had left as their pastor, conditions had deteriorated in many ways. All felt his absence and missed his presence.

One of Father Damien's immediate concerns was the food crisis on Molokai. The food that was brought by steamer from Honolulu was of a poor quality and was not sufficient to feed the large population at the settlement. In addition, the shipments of food were irregular. In stormy weather, when the turbulent seas prevented the boat from landing at the wharf in Kalaupapa, a food shortage throughout the settlement resulted. As a consequence, the lepers suffered from hunger and malnutrition. Father Damien had plans to build a storehouse to hold emergency food supplies for the times when the food did not arrive as scheduled.

The Board of Health initially thought that the lepers would raise their own crops and become a self-sufficient community. There was plenty of land on the island to do just that. But the fact was that at the Kalawao settlement, nobody worked. Many of the lepers were too sick to work and others had lost all hope and refused to work, feeling that their lives did not matter anymore, and in a sense, were already over.

Father Damien wrote numerous letters to the Board of Health in Honolulu asking for an adequate supply of food as well as clothing for the settlement. Fifty cents per week was allowed for each leper for food. Not even a tenth of the lepers were able to have a small daily supply of milk. Only those in Molokai's makeshift hospital received milk on a regular basis. Father Damien felt that the lepers needed the protein and the nutrition that milk supplied in order to maintain their strength.

Father Damien asked the Board of Health for a small daily supply of milk for each leper on the island and proposed an increase of dairy cows to one thousand head of cattle in order to supply the needed milk. He also asked for building materials so that he could build shelters for the lepers. Sometimes he requested, sometimes he entreated, sometimes he begged, sometimes he pleaded, and sometimes he demanded action from the Board of Health.

Each year, the men at the settlement received one pair of pants and one shirt while the women received one shirt and one dress from the Hawaiian Board of Health. Those who did not have a relative or a friend to provide an extra suit of clothing for the winter, suffered from the cold weather. Father Damien asked the Board of Health to increase the clothing allowance of the lepers from six dollars to ten dollars a year.

During his first months at Molokai, Father Damien returned to Honolulu twice. On one occasion, he traveled there in order to make his confession and on another occasion, he visited the Sacred Hearts Sisters in Honolulu on a quest for used clothing and blankets. He was happy to receive a large supply of both. He also asked the Sisters for food to take back to the lepers and was given a good supply.

The Hawaiian Board of Health was aware of Father Damien's two trips to Honolulu and they did not approve. They informed him that he was breaking the quarantine laws and he could no longer leave the settlement for any reason. Absolutely no exceptions could be made. Even though he did not have leprosy, the Board of Health was afraid that he could spread the disease due to his constant exposure to it.

Father Damien received an official letter signed by the Minister of the Interior forbidding him to leave the island. He was warned that if he did so, he would be arrested and imprisoned. In addition, no members of his religious congregation or anyone else for that matter would be allowed to go to the Kalawao settlement to visit him. Father Damien felt that the order was unjust and he was angry about it. The idea of never seeing the members of his religious congregation again or of making his confession was too much to bear. Furthermore, he was not afflicted with leprosy and he posed no danger to others. He told the Board of Health that he would travel to Honolulu whenever he pleased and there was nothing that they could do about it.

Four months after Father Damien took up residency in Molokai, the provincial, Father Modeste Favens was traveling between islands on the inter-island steamer. He knew that Father Damien had a great desire to make his confession and he wanted to give him that opportunity. He was also looking forward to having a visit with him.

When the steamer anchored at the landing wharf at Kalaupapa with cattle to drop off, Father Modeste prepared to go ashore. The captain told him that he had orders not to let him do so and that he would be arrested if he did not obey.

Father Damien got in a row boat and rowed out alongside the steamer but the captain would not let him on board. Father Damien knelt down in the row boat and shouted out his confession in French and was able to receive absolution from Father Modeste. People on the steamer stood on the deck and watched the strange incident with curiosity. Nevertheless, it was a humiliating experience for Father Damien and one of the many sacrifices that he was called to make in his life as a missionary.

Father Aubert Bouillon, one of the Sacred Hearts Fathers who served in Maui, worried about Father Damien's isolation and his loneliness. He decided to pay him a short visit. He changed out of his clerical garb, donned a straw hat and tied a red handkerchief around his neck and arrived in Kalawao in the middle of the night. He stayed only one day at the settlement. Father Damien was delighted to see his friend and the two priests had a wonderful reunion.

Father Aubert was certain that no one had noticed his presence at the settlement, but he was wrong. Right after he returned to Maui, the police came to his door informing him that a complaint had been filed against him. He had broken the quarantine laws by visiting Molokai and the incident had been reported to the Board of Health.

Bishop Maigret had been informed that the Board of Health had threatened to arrest Father Damien if he left the island and he was angry about it. Bishop Maigret spoke to the French Consul who then contacted the Minister of Foreign Affairs about the matter. As a consequence, Father Damien's freedom was restored, but only for a time.

The shortage of water on Molokai was one of the many crucial challenges that Father Damien faced. The lepers had to walk over a mile to the Waialeia Valley in order to obtain water and then hand-carry it back to the settlement in tins. Many were too ill to walk the distance and were drinking from a stagnant pool of water. A sufficient supply of water was also needed for wound care. The open skin ulcers of the lepers were exposed to dirt and flies and needed to be regularly cleaned and bandaged in order to prevent infection.

Father Damien mapped out his plans for the water system and asked the Hawaiian Board of Health to supply the water pipes. He and the more able-bodied lepers would provide all of the labor. With Father Damien's expertise, the reservoir was built and the water pipes were laid from the spring in the Waialeia Valley to the perimeters of the settlement. It provided fresh water for the eight hundred lepers who lived on Molokai. Not only was there enough water for everyone to drink, people could now bathe and wash their clothes as well. The water was also channeled to irrigate the fields since Father Damien planned to grow sweet potatoes and other crops as a back-up food source for the times when the steamer failed to deliver food to the island. The lepers who had been banished to the Kalawao settlement on Molokai had to deal with the boredom and idleness of their existence. There was nowhere to go and nothing to do. They passed their time playing cards, sleeping, dancing the hula, gambling and drinking *ki* which was made from the roots of a local plant. The *ki* root was cooked, fermented and distilled, making it a highly intoxicating liquor.

On Molokai, those who were stronger took advantage of the weaker ones. Robbery, rape, physical assaults and child abuse were all too common and drunken midnight orgies were prevalent. "Aole kanawai ma reia wahi" (In this place there is no law) was the common slogan at the Kalawao settlement.

Father Damien patrolled the settlement on a daily basis. Whenever he heard the sound of the uli-uli, the large gourd that was used as a drum, he would head in that direction. It was a signal that that the party was beginning, with plentiful *ki* for everyone.

Father Damien broke up the wild parties and the fights, often using his heavy walking stick to smash containers of home-brewed alcohol that the lepers tried to hide from him. One man said that Father Damien was the best policeman he had ever seen.

Because Father Damien was a member of the clergy, the lepers would not dare resist him when he confronted them. During the many years that he lived at the Kalawao settlement, he was never once accosted or attacked. He was respected and looked upon as the strongest moral authority on the island.

In addition to his many other endeavors, Father Damien dedicated much of his time to working in Kalawao's makeshift hospital. The hospital at the settlement was dark and dingy and sheltered those who were so ill that they could no longer care for themselves. The hospital had no doctors, no nurses, no beds and no medicine. Father Damien was determined to obtain medicine for those confined to the hospital as well as basic medicines for others who had various complaints like fever, pain, and diarrhea.

The hospital was damp and drafty and the roof leaked. The patients slept on thin mats on the hard, volcanic earth. Moreover, there were not enough blankets to keep the patients warm at night. During winter, the wind whistled through the cracks in the door. There were two tiny windows but they were too small to let in the light.

Conditions improved greatly when William Williamson, a leper, arrived to help Father Damien. William Williamson had been a doctor's assistant at the Kalihi Hospital on the island of Oahu when he was diagnosed with leprosy and sent to Molokai. William joined Father Damien in his work at the hospital and taught him many important nursing skills. He showed Father Damien how to apply salves and ointments, clean and bandage sores, sterilize wounds and even perform amputations.

Father Damien carried a thick black medical book around with him called *The Household Physician* and he studied it whenever he had the chance. He even did his own scientific research, hoping to find a cure for leprosy or at least a way to halt the progress of the disease.

Father Damien suffered from headaches when he worked in the hospital because of the stench that came from the patients' wounds and he found it very helpful to smoke a pipe in order to mask the horrible odor. He noticed that the graveyard at the settlement gave off the same suffocating stench.

William Williamson observed that Father Damien possessed a natural talent in caring for the sick. He bathed the patients, washed their linens and did everything he could to make them more comfortable. He would sit beside them and talk with them for hours, bringing them small gifts and good food to eat. In this environment of pain and even horror, Father Damien had a remarkable ability to comfort and console the patients. He even joked with them, to bring a smile to their faces.

Father Damien also made weekly visits to the sick who were confined to their homes. It took him four or five days each week to complete the sick calls. His pockets were always loaded with sedatives, remedies, Chinese medicine, pain pills, salves and any experimental drug he might be in possession of. Father Damien organized the Christian Burial Association at Molokai so that each leper who died could have a dignified and respectful burial. The Association also arranged a funeral with a Requiem Mass at St. Philomena parish. It was not unusual for Father Damien to preside at ten funerals a week. The excellent church choir sang at every funeral and flags were flown in tribute to the deceased. The funerals were marked by great religious solemnity and those who served on the Christian Burial Association considered it a privilege.

After the funeral, there was a procession to the cemetery led by the band which played the drum, flute, guitar and other instruments. Dressed in black, the women and girls walked behind the coffin. One group wore red scarves and one group wore white scarves, depending on which burial association they were a part of.

Father Damien ordered a wooden cross from Honolulu to be placed in the cemetery as well as several bundles of pickets. He built a picket fence around the cemetery in order to protect the graves from roaming pigs and other predators.

Every year, the steamer brought ten to twenty leper children between the ages of eight and fifteen years old to Molokai unaccompanied by their parents. They had no family members in Molokai to protect them from harm and were orphans in the true sense of the word. The policy of the government was to place the orphaned children in foster homes with adult lepers. It was not uncommon for the children to be sexually exploited. Many of them were used almost like slave labor and were made to clean, cook, and take care of the animals. As the children became more and more disfigured by their disease, the adults often threw them out of the house to fend for themselves.

To ensure the protection of the children, Father Damien built two orphanages, one for the boys and one for the girls. The orphanages proved to be a great success. The children were truly happy and thrived in their new environment. Many of the orphans still in foster care begged to be housed in the orphanage.

The expenses of the orphanage put a terrible strain on Father Damien's budget which was already stretched to the limit. He had to use creative ways to find the money to keep the orphanage operating. He raised sweet potatoes and cabbages which he sold in order to meet his expenses. Those who did the cooking and cleaning at the orphanage were paid for their services. Father Damien wanted to be able to pay them on time but it was often difficult to do so.

Father Damien sent the bishop a hand-written list with the names of all the orphans on it, stating that he had adopted them. He wanted to make sure that they would never go into foster care again. In his letter, he asked the bishop for financial help for the orphans and said, "I take the liberty of submitting to your Excellency the list of my orphan children whom I have adopted, begging you to help me to the measure of your resources in procuring for them what they need."

Father Léonor Fouesnel replied to the letter that Father Damien had sent to the bishop. He told Father Damien that no financial help would be sent for the orphans. He informed him that the needs of the orphans were the responsibility of the Board of Health and not the Catholic Missions. He accused Father Damien of exaggerating the harsh conditions at Molokai in an attempt to procure money.

Father Léonor never understood the great needs of the settlement. Father Damien wanted him to make a visitation to Molokai so he could see for himself the desperate situation of the lepers. Father Léonor would not consider it because he had a great fear of catching the disease.

When Father Damien contacted the Board of Health asking for help with expenses related to the children in the orphanage, they responded with the same cold reply that Father Léonor had. They informed him that their budget did not allow for assistance to the orphans and they let him know that his request for an increase in food and clothing for the needs of the entire settlement would not be granted either.

As time went on, the number of children at the settlement kept increasing. Father Damien tried to be both mother and father to them, and by all accounts he succeeded in an extraordinary way. In his spare time, he made wooden toys for them which they loved to play with. They also loved foot races, kite flying and playing marbles.

Father Damien truly considered the children that he had adopted to be his family. He took his meals with them as often as he could and also provided for their religious education. He supplemented their diet with fruits and vegetables from his own garden and eggs from his chicken coop.

Father Damien wanted the children at the settlement to have fulfilled and happy lives even though they were all living with a terminal illness. He also wanted them to get an education. He built two schools for the orphans, one for the boys and one for the girls and hired teachers who were paid a small salary for their services.

As part of the curriculum, the children learned to play musical instruments, many of which had been sent as gifts from well-wishers and some that Father Damien had made himself. Band practice was held every week. In addition, the boys were taught simple farming methods and the girls were taught cooking and sewing.

Father Damien called the orphans "my boys" and "my girls." Some of the orphans had been born at the settlement but their parents had died. Others had been abandoned by their parents who did not want them. Still others had come all alone on the steamer to Molokai from Honolulu after being examined by a government physician at the Kalihi hospital.

Joseph Manu, one of the orphans who lived at the settlement, was prone to getting into mischief on a regular basis. When Father Damien got a bad report about Joseph, he would take him aside to talk to him. To assure Joseph that there were no hard feelings, it wasn't long before Father Damien would reach into his pocket and hand him a piece of candy.

Joseph Manu often went with Father Damien to other parts of the island by boat. Before they got into the boat, Father Damien led a prayer for safe travel and when they came ashore, he asked Joseph to join in prayer with him once again. Joseph and the other children at the settlement saw Father Damien praying many times throughout the day.

Many people felt that the greatest work Father Damien did at the Kalawao settlement was what he did for the children. Some of the adults at Molokai who felt isolated and friendless, were aware of the happiness and contentment of the children who lived in the orphanage. They asked for permission to live in the orphan-age as well and Father Damien allowed some of them to do so.

When the orphans succumbed to their illness and died, Father Damien made their coffins with his own hands, dug their graves and lowered their coffins into the ground. He made the coffins for the adults at the settlement as well. Previously, the lepers who died at the Kalawao settlement were simply wrapped in a blanket and buried in the ground.

New leprosy victims generally arrived in Molokai every week. Whenever Damien heard the sound of the steamer, he fetched his horse William and loaded his buggy with blankets, hot food and coffee and headed toward the landing wharf at Kalaupapa. He stood at the shore and waited to greet each boatload of new arrivals. When they got to the settlement in Kalawao, Father Damien made arrangements for their lodging.

In addition to his many duties at the Kalawao settlement, Father Damien somehow found the time to build beautiful churches on the island of Molokai. It was a work that he loved and that he had a special talent for. He built Our Lady, Health of the Sick parish in Kalaupapa and later enlarged it. He also built St. Joseph parish in Kamalo, on Molokai's south shore.

Our Lady of Seven Sorrows parish which served the non-leper population in Kaluaaha, on the south side of Molokai, was considered one of Father Damien's finest architectural works. Built by the seaside, Our Lady of Seven Sorrows with its fifty-four-foot bell tower stood like a white silhouette against the emerald cliffs. People who visited the parish were awestruck by its beauty. Sunlight streamed in through the gothic windows, adding to the transcendent quality of the church.

Father Damien had been able to build Our Lady of Seven Sorrows on a very small budget and he built it in a surprisingly short period of time. He complained that he did not have the proper tools for the construction due to lack of funds. He had to make do with what was available but it did not appear to hinder what he had been able to achieve.

One priest who visited Our Lady of Seven Sorrows considered it an architectural masterpiece and was so stunned by its beauty that he wrote a letter to the bishop of Honolulu saying, "The church of Our Lady of Seven Sorrows is beautiful, truly beautiful. There are many parishes in Europe which do not have the like; the architect has surpassed his masters."

Father Damien was not only a master craftsman and builder of outstanding churches, he proved to be a true jack of all trades. At Molokai, he was a carpenter, farmer, mason, painter, gardener, school teacher, recreational director, housekeeper, pipe layer, undertaker, and gravedigger. To the lepers, Father Damien was their advocate, their confessor, their spiritual director, their priest, their doctor, their nurse, their father and their friend.

Word was sent to Father Damien that her Royal Highness, Princess Liliuokalani, the future Queen of the Kingdom of Hawaii was making plans to visit the leper settlement in Molokai. Hawaiians everywhere had a great love for their princess and with great joy, preparations were made for her arrival. Daily rehearsals were held for her special welcoming ceremony while

Father Damien and his helpers were busy whitewashing and cleaning every structure at the settlement.

The princess landed on Kalaupapa to the cheers of eight hundred lepers who stood on the beach and waved banners to welcome her as the band played the National Anthem of Hawaii. All of the lepers who were strong enough to walk to the landing were there to greet her, dressed in their very best and adorned with fresh flower leis.

Princess Liliuokalani arrived with her sister, Princess Likelike, the premier, Honorable Kapena, ladies in waiting, army officers, members of the Board of Health, and a number of journalists. Wearing a stately black dress with a long train, the princess passed under triumphal arches, escorted by a large number of lepers on horseback who wore red and black military-like uniforms.

Meanwhile, children from the settlement scattered flowers along the path of the procession. A choir of young girls in white dresses with bright red and blue sashes sang for the princess. They had been practicing for weeks. Some of the girls tried to conceal their hands which had festering sores and missing fingers. Others tried to turn their heads at an angle so that the disfigurement of their faces would not be noticed by the princess.

Father Damien then accompanied Princess Liliuokalani on the two-and-a-half-mile walk from Kalaupapa to the leper settlement at Kalawao. The princess was interested in seeing everything at the settlement. She was taken on a tour of St. Philomena parish, the free store, the whitewashed houses, each now complete with a wooden floor, the two orphanages and the rectory. Father Damien did not want to show her the hospital, thinking that it would be too shocking, but she insisted. An effort was made to usher her through the hospital quickly, but the trauma of seeing so many of the dying left its mark. She was not able to recover from the sadness that never left her for the rest of the day.

After the tour, the princess was led to a flower-decorated pavilion where the girls' choir sang for her once again. The princess then rose to make her speech. She told the people how proud she was of all of them and how brave they were in coping with their illness. Heartbroken at the plight of the lepers, the princess wept openly and was not able to finish the speech she had prepared. The premier, Honorable Kapena, stepped forward and read the rest of it for her.

As Princess Liliuokalani was departing, the entire community of lepers gathered on the shore and sang cherished Hawaiian songs to her while lepers with lighted torches stood at attention. Others carried lighted kukui nuts bound in ti leaves according to the long-standing tradition of honoring the royal family.

After the visit, Princess Liliuokalani returned to her palace in Honolulu and called a meeting of the King's cabinet. She reported on the details of her visit and was able to set in motion many relief measures for the settlement. She also wanted Father Damien to receive royal recognition for the important work he was doing. He received the highest honor in the Kingdom of Hawaii, the title of Knight Commander of the Royal Order of Kalakaua and was given a jeweled medal and decree signed by King David Kalakaua.

The Hawaiian press published the story of the royal visit as well as the great honor Father Damien had received from the King. Other countries reported on it as well. Although he never desired it, Father Damien was on his way to becoming an international star, a worldwide celebrity. Donations and gifts began to arrive at the settlement in abundance, sent by individuals, philanthropic institutions, and religious organizations worldwide.

Princess Liliuokalani asked the new apostolic vicar, Bishop Hermann Koeckemann to deliver the medal personally to Father Damien. Bishop Koeckemann, who had succeeded Bishop Maigret upon the latter's retirement, had a fear of leprosy. He had never been to Molokai and never intended to go there. He wanted Father Damien to come to Honolulu to receive the jeweled medal and the decree but he felt that he had to do what Princess Liliuokalani asked of him. He also feared the public reaction if he did not do so.

Bishop Koeckemann reluctantly made the journey to Molokai. Those who had the strength, walked the two-and-a-half-miles from Kalawao to Kalaupapa to greet him at the landing dock. He was escorted to the settlement by sixty-six lepers on horseback who held festive banners as the band played their very best musical selections for him.

At Kalawao, the entire settlement was present to witness the impressive ceremony and tribute to Father Damien. Afterward, everyone enjoyed an elaborate luau and dined on roasted pork, poi and a variety of fruits. Father Damien wore the jeweled medal only once, on the day he received it.

Father Damien knew that the visit of the princess and the gift of the medal and the decree signed by the King of Hawaii would not be received well by his regional provincial, Father Léonor. Father Léonor was jealous and resentful of Father Damien's immense popularity. The more the press praised him, the more severe Father Léonor became with him. He was of the opinion that the public acclaim made Father Damien proud and arrogant. However, those who knew Father Damien intimately said that nothing could be further from the truth and that he was a very humble man who shunned publicity and acclaim.

Matters had gone along smoothly for Father Damien when Bishop Louis Maigret and Father Modeste Favens were his superiors. Father Damien had a close and loving relationship with the two men and they supported him and encouraged him in all of his missionary endeavors. However, when they retired, everything changed. Father Damien's relationship with the new provincial, Father Léonor Fouesnel was never good but with the passage of time, it went from bad to worse. Father Damien later admitted that his interactions with Father Léonor were one of the most painful ordeals of his life.

Father Léonor was intelligent, artistic, well-organized and efficient but as a religious superior, he failed in many ways. He was considered a tyrant by many of the Sacred Hearts priests who described him as harsh, vindictive and lacking in compassion. Because of so many complaints about him by members of his own religious congregation, a critical report about him was eventually sent to the Superior General of the Order in Paris, Most Reverend Marcellin Bousquet.

The spiritual well-being of the lepers was always on Father Damien's mind. He trained a number of lepers to be prayer leaders and others to be prayer leader assistants. For those who were too ill to attend Mass, the prayer leaders visited them in their homes each Sunday, offering prayers and spiritual support. In that way, the sick were not left alone and they benefitted greatly from the attention and companionship of their visitors.

Father Damien set up three confraternities at the settlement whose purpose was to aid the sick. St. Joseph's Confraternity consisted of men who visited the sick in their homes. Our Lady's Confraternity was made up of women who helped those who had become isolated and neglected. The Holy Childhood Confraternity was made up of children who were trained in a special way to help the sick at the settlement.

At the settlement, many of the lepers who were Catholic had a love for the traditional Catholic devotions. Devotions to Our Lady of Sorrows as well as to the Stations of the Cross were very popular. The Stations were displayed in the church of St. Philomena for both private and public devotion.

Since perpetual adoration was such an important part of the apostolate of the Sacred Hearts Congregation, in 1879, Father Damien instituted the Perpetual Adoration Association at the settlement. Twenty-four hours a day, seven days a week, lepers took half-hour shifts in the church in order to spend time in prayer and silent adoration before the Blessed Sacrament. When the lepers were too ill to walk to the church for their allotted half-hour of adoration, they completed their prescribed prayer time in their house.

The Board of Health owned a small store at the Kalawao settlement on Molokai where the lepers could buy food and clothing, but only a minority of the lepers had the money to do so. In addition, the items for sale were all overpriced. Later, when inspectors paid a visit to the store, they found that the sugar was dark and dirty and the bread was of a very poor quality. It was even inferior to the bread that was served to the prisoners at the Oahu jail. In addition, the salmon that was for sale was moldy and unfit for human consumption.

The lepers were required to buy vouchers in order to purchase food and other items from the store. On one occasion, Father Damien had volunteered to buy food for some of the sick lepers who were too weak to walk to the store. He had misplaced their vouchers and was frantically searching everywhere for them. He was so upset that he was crying. Vouchers that were lost or stolen could not be replaced. The strict policy was enforced by the Board of Health and they would not bend the rules for any reason. Without a voucher, no food could be obtained from the store.

From donations that came in, Father Damien decided to set up a store where everything was free. He wanted the lepers to have special foods that they would enjoy as well as a good supply of nutritious food. In the free store, the lepers could get chicken, biscuits, rice, sugar, bread, eggs, tobacco, candy and other items.

When Father Damien arrived in Molokai, the church of St. Philomena had been neglected for a long time and was in great need of cleaning and repair. It had been built one year before he had arrived at the settlement. He set about to make the necessary improvements, doing his best to turn St. Philomena into a sacred place, a house of God. He painted the interior in bright colors according to the Hawaiian tradition and did restoration work throughout.

At the Mass, Father Damien used the lovely chalices of gold that had been sent to him as a gift for the settlement from the superior of the church of St. Roche in Paris. On Sundays, the altar was ablaze with candles and splendid bouquets of fresh flowers. Father Damien wore beautiful priestly vestments of the finest quality. The parishioners came dressed in their Sunday best and all wore the traditional fresh flower leis around their necks. The men wore calico shirts and white pants and the women were decked out in bright colored full-length dresses and straw hats decorated with ribbons. The parishioners participated fully at the Mass, listening to the homily with attention and reciting the Mass prayers with devotion and reverence. Visitors who came to St. Philomena for Sunday Mass were deeply impressed. Through Father Damien's efforts, St. Philomena had become a model Christian parish.

Sunday Mass at St. Philomena's was known for its outstanding music sung by a large adult choir. The music was so excellent that it achieved international fame. Father Damien also organized a children's choir. The organist played beautifully at all the Masses even though some of his fingers were missing on his left hand due to leprosy. He tied a piece of wood to his arm which enabled him to hit all the low notes without skipping a beat.

Few Catholics missed Sunday Mass at St. Philomena as it was the highlight of the week. Father Damien knew all of his parishioners by name and if any of them were absent from Sunday Mass, he would visit them first thing Monday morning to see if they were all right.

Attendance at Mass became so large that the church could not contain all the people. The overflow remained outside, looking in through the windows. Father Damien enlarged the church two times due to ever growing numbers. Non-Christians and Protestants also attended Sunday Mass, attracted by the excellent music and the pageantry. The drunkenness and immorality that Father Damien had encountered on his arrival at the settlement was now only a distant and fading memory.

Father Damien had an important message to deliver each Sunday morning and he repeated it again and again. Although all of his parishioners had been given a death sentence due to their illness, Father Damien stressed to them that death was not an end, but a beginning. Death was not to be feared for it was the portal to eternal life. He once said to his parishioners, "Earth is only a place we are passing through, an exile. Heaven is our real homeland. We lepers, we are sure of going there soon. We will be repaid for all of our miseries. . . We will be changed and will be happier and more beautiful, the more patiently we have borne our suffering here below." As one person observed, "It was Father Damien's daily job to get souls ready to appear before God."

Death was omnipresent on the island of Molokai. Regardless of their faith or lack of it, almost all of the lepers asked to see Father Damien on their death beds. At that time, the majority of those who had not been baptized, then requested it.

Father Damien did not want the lepers to be idle but instead to have healthy and enjoyable activities to participate in at the settlement. He organized public games and sporting events and those who were strong enough took part. He arranged luaus, foot races, festivals, processions, and a variety of celebrations. He encouraged the people, despite their illness, to get regular exercise, to raise flowers, to go horseback riding, to join the church choir, to learn a musical instrument and to join the band.

Some of the musical instruments for the band arrived as gifts from well-wishers. Father Damien made some of the musical instruments himself. He fashioned flutes for the people out of old coal oil cans. Even those who had only two or three fingers due to their disease were able to play the hand-made flutes very well. Father Damien purchased bugles, clarinets, trombones, cornets, and a bass drum for the band with gift money. When visitors came to the settlement, they were sometimes serenaded by a choir of one hundred people afflicted with leprosy while the band played. In Molokai, the band played at all events, both large and small. Father Damien found great pleasure in listening to the music.

Father Damien encouraged the lepers to have their own vegetable gardens, believing gardening to be a very healthy occupation. With his prompting, in time, the number grew from ten percent to ninety percent of the lepers who were cultivating the land and growing sweet potatoes, onions and cabbages. He asked the Board of Health to purchase their crops and they agreed to do so. Father Damien reasoned that with so many lepers engaged in growing vegetables, on the occasions when bad weather prevented the steamer from landing at Kalaupapa with a shipment of poi and other staples, the settlement would always have a supply of food.

As time went by, for an unknown reason, Father Damien began to let his guard down regarding protecting himself against close contact with those confined to the settlement. By his carelessness, he was exposing himself to the disease. He occasionally let the lepers take a puff on his pipe and he allowed them to prepare his meals. There was always a lot of traffic inside and outside of his residence. His house was nicknamed "Kalawao Family House and Lepers' Rest" because so many lepers visited him there. His door was always open and no one was ever turned away.

On one occasion, the steamer approached the Kalaupapa landing dock but was not able to drop off the lepers due to rough seas and stormy weather. The captain ordered the twenty-one lepers thrown overboard to swim ashore. Father Damien and several others happened to be standing by the landing dock that day and witnessed the terrible event. They jumped into the heavy surf and swam toward the steamer, risking their own lives in the process. Two of the lepers died on the beach that day, one in the arms of Father Damien.

The tragic incident was written up in the Hawaiian press and the outcry was immediate. Articles that were published stated that the poor lepers were treated like "dogs thrown into the water" and that according to the authorities, their lives had no value. The incident nearly led to a revolt. The citizens of Hawaii were furious and demanded change. They wanted the settlement closed down permanently and threatened the government that plantations would be set on fire and other forms of violence would follow if no action was taken. Blame was laid on the Board of Health for their inhumane treatment of the lepers.

Government officials in Hawaii felt the pressure to respond to the public outcry. A decision was made that those who were suspected of having leprosy would no longer be deported immediately to Molokai. Instead, they would stay at the Kakaako Branch Hospital in Honolulu where they would receive expert nursing care from professionally trained nurses. They would also be allowed to receive regular visits from their family.

Bishop Koeckemann became involved, hoping for improved conditions for all leprosy sufferers. Due to budget constraints, it would be difficult to pay for the services of trained nurses. Bishop Koeckemann asked Father Léonor to contact Catholic religious congregations in North America and make a plea for nursing Sisters to come to Hawaii and work at the Kakaako Branch Hospital. Traditionally, Catholic Sisters worked free of charge, receiving only a very small monthly stipend.

Father Léonor wrote letters of appeal to fifty heads of religious institutions in the United States and Canada. Half did not respond to his letter and the rest wrote back to say no to his request. However, Father Léonor did receive one positive reply. It was from Mother Marianne Cope, the provincial superior of the Sisters of the Third Order of St. Francis at St. Anthony's convent in Syracuse, New York. She wrote back saying that it would be an honor to serve the sick in Hawaii and that she and her Sisters were willing and able to do so. Mother Marianne was forty-five years old.

Mother Marianne had entered the Sisters of the Third Order of St. Francis when she was twenty-four years old. After teaching for ten years, she became the chief nurse and administrator of St. Joseph's Hospital in Syracuse, New York and was elected superior of the Order.

In addition to her deep faith and piety, Mother Marianne was intelligent, resourceful and filled with good common sense. Nothing was too hard for her, no work too daunting. Some of the alcoholic priests that were patients at St. Joseph's Hospital in Syracuse said that the loving care and kindness they received from Mother Marianne was truly edifying. They said that they thought she should be canonized for her acts of charity toward them.

After Mother Marianne had accepted Father Léonor's invitation to work at the Kakaako Branch Hospital, he had to tell her a piece of information that he had not included in his letter. The sick whom the Sisters were asked to help, all had leprosy. Mother Marianne assured Father Léonor that she and her Sisters were still willing to come.

Mother Marianne along with six other Sisters arrived in Honolulu in 1883. Mother Marianne's desire was to remain in Hawaii just long enough to help the Sisters begin the work at the Kakaako Branch Hospital. As provincial superior of her Order, she was needed at the motherhouse in Syracuse and was responsible for many administrative tasks there. She assumed that she would return to New York in a year's time.

The Kakaako Branch Hospital in Honolulu that the Sisters would manage was a grim and cheerless place. It often flooded due to the fact that it had been built on a salt marsh. Surrounded by a high wooden fence and locked gates, it had an oppressive, prison-like appearance. Some said that it reminded them of an insane asylum.

When the Sisters were taken on an initial tour of the hospital by an administrator of the Board of Health, they found the conditions shocking. Two hundred lepers were crowded into an area meant for no more than one hundred. The hospital kitchen was nothing more than a shed where a few firepits had been dug. Rats nibbled freely at crumbs on the ground. Flies swarmed in the room where the patients took their meals and thick layers of dirt and grime were everywhere. The wards were infested with bedbugs and lice. The patients slept on straw mattresses on the floor with dirty grey blankets to cover themselves. Since there was no furniture in the hospital, the children sat crowded together on the floor, looking utterly despondent. There was not a smile or a word from any of them. The conditions at the Kakaako Branch Hospital were polar opposite to the thoroughly clean and modern St. Joseph's Hospital in Syracuse, New York where the Sisters had worked just a month before.

The Sisters' first priority was to clean and sanitize every room in the hospital. Working long hours, they gradually made progress. They provided expert nursing care to the lepers, cleaning and bandaging their painful wounds and dispensing medication to them. The Sisters planted grass and flowers in the front of the hospital to give it a homey and welcoming feeling for the new leprosy patients who were regularly admitted.

Father Damien was overjoyed when he got word that the Franciscan Sisters had come to the Hawaiian Islands to assist the lepers. For years, he had prayed that Catholic Nursing Sisters would come to Molokai. He even circulated a petition at the settlement, asking all of the lepers to sign it, requesting nursing help from Catholic Sisters.

Father Damien naturally assumed that some of the Sisters would be sent to help him at the settlement's hospital. There were five times as many lepers in Molokai as in the Kakaako Branch Hospital on Oahu. He was very disappointed to learn that there were no plans to send the Sisters to Molokai. He did not give up however, but continued to pray and to plead for helpers to assist him in the work.

There were a number of healthy children who were born at the Kalawao settlement in Molokai whose parents had leprosy. The children were at great risk of catching the disease due to the constant exposure. Mother Marianne, Father Damien and Dr. Edward Arning had lengthy discussions on how the children could best be protected. All agreed that it was necessary to separate them from their parents so that they would not contract leprosy.

The healthy girls and babies at the settlement were transported by steamer to Honolulu where Mother Marianne and her Sisters cared for them lovingly at the Kapiolani Girls' Home on the grounds of the Kakaako Branch Hospital. The girls also attended school there. The Kapiolani Girls' Home had been instituted two years after the Sisters arrived in Honolulu and was named after Queen Kapiolani who made it possible by her generous financial support.

Mother Marianne and the Sisters taught the girls how to sew and to make lace which they sold to members of the community. They baked cakes and cookies for the girls which they gave to them as a special surprise. During the holidays, the Sisters bought Christmas presents for the girls from the $20.00 a month stipend they each received from the Board of Health.

In 1884, at the request of the Hawaiian government, Mother Marianne established the Malulani Hospital (Protection of Heaven) in Wailuku, on the island of Maui. It was the first general hospital on Maui. Mother Marianne was then called back to her work at the Kakaako Branch Hospital in Honolulu. Twelve Sisters in all served on both Maui and Oahu.

As time passed, the Hawaiian government as well as the Board of Health placed their full trust in Mother Marianne. She had only intended to spend one year working in Honolulu before returning to her duties in New York. She proved to be such an outstanding administrator of the Kakaako Branch Hospital that the government as well as the church authorities did all in their power to block her from leaving.

As Father Damien kept up his intense work schedule at the Kalawao settlement, he began to experience violent pains as well as inflammation and swelling in his left leg. As time passed, he dragged his leg and could barely walk. After prolonged exposure to leprosy, the telling signs gradually began to appear on his body.

Dr. George W. Woods was a medical inspector in the U.S. Navy and visited Molokai in July, 1876. At the time of his visit, he was working on a report on leprosy for the Bureau of Medicine and Surgery. Father Damien showed him the settlement and told him, "This is my work in this world. Sooner or later, I know I will become a leper but I ask God that it may not happen before I have come to the end of my ability to help these poor children."

In addition to the pain in his leg, Father Damien noticed that his foot was becoming increasingly numb. One day, he placed his foot into scalding water by accident. His skin blistered but he felt no pain. He also noticed dry, yellowish spots on his back and arms.

Dr. Edward Arning gave Father Damien a thorough examination in 1884. He probed his foot and leg with an electrically charged platinum needle and found damage to the sciatic nerve in his lower leg as well as atrophy of the skin on his foot. Dr. Arning told him the sad news, that he had contracted leprosy. After the diagnosis, Father Damien would live for four more years.

Father Damien wrote a letter to his brother, Father Pamphile, and told him that he had been diagnosed with leprosy. He asked him not to tell his aging mother. He also wrote to his mother, but in order to spare her the pain, he did not mention it to her.

The news that Father Damien had contracted leprosy spread like wildfire. Newspapers world-wide carried the story. Expressions of heart-felt sympathy as well as gifts and monetary donations were sent to Father Damien from all parts of the world.

As the disease progressed, Damien's eyesight began to fail and the bridge of his nose collapsed. His eyebrows fell off, his face became puffy and covered with sores and he had great difficulty breathing. His arm became so swollen that he had to wear it in a sling. The pain in his legs became almost unbearable. When it became too difficult to walk, he rode on horseback or in a wagon. In a letter, he described the agony of his condition and said, "I am disabled, probably for life. . .I drag my leg when I walk. When I go to or from the hospital, a mere five-minute walk, I cry all night from the pain." Far from lessening his desire to work, his illness seemed to motivate him to work even harder.

Father Damien's attitude about his condition can only be described as heroic. He wrote to his bishop and said, "Soon I shall become completely disfigured but I stay calm, resigned, and quite happy in the midst of my people." Once a person asked Father Damien if he would like to be healed of leprosy. "No, not if the price was leaving Molokai and abandoning my work," he answered.

Bishop John Joseph Scanlan, the second bishop of the diocese of Honolulu said, "We know that the motivation which inspired the supreme involvement of Damien in the suffering and despair of Kalawao springs only from a greatness of soul which most of us do not have." And author Gavan Daws said, "Damien de Veuster was an ordinary man who made the most extraordinary moral choices again and again and again."

After he learned that Father Damien had contracted leprosy, Father Léonor, his immediate superior, never reached out to him or spoke to him about his diagnosis. His focus was always on his various projects at the Capital in Honolulu. To many, Father Léonor seemed incapable of ordinary human empathy. In the sixteen years that Father Damien worked at the Kalawao settlement, Father Léonor did not visit him once.

Reverend Hugh B. Chapman, a Protestant minister of the church of St. Luke in London, England read an article about Father Damien in the paper and was deeply inspired. He said that Father Damien's life made his own life seem easy and selfish in comparison. He wrote to Father Damien and said, "You have taught me more by the story of your life than all the commentaries I have ever read." On another occasion he wrote to him and said, "Your example can make more converts to Catholicism than any sermon." He always signed the letters, "Your friend who loves you."

One Sunday morning, Reverend Chapman spoke from the pulpit to his congregation about Father Damien and his work with the suffering lepers in Molokai. He asked those who could, to give a donation and he asked them to be generous. His congregation was made up mostly of poor people who struggled just to make ends meet. He was well-aware that they would have little extra money with which to donate. He encouraged his congregation by saying, "It is a great honor for us to give a donation to such a great and brave man as Father Damien." When Reverend Chapman took up a collection, he was astonished at the great generosity of his congregation.

Reverend Chapman also wrote an article describing Father Damien's work in Molokai along with a request for donations and submitted it to the widely-circulated London newspaper, *The Times*. His article was published and soon generous donations from all over England began to pour in. Reverend Chapman was able to send a very large check to Father Damien.

With the money, Father Damien purchased large quantities of thread, fabric, sewing needles and other sewing supplies from Honolulu. He hired people to sew the clothes for the lepers who did not know how to sew or were too sick to do so. All of the other lepers sewed the clothing themselves. From the donations that were sent from England, over five hundred lepers received two articles of warm clothing for the approaching winter season.

Father Léonor was indignant about the latest turn of events. He disapproved of the recent gift of the clothing to all the lepers and wrote a letter of complaint to the bishop informing him that Father Damien had "resorted to fundraising" and that "hardly did he have the money in his hands but he made a gift of a full set of clothing to every leper." He felt that Father Damien was casting the Catholic Missions and the Board of Health in a bad light and implying that they were not taking care of the lepers adequately.

Charles Stoddard, an American writer and journalist, visited Molokai in 1868, five years before Father Damien's arrival. He returned to the settlement again in 1884 and could barely recognize it. It was no longer a place of poverty, crime, and hopelessness. It had also lost the appearance of a government run prison where outcasts were left to die. Rather, it had become a place of beauty, joy, and human dignity.

The settlement at Molokai had completely transformed. Replacing the thatched huts were rows of whitewashed wooden houses that were clean and neat, with a flower garden in front of each. Two large and fully functioning orphanages had been built and the boys and girls who lived there were genuinely happy even though all were afflicted with leprosy. The adults were enjoying life as well. Most days found them out in the fresh air enjoying a horseback ride or taking a walk.

There was now a cemetery surrounded by an attractive white picket fence where the dead were buried with religious reverence. There were cultivated fields, vegetable gardens, lush tropical trees and well-maintained roads. Father Damien had brought order out of the chaos and lawlessness he had encountered when he first arrived at the settlement. He had also been able to transform a dangerous group of condemned outcasts into a close-knit supportive community, a family.

Edward Clifford, a Protestant from England, made a trip to Molokai and described the island as being so beautiful that it "looked like paradise." There was music, joy and contentment at the settlement. Edward Clifford said, "I had gone to Molokai expecting to find it scarcely less dreadful than hell itself, and the cheerful people, the lovely landscape, and the comparatively painless life were all surprises. These poor people seem singularly happy." Edward brought many gifts with him from the citizens of England for the lepers at the settlement.

Edward Clifford asked the lepers if they missed being back home with their relatives and friends and the life they had known before they were sent to Molokai. The lepers told Mr. Clifford that they were not homesick for their former way of life. "Father Damien takes very good care of us," the lepers said. "We lack for nothing. We would never want to leave Molokai if it meant that we had to leave our Father Damien." Father Damien had promised them on numerous occasions that he would never leave them.

Dr. George Woods had been so impressed by what he had seen when he visited Molokai that he spoke to the Board of Health in Honolulu, praising Father Damien's compassionate care of the lepers. Dr. Woods said, "Having visited all the places on earth where leprosy is endemic, I can testify that in no other part of the world are the lepers so happy and so well cared for as in the Hawaiian Islands." Dr. Woods also remembered fondly that when he visited Molokai, Father Damien introduced some of the children to him by saying proudly, "These are my boys."

Monetary donations, care packages and religious articles continued to be sent to the Kalawao settlement by well-wishers from many parts of the world. A pastor from Boston, Massachusetts sent a beautiful harmonium to the settlement while large and ornate plaques of the Stations of the Cross were sent from England. A grind organ which could play forty songs by the turn of a handle was a favorite gift among the children and adults alike. Another favorite was a magic lantern with illuminated images of the gospel stories. Father Damien used it to instruct the children in their catechism classes. Bankers in Portland, Oregon contacted Father Damien and offered him interest-free loans upon request.

In addition, Queen Kapiolani arranged for gifts to be sent to all of the lepers at Kalawao. Father Damien went to great pains to see that a gift package addressed individually to each man, woman and child at the settlement was received by them, compliments of the queen.

As the years passed, the physical and mental isolation of life on Molokai became more oppressive to Father Damien. He felt cut off from the world and deprived of the friendship of his peers. He loved the members of his religious community and missed seeing and communicating with them. In his loneliness, he spoke of the settlement as "a tomb." He wrote to the secretary of the Father General of the Order and said, "Being deprived of the companionship of my colleagues of our dear congregation is more painful to bear than leprosy." He said that the only way he could cope, was to recall his ordination day when he had dedicated his life completely to God. He used to say, "Without the Blessed Sacrament, a position like mine would be unbearable."

Many times, Father Damien prayed that the Lord would send him a friend and companion, a fellow worker at the settlement. On numerous occasions he asked his superiors to send one of the Sacred Hearts missionaries to help him. Most of the time, the shortage of priests made it impossible for them to send him a helper. However, through the years, they managed to send several priests. Unfortunately, those who came were often too ill to work. Others that were sent were priests that the Sacred Hearts Congregation could barely tolerate because they were impossible to get along with. For ten of the sixteen years Father Damien served at Molokai, he was completely alone.

The unexpected arrival of Ira Barnes Dutton to the settlement in 1886 was truly an answer to Father Damien's prayers. Ira Dutton was born in Stowe, Vermont on April 27, 1843. Later, the family moved to Janesville, Wisconsin where Ira received an excellent education, attending Milton Academy and Milton College.

During the Civil War, Ira served with distinction as a First Lieutenant in the Union Army. He fell deeply in love with a woman and married her, even though some of his friends advised him not to. She proved to be unfaithful to him and later left him after spending most of his money. Ira was broken-hearted and made an effort to reconcile with his wife but to no avail. He called the marriage his "first serious mistake." After a painful divorce, he tried to drown his problems by drinking heavily and he continued in the destructive pattern for ten years. Finally, with a desire to get his life back on track, he took a pledge never to drink again and he kept the pledge for the rest of his life.

After the war ended, Ira worked in Alabama and later in Tennessee in various civil service posts. He possessed remarkable leadership and administrative skills and achieved success in every field of endeavor that he pursued.

Ira, who was raised in the Episcopal church, became interested in Catholicism, and after making the required preparation and study, was received into the Church on his fortieth birthday. At that time, he changed his name to Joseph, in honor of St. Joseph, the father of Jesus. Not long after, he was accepted as a lay brother at the Trappist monastery of Our Lady of Gethsemane in Gethsemane, Kentucky. Although he did not take religious vows, he lived at the monastery with the Trappist priests and brothers, working alongside of them. Observing the Rule of St. Benedict, they lived in poverty, seclusion, silence and strict discipline and followed a schedule of manual labor, prayer, and spiritual study.

The Trappists are members of the Cistercian Order of the Strict Observance. As a cloistered religious congregation, they live an austere and penitential life, never leaving the monastic enclosure. After living and serving in the community for two years, Joseph Dutton felt that his calling lay elsewhere and he left with the blessing of the Abbot.

After Joseph left the Trappists, he was interested in learning more about other religious congregations. He found that he was drawn to the active life of a missionary more than to the contemplative life of a cloistered monk. When Joseph read a brief account of Father Damien and his work with the lepers in a Catholic publication, he knew that he had found his vocation. His next step was to find out where Molokai was and how to get there.

At age forty-three, Joseph Dutton gave away all of his possessions and made arrangements for his army pension to be sent each month to the Trappist monks in Kentucky. He made a trip to Wisconsin to say goodbye to his elderly mother and gave her part of his estate.

Less than two months after he had first read the article about Father Damien, Joseph Dutton set sail from San Francisco to Hawaii. He viewed the long sea voyage as a pilgrimage and he planned to use the time on board the ship to prepare his heart and his mind for his new life, his new beginning. He also had a great desire to do penance and to atone for his wasted years.

Joseph Dutton arrived in Honolulu unannounced. He visited the bishop in Honolulu and presented his letters of introduction and his references. He made a good impression on the bishop who gave him his full support and encouragement. The bishop referred Joseph to the president of the Hawaiian Board of Health who granted him permission to work at the settlement and even offered him a full-time salary. Joseph declined the salary and explained that he had the desire to offer his services free of charge.

From Honolulu, Joseph Dutton took the inter-island steamer and arrived at the Kalaupapa landing dock on July 29, 1886. Father Damien, who had been told he was coming, was waiting on the shore to greet him.

Joseph introduced himself to Father Damien and handed him the written permissions from the bishop and the Board of Health of Hawaii as well as his formal letters of introduction. Father Damien was elated that Joseph Dutton wanted to help him in his work with the lepers. He told him that he had always wanted brothers and priests to join him at Molokai and had made the request many times to his superiors. Perhaps that was why he called him "Brother Joseph" from the first day of their meeting. The bishop later said that he believed God had led Joseph Dutton to Hawaii. Father Damien would live for three more years.

In his old horse-drawn buggy, Father Damien took Brother Joseph on the two-and-a-half-mile journey to the Kalawao leper settlement. Father Damien spoke of the hopes and dreams he had for his lepers as well as the building projects he was anxious to complete. He took Brother Joseph to St. Philomena church and showed him all of the improvements he had made. Brother Joseph was impressed with the beauty and cleanliness of the church.

Dr. Arthur Mouritz happened to be at the settlement on the day that Joseph Dutton arrived and had lunch with him that afternoon. Dr. Mouritz noted that the former army officer was reserved and dignified in manner and that his presence commanded a certain respect.

Joseph had nothing to say to Dr. Mouritz about why he was seeking work as well as seclusion at Molokai. He made no mention of why he was turning his back on the world. Later, someone asked him directly about his reason for coming to Molokai. He said that his only motivation was a desire to help relieve the suffering of the lepers and to do "as much good as he could."

Father Damien appointed Brother Joseph to be the official sacristan at St. Philomena parish as well as at the parish at Kalaupapa. Father Damien said Mass at both parishes every Sunday. Brother Joseph had resolved when he came to Molokai to do any work that was asked of him and to get along with everyone he came in contact with.

Father Damien tutored Brother Joseph in the Hawaiian language and in only a few months, he was able to speak the language quite well. He also built a small cabin for Brother Joseph right next to his own. Brother Joseph's cabin, which was ten feet by fourteen feet, connected with a passageway to St. Philomena church. Brother Joseph said, "I live near the Blessed Sacrament. Without this and hearing Mass daily, I would be lost."

The front of Brother Joseph's cabin had an amazing view of the vast and endless blue ocean. For Brother Joseph, the ocean was a symbol of eternity and he loved to gaze at its vastness and beauty. The back of his house looked out on to the cemetery which contained about two thousand graves. There were another one thousand graves elsewhere on the island. For Brother Joseph, the view of the cemetery was a valuable and sobering meditation on the brevity of life.

Brother Joseph was up at four o'clock every morning to begin his day with meditation and prayer. At five o'clock he rang the Angelus bell and then wakened all the boys in the orphanage to get them ready for morning Mass at six o'clock. Four of the young boys in the orphanage were blind. Of the four, one took it upon himself to lead the others and to try to keep them safe from falls and accidents.

Brother Joseph and Father Damien usually started their work very early in the morning and did not finish until ten or eleven o'clock at night. They built chapels, made cottages for the lepers, repaired buildings and visited the sick in their homes. After a time, Brother Joseph, who was an outstanding administrator, was put in charge of the day to day operations of the settlement. He also took care of the children and coached their ball games.

Brother Joseph asked to be taught how to care for the lepers who were confined to the hospital because he wanted to lighten Father Damien's workload. He did not have any fear of catching the disease. He first assisted the children who were in the hospital. He learned how to administer the carbolic acid baths which were used to disinfect and clean the open sores, how to dress and bandage the wounds, and how to remove dead and decaying bone when necessary. He had a small music box and he liked to listen to Strauss waltzes while he bandaged the sores.

Brother Joseph accepted the most repulsive nursing tasks at the hospital and performed them well. He learned quickly and as someone observed, "Whatever Brother Joseph undertook to do, he did with perfection." Eventually he had so many patients to attend to that they waited in line for four or five hours to be treated by him. He cared for the sick in their homes as well. He never spoke about himself or made any mention of his life before coming to Molokai.

Brother Joseph became the friend that Father Damien had always yearned for. At sunset, they would meet on the porch of the rectory in order to discuss in detail all of the work they had accomplished that day as well as what they hoped to do the following day.

Brother Joseph was gentle, devout, humble, and soft spoken. No one ever saw him angry or moody. At the settlement, he made friends easily. He never showed even the slightest annoyance but was exceptionally calm in all circumstances. As Dr. Mouritz said, "Brother Joseph had a divine temperament. Nothing could ruffle him." He was extremely neat and clean in appearance, each day wearing a long sleeve denim shirt and denim jeans.

Father Damien treasured Brother Joseph's friendship and loved him as a brother. The lepers loved him as well. He was courteous and discrete in his dealings with everyone. He worked long hours, day in and day out, and he asked for nothing in return. The list of his virtues could go on and on.

In addition to his friendship with Brother Joseph, Father Damien's life was to be blessed with another wonderful friend, companion, and advocate for lepers, Father Louis Lambert Conrardy. Father Conrardy, like Father Damien, was a native of Belgium. After ordination, Father Conrardy served as pastor in Stavelot, Belgium. In 1869 during the cholera epidemic, he devoted his time to nursing the sick poor in the area, taking caring of them with extraordinary sensitivity and love, even offering his own bed to them.

Father Conrardy applied to the Foreign Missions, asking to serve in China but his repeated requests were ignored. He served as a missionary in India for several years and later was sent to Portland, Oregon in the United States. He was assigned to a mission on the Umatilla Indian reservation where he worked with the Native American Indians. The territory that he was responsible for was so large that it took him three months to cover it. He built churches, taught catechism and performed numerous priestly functions. He spent fourteen years living in isolation, far from civilization, and seemed perfectly suited to the rugged existence of missionary life among the Indian tribes.

Father Conrardy was a peacemaker and was determined to have good relations with the Native American tribes. He traveled alone on foot or horseback and was regularly confronted by hostile Indian tribes. Exposed to danger, he never carried a gun, a knife or a weapon of any kind for protection. Ice, wind, and heavy snow did not deter him on his missionary journeys. In many ways, he seemed invincible. Father Conrardy's archbishop, William Gross of the archdiocese of Portland, Oregon held him in the highest esteem and praised him for his stability, his courage, and his "noble and heroic character."

It was common knowledge among the Native American tribes that Father Conrardy was not afraid of them. They admired him for his bravery and his strength of character. By showing his commitment to nonviolence and his lack of fear, Father Conrardy earned the respect and admiration of many of the native people and maintained good relations with them.

Father Conrardy first learned about Father Damien when his superior, Archbishop William Gross spoke to him about the important work Father Damien was doing on Molokai. Father Conrardy and Father Damien began to correspond through letters. Father Conrardy had a great desire travel to Molokai to help Father Damien with his work but there were many people who needed him in the Oregon territory where he was assigned, so he remained there.

Ten years later, when Father Conrardy got word that Father Damien had contracted leprosy and did not have a priest to assist him, he asked for permission to go to Molokai. Father Damien wrote a letter to Father Conrardy saying, "I beg you from the bottom of my heart to come to join me, to help me, and to replace me."

Father Damien also wrote letters to his own superiors, pleading with them to allow Father Conrardy to help him at the settlement. He reasoned that Father Conrardy would be ideal for the job. He was used to the strenuous life of a missionary and would be able to do the hard work that was required. Father Damien knew that his time was short and he wanted Father Conrardy to carry on after his death. He had no other offers of help.

Archbishop William Gross had only praise for Father Conrardy and approved his request to work in Molokai. He felt that Father Conrardy's life of privation and isolation on the Oregon prairie had been a perfect preparation for the life he would lead at the leper settlement. Father Conrardy, who was fortyseven years old, wrote to Father Damien and told him that he felt he could work for at least twenty more years.

Father Damien was there at the landing wharf at Kalaupapa to meet Father Conrardy on the day of his arrival, and with great joy, he welcomed him. They traveled the two-and-a-half-mile trek to the Kalawao settlement in Father Damien's rickety old buggy with his horse William leading the way.

Father Conrardy was shocked by the terrible disfigurement of Damien's face and body due to his leprous condition. Festering sores, like boils, covered his face, neck and hands and they gave off a horrible stench. His nose was somewhat sunken. His ears were three times their normal size and his hands were deformed and grossly enlarged. The disease had invaded his windpipe and reduced the sound of his voice to a rough whisper. That afternoon, after the two priests toured the settlement, Father Damien prepared lunch for Father Conrardy but Father Conrardy could hardly eat.

Father Damien put Father Conrardy in charge of the boys' orphanage. At the time, there were eighty boys living there. The new priest did exemplary work, showering his affection, concern and tender care on the children and the adults as well. The residents of the settlement loved Father Conrardy. He also helped at the hospital, assisted at Mass and visited the sick in their homes. In his spare time, he studied the Hawaiian language until he became fluent.

Father Conrardy was impressed that Father Damien, as sick as he was, was still able to do a great deal of work each day. At the time, Father Damien was preoccupied with trying to find the money to pay for building repairs and had even started construction on two new dormitories for the boys. Father

Conrardy was also impressed by Father Damien's upbeat and optimistic attitude. He had a wonderful sense of humor and enjoyed telling jokes and laughing.

Father Conrardy could not help but wonder if he too would catch leprosy and he came to the conclusion that in all likelihood he would. He shared living quarters with Father Damien and sat next to him at all of their meals. Lepers cooked and served their food and baked their bread. Their daily fare consisted of rice, meat, ship biscuits and coffee, with leftovers in the evening.

Considering the day to day life at the settlement, contact with the lepers came in a thousand different ways. Because Father Conrardy was so worried about exposure to the disease, he was not able to relax. He began to suffer from continual headaches. The thought came to him that even the chickens might be contaminated. He saw them scratching around and pecking in the garbage by the hospital where some of the patients' bandages had been discarded and he feared eating the eggs that were served to him. Father Damien assured him that the eggs were completely safe and that chickens were immune to leprosy. Father Conrardy still felt uneasy about it. Shortly after he arrived at the settlement, eleven people died in one day. He prayed that God would protect him and he asked others to pray for him so that he would be able to persevere in his work on Molokai.

Father Conrardy had been deeply religious his entire life. He had read the lives of the Christian martyrs, those who had sacrificed their lives for the faith, and it stirred something deep within him. He had once been offered a coveted assignment at a fine parish near Buenos Aires in Argentina. He was promised a good salary and plenty of leisure time but he was not the least bit interested. He had never felt compelled to seek an easy or comfortable life. He had prayed daily to be stationed in the worst place in the world.

Serving at the Kalawao leper settlement in Molokai could easily be considered the worst priestly assignment in the world. There were many good reasons why the settlement was referred to as an "earthly hell" and a "living graveyard." Father Conrardy believed that life among the lepers would be worth more than all the temporal comforts and benefits the world had to offer. Eventually his terrible headaches subsided and his appetite returned.

Howard Crouch of New Jersey, who founded the Damien-Dutton Society for Leprosy Aid, shared a beautiful story of an exchange between Father Conrardy and Brother Joseph Dutton. Father Conrardy told Brother Joseph that he noticed that Brother Joseph was completely at ease at the dinner table with Father Damien. Father Conrardy on the other hand, found it difficult to eat with him. Father Damien's grotesque physical appearance as well as the stench from his open sores made Father Conrardy feel nauseated. He made a great effort not to show signs of disgust but he had a hard time swallowing his food during meals with Father Damien. He asked Brother Joseph how he could be so relaxed during the meals.

Brother Joseph told Father Conrardy that in the beginning he too had a hard time sharing meals with Father Damien. "I looked into Father Damien's eyes and I imagined I was looking into the eyes of Christ," Brother Joseph said. "His eyes would be like Damien's. Then I remembered all the things that Christ did during his life here on earth. I remembered that when he was to open Lazarus' tomb, the disciples told him not to do it for the stench would be overwhelming, but Christ opened the tomb and Lazarus came forth. When the lepers touched his garments, he did not shrink but blessed them and then he cured them. If Christ had leprosy, I would feel it an honor to eat with him at his table. I am not aware of Damien's odor nor does his appearance bother me anymore," Brother Joseph said.

Father Damien and Father Conrardy worked well together and became very close friends. Father Conrardy was jovial, friendly and well-liked by those who lived at the settlement. Father Damien was grateful that Father Conrardy was able to hear his confession on a regular basis, something that he had been deprived of due to the isolation of his life on Molokai. Father Conrardy had assured Father Damien many times that he would never leave him. Father Damien described him as "a friend, a consoling angel, and a true brother."

Father Conrardy was outspoken when it came to the rights of the lepers at Kalawao. He was not afraid to challenge the Board of Health and he did so on numerous occasions. Hoping for change, he spoke to the newspapers in his frank and forthright manner, bringing to light what he believed to be grave injustices committed by the Board of Health. His comments embarrassed the members of the Board and they resented him for it. "Father Conrardy was one of the most difficult, determined, stubborn, independent, and controversial persons who ever resided at the settlement. In other words, he was much like Father Damien," someone observed.

Father Damien tried to do little things to please Father Conrardy and brought him special things to eat whenever he could. Once, Father Damien brought a surprise to Father Conrardy - a bag of candy and a bag of oranges. Father Damien said, "Don't worry. You can eat these with no fear at all. I made sure that no leper has touched them!" Evidently Father Damien had momentarily forgotten that he too was a leper and that he had touched them.

Father Damien learned about a Chinese medicine called Hoang Nan which was used at the time to treat leprosy, snake bites and skin diseases. It was a remedy that was extracted from a species of ivy. He ordered a large quantity of the Hoang Nan pills and felt that many people in the settlement who took it were helped. He believed that it prolonged the life of some and enabled others to regain their bodily strength and energy. He wanted the Board of Health to supply it to those at the settlement. If they would not do so, he planned to make his request to the Hawaiian parliament.

Father Damien was also interested in the Goto hot bath therapy for leprosy victims which was reportedly more promising than the Hoang Nan pills. It was the scientific work of a Japanese doctor named Masanao Goto who had devoted his life to leprosy patients. He advocated proper diet and two daily hot baths infused with herbs and medicines for sufferers of leprosy. It was not considered a cure, but for many, it greatly relieved the painful symptoms of the disease.

When Father Damien learned that the Goto baths were available at the Kakaako Branch Hospital where Mother Marianne and her Sisters worked, he asked his superior, Father Léonor for permission to travel there in order to receive the treatment. During the many years he served at the Kalawao settlement, he had only made the trip to Honolulu a few times and those were on occasions when he had business to conduct.

Father Léonor wrote back and told Father Damien he would not grant permission for him to receive the Goto therapy at the Kakaako Branch Hospital. He was a leper and he was no longer welcome in Honolulu. Father Léonor added in his letter that Father Damien's presence would be an embarrassment to the entire Catholic mission there. For a long time, Father Damien had felt abandoned and forgotten by his religious congregation and receiving such a letter from his superior only confirmed his feelings.

Dr. Arthur Mouritz then wrote a letter to the bishop on Father Damien's behalf, requesting that he be allowed to travel to the Kakaako Branch Hospital for the Goto therapy. He explained that Father Damien's leprosy was progressing rapidly. Although he was sick, he still had a very heavy workload. He would benefit from the rest as well as from the Goto hot baths. Surrounded by constant death and dying, life at the settlement could be grim. Dr. Mouritz wrote that a short time in Honolulu would be of great advantage to Father Damien and he encouraged his superiors to reconsider.

Although he did not receive official permission to make the trip, Father Damien decided to go anyway. Mother Marianne and the Sisters were elated to receive him as a patient at the Kakaako Branch Hospital. They were well aware that he had sacrificed his life for the lepers at the settlement and they revered him as a saint. Mother Marianne asked Sister Crescentia to be in charge of his care during his stay at the hospital.

Sister Crescentia noted that Father Damien spent all of his spare time at the hospital encouraging the other lepers and talking to them about spiritual matters. His cheerful presence lifted their spirits. He talked a lot to Sister Crescentia about the lepers in Kalawao and how much he loved them and desired to ease their suffering. He never talked about himself. Although he was suffering the terrible effects of his disease, he radiated joy. The day before Father Damien left the hospital in order to return to the settlement, he was visited by King David Kalakaua as well as Walter Gibson, the Prime Minister of Hawaii, and Bishop Koeckemann, Hawaii's third missionary bishop.

Father Damien felt that he had benefitted from the Goto baths and had regained a lot of his energy and vigor. The movement in his hands and fingers had also improved significantly. He wanted the warm-water Goto baths to be available to the lepers at the Kalawao settlement just as they were available to the lepers at the Kakaako Branch Hospital. He asked the Board of Health to provide the Goto baths for those at the settlement but they would not approve it, stating that it would be too expensive.

Father Damien, through his ingenuity, was able to bring the Goto treatment to Kalawao on a modest scale. He purchased empty bread boxes from the settlement store and used them as bathtubs. Recruiting other men to help him, Father Damien cut down kukui trees on the island and used them for firewood. In addition, he ordered a large supply of coal. The water was heated to the required temperature and the Goto baths became available to the lepers.

Five years after the Franciscan Sisters arrival in Hawaii, Father Damien's prayers were finally answered. He got word that three of the Sisters were coming to Molokai to help him in the work. He received the good news just months before his death.

Mother Marianne Cope, Sister Leopoldina Burns, and Sister Vincentia McCormick traveled by the inter-island steamer from Honolulu to Molokai along with forty lepers who were being deported to the settlement. Police herded the lepers up the gangplank to a barricaded pen, a corral that was used to transport cattle to Molokai. They were confined there for the overnight journey with no protection from the elements. The Sisters observed sadly that those who were afflicted with leprosy were shunned completely for the duration of the trip and that animals generally received better care than the lepers did.

The Sisters landed on Molokai on November 14, 1888 and were the first professionally trained nurses to work at the leper settlement. Father Damien had been sick with a high fever and confined to his bed for six weeks. On the day of the Sisters' arrival, he managed to get out of bed and go to the landing wharf at Kalaupapa to welcome them. The Sisters were surprised to see how frail and thin he was. Sister Leopoldina and Sister Vincentia said that he looked "like death." Even so, he was cheerful and filled with joy to see the Sisters.

Father Damien had a desire to continue working at the settlement as long as he had the strength to do so. When a severe storm tore the steeple off St. Philomena church and blew it to the ground, Father Damien immediately began to plan for its reconstruction and repair. Although Father Damien's hands were swollen and grossly enlarged, he still had some movement left in them. He felt that with help, he would be able to do the repair work to the steeple. At the same time, he decided it was the right time to enlarge the church as well as add a more attractive edifice to the front.

Father Corneille Limburg, a Sacred Hearts missionary, had come to Molokai temporarily in order to help Mother Marianne and the Sisters begin their new work. One day, Father Corneille was shocked to see Father Damien up on the sheet metal roof of St. Philomena, doing the repairs and supervising the stonemasons, carpenters, and laborers, all of whom were lepers. Father Damien's face was puffy, his eyes were bloodshot and his ears were swollen. He was in the final stages of leprosy. To Father Corneille, it seemed impossible that Father Damien would be able to do the repair work, given his condition. However, he was in good spirits and working as though he was not sick at all.

At the Kalawao settlement, Father Damien took the Sisters on a tour of the two orphanages. At the girls' orphanage, he gathered the children together and introduced Mother Marianne to them. He told the girls that she was going to be their new mother. "I will soon be going to heaven," he said. "That is why I asked Mother Marianne to come here. She is going to take very good care of you." The girls began to cry and to cling tightly to him.

Father Damien showed the Sisters the boys' orphanage and instructed them on how to make their clothing. The Sisters noticed that three separate times during the course of the day, Father Damien asked them if they would care for the boys after he was gone. Three times they promised him that they would. Father Damien lifted his hands to heaven and thanked God that help had finally come. At that time, there were more than one hundred children in his care and the number of leprosy patients at the settlement had risen to over one thousand. He told the Sisters that he had a great desire to finish the needed repairs to the buildings at the settlement and he knew that would be his last work.

Father Damien realized that it was time to set his affairs in order. He had few earthly possessions and he left all of them to Brother Joseph Dutton to distribute as he wished. As for his beloved horse William, he sold him to Father Conrardy for a very small fee, knowing that he too was a lover of animals and that he would take good care of him. Father Conrardy received the bridle and saddle as well.

James Sinnett, a registered nurse from St. Louis, Missouri arrived at the settlement eight months before Father Damien's death. Inspired by Father Damien's life, he wanted to offer his nursing services at the settlement and received permission to do so by the Hawaiian Board of Health. He had previously worked at Mercy Hospital in Chicago, Illinois.

From the beginning, James Sinnett was called Brother James by Father Damien. Father Damien asked him to help Brother Joseph with bandaging and dressing the wounds of the boys in the orphanage. He also asked Brother James to help with the English correspondence and letter writing. Like the others who served at the settlement, Brother James was soon overwhelmed with work. During the final months of Father Damien's illness, Brother James served as his private nurse and took expert care of him.

Father Damien became bedridden on March 28, 1889. Father Conrardy, Brother James Sinnett and Brother Joseph Dutton remained close by at all times. The lepers from the settlement were almost always in his room. Brother James had the thin straw mat Father Damien had been laying on replaced by a firm mattress with clean sheets and a pillow. He did not protest and he had not slept on something so comfortable since childhood.

Late in the evening, Father Conrardy would go to the church and take out a consecrated host from the tabernacle so that Father Damien could receive Holy Communion. Brother James Sinnett would follow behind Father Conrardy, ringing a bell and carrying a lighted candle as they walked from the church to Father Damien's bedside.

During the last weeks of Father Damien's life, Father Wendelin Moellers visited him often. A Sacred Hearts of Jesus and Mary missionary, Father Wendelin had arrived in Molokai shortly after the Sisters. He was assigned to be the Sisters' chaplain and confessor and would also serve as the pastor at Kalaupapa.

Father Wendelin heard Father Damien's general confession on March 30 and together they renewed their priestly vows.

"How happy I am to die a child of the Congregation of the Sacred Hearts," Father Damien said. He said, "I thank God that I have lived long enough to see two priests at my side and the Franciscan Sisters at the settlement. I know that the work for the lepers is in good hands now." Father Damien was at peace.

Father Wendelin revered Father Damien as a saint and wanted to have a relic. He asked Father Damien if he could have his heavy black cloak. "What good would it be to you?" Father Damien asked. "It is full of leprosy."

Father Damien received the Last Rites from Father Conrardy on April 2, 1889. Those closest to him said that it was truly edifying to see him in his final days because he seemed so happy. "I am happy that I can celebrate Easter in Heaven," he said. A short time before his death, Father Damien was asked where he wanted to be buried. "Under the same pandanus tree where I first slept when I came to the settlement," he replied. He was assured that his desire would be fulfilled. "This is another one of my wishes that our Dear Lord has granted me," Father Damien said thankfully.

When Father Damien was close to death, Father Conrardy knelt beside his bed and recited the prayers for the dying, *"From the realm of death deliver my soul, O Lord. Once I was dead but now I live forever and ever. I hold the keys of death and the nether world. Come, let us return to the Lord."*

After serving sixteen years on the island of Molokai and twenty-five years altogether as a missionary in the Hawaiian Islands, Father Damien died peacefully in the arms of Brother James Sinnett and Father Conrardy on April 15, 1889. Brother James said that it was the most peaceful death he had ever witnessed. It was the first day of Holy Week, the Monday before Easter. Father Damien was 49 years old.

When Mother Marianne and the Sisters were told of Father Damien's death, they quickly set out for his residence. When they arrived, Father Conrardy was there to greet them. With tears streaming down his face and overcome by emotion, he was unable to speak.

Father Wendelin presided at the funeral Mass the following day. Afterward, the funeral procession made its way to the cemetery. The cross bearer led the procession followed by the band, then the members of the funeral association, the Sisters, the women and girls of the settlement, the coffin carried by eight lepers, Father Wendelin, Father Conrardy, Brother Joseph Dutton, Brother James Sinnett and finally the men and the boys of the settlement.

Although he did not wear it in his lifetime, Father Damien was buried with the jeweled medal of honor given to him by King David Kalakaua. A large black marble cross was placed over his grave with the words: "Sacred to the memory of Reverend Father Damien de Veuster who died a martyr to charity for the afflicted lepers, April 15, 1889."

Fifteen days after Father Damien's death, at the solemn funeral Mass in the Cathedral of Our Lady of Peace in Honolulu, Bishop Hermann delivered the eulogy and said:

We are assembled here to honor the memory of a man whose fame has spread over the whole globe. There is perhaps not a city, small or large, in the civilized world where the name of Father Damien is not known and blessed by all sympathetic hearts. Every good man has a right to our respect, but there are degrees in the merits of good men.

A good Christian is justly honored by his fellow Christians; a generous benefactor is entitled to the gratitude of those who have received his benefits; a zealous propagator of the Gospel of Christ who works honestly for the salvation of souls, and who practices himself the works of charity he preaches to others, will always earn the admiration of fair-minded people.

Father Damien unites all these claims to our admiration in an eminent degree, and even many others in addition. But he has two more glorious titles which raise him above the rest of good men - he is a hero and a martyr of Christian charity.

History points out to us many heroes of different kinds. The most celebrated are perhaps those brave men who risked their lives on the battlefield for the defense of their country, with the firm resolution to conquer or to die in the attempt.

Father Damien seems to me to have been a hero more glorious than he who falls on the battlefield, sword in hand. At about the age of thirty-four, in the full strength of youth and in perfect health, he offered to share the fate of those unfortunate ones, separated from their families and friends. He asked, as a favor, the permission to live at the lazaret, in order to console and to comfort, physically and morally, the suffering portion of humanity assembled there through inevitable necessity.

His hierarchical superiors, with joy and admiration for his singular merit, accorded him their consent for his voluntary immolation. He not only exposed himself to the loathsome disease, but he faced the danger with a supernatural Christian indifference, perhaps with more hope than fear to fall a victim of his charity.

Without doing harm to anyone, he has like Christ, conquered by means of his death. For many years he suffered all the symptoms of leprosy. During these last two years, it had become evident that the disgusting sickness had taken hold of his body. Nevertheless, he still continued his arduous work as long as the least ability remained, until God called him to his reward, a real martyr of his devotion to the work of Christian Charity...

People could hear the heart-rending cries of those outcasts of humanity, forcibly thrust on this island in the ocean. They admired the man who voluntarily buried his youth among them. He did not fold his arms and mouth platonic consolations. He could have allowed himself to be fired with a flame of heroism that would be quickly snuffed out. On the contrary, they saw him there in that living graveyard - serious, solid, willing, positive, paying the price with his very own person. He did not allow himself any let up during the innumerable minutes and interminable days, poignant in their incessant renewal of a sixteen-year sojourn. He was as ardent on the last day as he had been on the first. And thus did he take his place among the purest heroes of history and legend. . .

He deserves to be revered as a real disciple of Christ and a man who is a credit to humanity. Up to his time, people pretended to forget that lepers were human beings. His example inspired shame for the continued neglect of essential duties toward them, and for the cruel egoism practiced toward them. Since his time, lepers are no longer treated as pariahs. The world has been brought to realize that they have as much right to help as other suffering persons. . .

After Father Damien's death, numerous organizations dedicated to improving conditions for the sick poor sprung up worldwide including the Damien-Dutton Society, Friends of Father Damien in the Belgium Congo, the Damien Foundation in Korea and many more. When Father Damien cared for the lepers in Molokai, there were few other leper colonies where Catholic priests and nuns served. After his passing, dozens of leper colonies run by Catholic missionaries opened in Africa and Asia as well as many other parts of the world. In the ten years after Father Damien's death, vocations to the Sacred Hearts of Jesus and Mary Congregation increased by more than 70 percent.

Father Damien's death left a great void in the hearts of the people at the settlement and an emptiness that no one else could fill. After his passing, a number of the lepers reverted to their old lawless ways, to drunkenness and debauchery similar to the chaos and discord Father Damien had encountered when he first came to the settlement. There was a revolt and the resident administrator of the Board of Health was captured and tied up. They threatened to do the same to Father Conrardy. Two fatal stabbings occurred at the Kalaupapa landing wharf and a death threat was made against Mother Marianne as well. Fifteen armed police officers were called to the settlement to restore order. As the situation grew more tense, some of the troublemakers barricaded themselves in their homes, refusing to submit to the authorities.

After Father Damien's passing, Mother Marianne remained on Molokai for the rest of her life. She was sick during most of her years on the Islands, but continued to work in spite of it. Her deep spirituality inspired hope in the lepers who loved her as a mother and a friend. She taught her Sisters that their primary duty in life was "to make life as pleasant and as comfortable as possible" for those with leprosy.

Mother Marianne served the lepers in the Hawaiian Islands for thirty-five years. Due to her heavy workload, she was never able to take a vacation in all those years. Quiet and unpretentious, Mother Marianne never sought to be in the spotlight and she shunned publicity of any kind. Nevertheless, her influence was profound and the Hawaiian people revered her. She was described by many as having an angelic nature. Her own Sisters felt that she was a saint. Mindful of the purity of her character, Sister Leopoldina described her as a "beautiful white lily." Mother Marianne died on August 9, 1918. She was eighty years old.

On May 14, 2005, at Mother Marianne's beatification ceremony in Rome, Cardinal José Saraiva Martins said of her,

"She saw in the lepers the suffering face of Jesus. Like the Good Samaritan, she became their mother." Mother Marianne Cope was canonized by Pope Benedict XVI in 2012.

After Father Damien's death, Brother Joseph Dutton's workload increased at the settlement as he assumed many of the duties that Father Damien had formerly done. In honor of his beloved friend, Brother Dutton sent leaves and pieces of the bark from the pandanus tree above Father Damien's grave as souvenirs to those who were devoted to the saintly priest. Brother Joseph received an invitation to a reunion party and celebration with the members of his old army regiment but he declined it. He sent a letter in reply saying, "I have entered another army since seeing you all, enlisting for life or rather death.

Brother Joseph received numerous letters from people who asked him if they could come to Molokai and work with him. He felt that many who inquired seemed to have a highly idealized and almost a romantic idea of the missionary work at the settlement. Brother Joseph wrote back to each one of them and said, "I wish to guard you against having too high an estimate of the work here. Work performed with a good intention to accomplish the will of Almighty God for his glory is the same in one place as another. One's Molokai can be anywhere."

In the evenings, Brother Joseph worked late into the night, by candlelight and oil lamp, trying to answer the hundreds of letters that were sent to him from all over the world. He also spent time in the evenings studying books on medicine to help him in his care of the lepers. He was offered a typewriter as well as electricity for his little cabin, but he refused both.

Brother Joseph Dutton became widely known by many important figures in the United States and abroad. In 1908, President Theodore Roosevelt, who admired Brother Joseph and considered him a great humanitarian, ordered the Pacific Fleet of the U.S. Navy, as it was circling the globe, to divert from its course and pause at the island of Molokai in order to salute the former Army officer. With a volley of gunfire, they acknowledged Joseph Dutton's years of service to the lepers and thanked him. The lepers of Molokai gathered on the shore to witness the historic event and to watch as each of the sixteen vessels passed. The event received wide coverage in the press. In 1923, President Harding sent Brother Joseph a personal letter praising his work. President Coolidge wrote to him in 1928, thanking him for his dedication to the lepers. He also received words of praise from President Woodrow Wilson. Pope Pius XI sent his apostolic blessing to Brother Joseph in 1929. The Hawaiian Parliament honored him as well.

In 1930, Brother Joseph's health was in a state of decline. He also had an eye ailment which required surgery. It was necessary for him to go to the hospital in Honolulu for the operation. Brother Joseph was now eighty-seven years old and had not left Molokai since his arrival in 1886. He had only traveled the two-and-a-half miles to Kalaupapa three times in the last forty-four years. He was very resistant to the idea of going to Honolulu. Those close to him insisted that he go and he was finally convinced to do so.

When Brother Joseph arrived in Honolulu, he was too feeble to walk. Numerous reporters were waiting for him at the dock and were very excited to meet him. They were anxious to ask him questions about his forty-four years serving at the Kalawao leper settlement.

Brother Joseph Dutton received excellent care at the St. Francis Hospital in Honolulu but was too weak to return to Molokai. He died on March 26, 1931. His last wish was that he be buried next to Father Damien and his wish was granted. He had left behind very few possessions. It was discovered that there were 400 letters in his desk which had not yet been answered. At the end of his life he said, "I have had a happy life. Molokai is a happy place."

At the news of Brother Joseph Dutton's death, President Herbert Hoover made a public statement describing him as "a pioneer, a soldier and a great humanitarian." The President said, "It is a privilege to pay tribute to his memory."

Like Brother Joseph Dutton, after the death of Father Damien, Father Conrardy continued working at the Kalawao settlement in Molokai. He served the lepers there for six more years. Later, he visited Canton, China and observed that the lepers in the area were completely neglected and living in appalling misery. The government was not willing to assist them in any way. Father Conrardy wanted to found a leprosarium in China but was told by the Chinese government that he would need to be a licensed medical doctor before doing so.

Father Conrardy went back to the United States and at fifty-five years of age, he began his study of medicine at the University of Oregon's medical school in Portland, Oregon. After graduating, he spent the next eight years preaching, lecturing and fundraising, requesting donations to purchase land in China to build his leper colony. In his spare time, he studied Chinese. He said that if God would allow him ten years to serve the lepers in China, he would be a happy man. He would be satisfied.

Each day, the lepers in China were forced to beg for the small amount of rice they subsisted on. If they became too weak or ill to go out and beg for their food, they would likely die from starvation. No one was helping them or advocating for them. Conditions for the lepers in Molokai were much better than for the lepers in China.

Bishop Jean-Marie Merel, the Bishop of Canton, China wrote to Father Conrardy and told him that one day a group of lepers knocked on the door of his residence. They told him they had heard that a priest was planning to come to China to help them and they wanted to know if it was true. Bishop Merel told them that it was indeed true. Father Conrardy was coming as soon as he was able to raise the money and he planned to build a leper colony where the patients would receive food, shelter and medical attention. Bishop Merel added in his letter that the lepers were overjoyed to hear the news and were waiting for Father Conrardy with great anticipation.

In the United States, Father Conrardy made his appeal at churches in Brooklyn, Newark, Baltimore, Philadelphia, Boston,

Syracuse and more. He preached every Sunday morning and evening as well as two or three times during the week.

Father Conrardy wrote articles in the newspapers, went door to door, and engaged in an extensive speaking tour in order to raise public awareness about the plight of the lepers in China and to ask for donations. He did not confine his speaking tour to churches but lectured in secular institutions as well. He experienced what he called "the generosity of the American spirit." He also preached and lectured in Canada as well as in Italy, France, and England. On one occasion, a robber stole a portion of the money that he had been given for the China mission. Another time he was arrested and charged with being a swindler but later released when his innocence was proven.

By 1908, Father Conrardy (Dr. Louis Lambert Conrardy) had raised thirty thousand dollars. At sixty-seven years of age, he returned to China, purchased twenty acres of land and founded St. Joseph's leper colony on the island of Shek Lung between Hong Kong and Canton. As it had been stated on many occasions, "Father Conrardy had a great capacity for achieving the impossible."

Father Conrardy went through the city searching for lepers and inviting them to come to St. Joseph's. Right away, he had seventy lepers in his charge. Since he was unable to find anyone to help him, he did all of the work himself. He provided medical assistance to the lepers, bandaged their wounds and saw to their every need. With the skills he had learned in medical school, he achieved wonderful results. St. Joseph's leprosarium became known as the "second Molokai."

The sick who resided at St. Joseph's leper colony had profound love and gratitude for Father Conrardy. He did all that he could to comfort them and to relieve their pain. At their bedside, he was not afraid to hold their hand or to embrace them with fatherly affection. They said, "Make no mistake about it. We have never before and will never again meet so great a man as Father Conrardy. We are ten times more indebted to him than to our own fathers!"

Impressed with all the good that Father Conrardy was doing on Shek Lung, in 1913 the Chinese government gave St. Joseph's leper colony its formal approval and full support. Later, St. Joseph's grew to be home to seven hundred lepers. Five nuns with nursing degrees who belonged to the Missionary Sisters of the Immaculate Conception of Montreal eventually came to the leper colony to help Father Conrardy. Two priests, one Chinese and one French, came to serve there as well. St. Joseph's soon became the largest Catholic leprosarium in the world.

Father Conrardy died of pneumonia in Hong Kong on August 24, 1914. He was seventy-three years old. He was buried according to his desire, rolled up in a mat between two lepers. He made all the necessary provisions so that St. Joseph's leper colony would continue to function long after his death. Approximately two hundred missionary vocations are attributed to the inspiration of Father Louis Lambert Conrardy's exemplary life.

In 1936, King Leopold III of Belgium, asked and received permission from President Franklin D. Roosevelt for the permanent transfer of Father Damien's body to Belgium. On the day of his transfer, the band of the 20th Artillery Regiment played while his remains were taken by military escort to the U.S. Army troop ship, the *U.S.S. Republic*. He was given the honor that the United States Army reserves only for its greatest heroes. Overhead eight bombers flew. The Belgian navy ship *Mercator* was waiting to receive Father Damien's body in Panama.

The Secretary of State to Pope Pius XI, Eugene Cardinal Pacelli, the future Pope Pius XII sent the following message: "The sublime devotion of this religious, consuming his life on the far-off islands of Hawaii in the service of the lepers to whom he abundantly gave all spiritual and corporal comforts, will remain one of the most beautiful examples of apostolic activity of our times."

In Antwerp, Belgium on May 2, 1936, the King, the King's cabinet, high government officials, members of the Catholic episcopate and hundreds of thousands of Belgian citizens were waiting for Father Damien's arrival. When the *Mercator* dropped its anchor, amidst great pomp and circumstance, the cannons sounded, the trumpets blared, and all the bells in the city of Antwerp began to ring. Soldiers, in unison, lifted their guns in an impressive military salute. Members of Father Damien's religious congregation, the Sacred Hearts of Jesus and Mary, formed a Guard of Honor. The casket was placed before the platform where King Leopold III stood. The king then stepped forward and saluted Father Damien with great reverence.

A hearse, drawn by six white horses, carried Father Damien's casket to Our Lady's Cathedral where a solemn pontifical Mass was then celebrated in the presence of the highest civil and religious figures in Belgium. The Archbishop of Mechelen-Brussels, delivered the eulogy.

Late in the evening, the hearse carried Father Damien's body to Louvain. He was laid to rest in a crypt in St. Joseph's Chapel in the National Shrine dedicated to St. Joseph and directed by the Fathers of the Sacred Hearts of Jesus and Mary.

After his beatification in June 1995, part of his remains were taken back to Molokai and reinterred in his original grave. In 2005, Father Damien was voted "the greatest Belgian" in the nation's history. He was named the patron saint of lepers and outcasts as well as the patron saint of the diocese of Honolulu and of Hawaii.

In 1984, Mother Teresa of Calcutta, the founder of the Missionaries of Charity in India, wrote a letter to Pope John Paul II, urging him to declare Father Damien a saint. Mother Teresa had a great devotion to Father Damien. In her letter to Pope John Paul II she said:

> Dear Holy Father, as you know we are working among thousands of lepers in India, Yemen, Ethiopia and Tanzania through mobile clinics and

rehabilitation centers built on land given by different governments. To be able to continue this beautiful work of love and healing, we need a saint to guide and protect us. Father Damien could be that saint. Holy Father, our lepers and each one throughout the world beg you for this gift – a saint and martyr of great love and a beautiful example of obedience...

Father Damien was raised to sainthood on October 11, 2009. The unexplainable cure of Audrey Toguchi of Aiea on Oahu's south shore, provided the needed miracle for his canonization.

In January 1998, Audrey had a biopsy of a large lump on her hip which revealed that she had *pleomorphic liposarcoma*, an aggressive and rare form of cancer of the fat tissues. The mass was removed and Audrey underwent radiation to stop the spread of the disease but three months later the cancer had metastasized and had spread to both lungs.

Dr. Walter Chang, her doctor, told her that she had at the most, six months to live. In cases of *pleomorphic liposarcoma* spreading to other parts of the body, 80 percent of patients die within six to twelve months. Memorial Sloan-Kettering Cancer Center in New York reported that out of 135 patients with the same type of cancer as Audrey's, three years after their diagnosis, all 135 patients had died.

Dr. Chang recommended chemotherapy but explained to Audrey that there was no cure for her condition, that it was terminal. He said to her, "Nobody has ever survived this form of cancer. It is going to take your life." Audrey decided against having chemotherapy. If she was not going to get well, she saw no reason to take the anti-cancer drugs.

Audrey's parish priest encouraged her to pray to Father Damien and to ask for his intercession, which she did. With all the sincerity of her heart, she prayed to Father Damien, asking to be healed of cancer. Audrey remembered the day when she stood on Honolulu's shore with hundreds of others in order to watch as

Father Damien's earthly remains were carried to the *S.S. Republic* ship enroute to Belgium. Audrey was seven years old at the time. Some of her relatives who had been stricken with leprosy had lived and died on Molokai when Father Damien served there. Dr. Chang was shocked sometime later, when x-rays showed that the tumors in Audrey's lungs had shrunk significantly. Several months later, her cancer had disappeared completely. Dr. Chang said that as far as he knew, Audrey's was the only documented case where *pleomorphic liposarcoma* had spontaneously regressed and disappeared without any treatment. A number of doctors who were consulted all agreed that Audrey's cure was unexplainable by medical science.

Pope Benedict XVI canonized Father Damien at St. Peter's Basilica in Rome on Rosary Sunday, October 11, 2009. King Albert II and Queen Paola of Belgium were in attendance as well as a number of leprosy patients from Hawaii and thousands of admirers from all parts of the world. St. Damien de Veuster's feast day is celebrated each year on May 10.

It is in time that I am able to do good to my neighbor, that I am able to love and help him... It is only along the path of my passing days that I am able to meet the suffering soul and to give a word of comfort and hope. Time is valuable, because it offers me the possibility to do good. Certainly, upright Christian sentiment, knowledge, love and praise of God will continue in eternity, but they will be proportional to our knowledge, love and praise in time. . .Time is valuable because it offers me the possibility to prepare myself for eternity.
- Father Gerardo di Flumeri

Chapter 4

Saint André Bessette

Alfred Bessette (Saint André Bessette) was born on August 9, 1845 in a one room wooden cabin in the village of Saint Grégoire Iberville, about thirty miles southeast of Montreal, Canada. He was so sickly and weak at birth that the midwife decided to baptize him immediately, fearing that he would not live more than a few hours. The next day he was taken to church and formally baptized by the parish priest.

Alfred's childhood was one of poverty and deprivation. His father, Isaac was a carpenter and woodcutter by trade and was not able to find sufficient work in the isolated village where they lived. On more than one occasion, the Bessettes had to pack everything up and move as Isaac sought work to support his ever-growing family.

Alfred's mother Clothilde, was very pious. She taught her children their prayers and gathered them together every evening for family devotions. Alfred adored his mother and throughout his life, he remembered her beautiful smile. Alfred used to say that after his mother's death, he often saw her smiling at him.

Clothilde passed on her great devotion to St. Joseph to her children. Two of her distant cousins, Marie Rose Durocher and Marguerite d'Youville were very holy women. Marie Rose Durocher who founded the Sisters of the Holy Family of Jesus and Mary was beatified in 1982 and Marguerite d'Youville who founded the Sisters of Charity of Montreal was canonized in 1990.

Because Alfred was frail and sickly, his mother gave him special attention. She worried about his health and tried to give him nourishing food to build up his strength. Every evening when the family prayers were recited, Alfred sat next to his mother.

When Alfred was nine years old, his father passed away in a tragic accident. Isaac was cutting down a tree when it fell the wrong way and crushed him, killing him instantly. His son Isaïe was nearby and witnessed the terrible accident. He was so traumatized that he was unable to speak for days.

Clothilde tried to the best of her ability to support the family and keep everyone together but she never really recovered from the shock and sadness of losing her dear husband. Her neighbors pitched in and tried to help her by providing food and other necessities for the children but the family remained destitute.

When Clothilde was diagnosed with tuberculosis, her strength began to gradually ebb away. Alfred, Léocadie, Marie and the younger children remained with her and the four oldest boys went to live as hired hands on nearby farms. Clothilde knew that Alfred needed to avoid heavy manual labor because of his poor health. She wanted him to seek an apprenticeship and learn a trade but a fee was required which she could not afford. At the age of eleven years, Alfred lived at home and worked as a day laborer on the nearby farms.

In the province of Quebec at that time, there was no public school system. However, families who had money could send their children to private schools if they wished. Since there was no free public education, Alfred did not have the opportunity to attend school.

One day, Clothilde received the news that her son Joseph had disappeared. Joseph was fifteen years old and had been living on a nearby farm working as a field hand. Clothilde learned that he had been severely abused by the family who had taken him in.

Joseph had stowed away on a boat headed for the United States. A cook on the boat discovered the frail and fragile boy and felt very sorry for him. When the boat docked in Plattsburgh, New York, the cook supplied Joseph with food and told him where he could find a job in the iron mines. It was many years before Joseph was reunited with his family.

When Clothilde was forty-three years old, her health took a turn for the worse. She gathered her children around her bedside and said goodbye to each one of them. She told them that she wanted them to always attend Mass on Sundays and to remain strong in their faith. She died on November 20, 1857.

Alfred then moved in with his mother's sister, Rosalie and her husband Timothée Nadeau who along with their five children, lived in the town of St. Césaire. Alfred's oldest siblings - Isaïe, Napoleon, Claude, and Marie all went their separate ways after the death of their mother. The three youngest siblings were cared for by Léocadie, Alfred's older sister.

Rosalie and Timothée were able to send twelve-year-old Alfred to school for a short time. It was his first and only opportunity to get an education. He was very grateful to his aunt and uncle and proved to be a good student. At the same time, Alfred was being prepared for his first Holy Communion. Rosalie and Timothée bought Alfred a blue suit for his first Holy Communion and he had his picture taken on that very special day.

Alfred's Uncle Timothée knew that Alfred's health was poor but explained to him that he needed to get a job and help contribute to the family's income. Alfred was twelve years old at the time. Uncle Timothée arranged for Alfred to learn to be a shoemaker. Although he made the effort, Alfred did not do well as an apprentice to the village cobbler. Striking a hammer all day and kneeling down to make the shoes required more physical strength than he was capable of. His chronic stomach problems flared up as his strength failed. He loved his Aunt Rosalie and Uncle Timothée very much and felt that he was a disappointment to them.

After leaving the shoemaking trade, Alfred tried his hand as a tinsmith, but did not do much better. After that, he found a job as a baker's assistant. The work was lighter and he was much more suited to it. He enjoyed working in the bakery, kneading the dough and preparing the loaves of bread.

In 1860, Timothée Nadeau decided to join the "gold rush" to California, hoping to find his fortune prospecting for gold. Before he left, he moved his family to the town of Farnham. Fifteen-year-old Alfred was then expected to fend for himself. Alfred found a job as a blacksmith and later moved to Sainte Brigide where he found work hauling wood. Later, he traveled to Sainte Angele where he was hired as a construction worker. He worked twelve hours a day, six days a week for wages that were generally not much more than one dollar a day. He then returned to St. Césaire where a farmer, Louis Ouimet, hired him on as a field hand.

Louis Ouimet was aware that Alfred was a very pious young man. On one occasion, Louis purchased a wooden crucifix at an auction and gave it to Alfred. Alfred treasured the crucifix and hung it up in the barn. He began to spend all of his free time there, praying before it. Alfred loved to pray the Rosary of the Sacred Wounds as well as the Rosary of the Seven Sorrows and Seven Joys of St. Joseph. He also loved novenas and vocal prayers.

As a teenager, Alfred made a good impression on his many employers. One of them observed, "Nobody was more pious than Alfred." Another said, "He was a very sickly young man. He could digest practically nothing. He rarely went out but he was very kind and he was always praying." His employers as well as his friends and associates spoke of the excellence of his character.

In 1863, Canada was experiencing an economic depression. Alfred was barely able to make a living and realized that that he was getting nowhere in life. He believed there was no future for him in the poverty-stricken farm towns he had been working in. He had heard that jobs were plentiful in the United States where people enjoyed greater opportunity and prosperity. A number of Alfred's good friends as well as his relatives had already relocated to the United States in search of work.

Alfred asked Father Edward Springer, the parish priest at Farnham, for advice. Father Springer encouraged him to move to the United States saying that the climate would certainly be better for his health and there would be greater opportunities for work.

Most of Alfred's brothers and sisters were living in different parts of New England. Alfred left for the United States with great excitement and anticipation. Although he was twenty years old, he looked more like a young man of fifteen or sixteen years of age. He took a train to Nashua, New Hampshire and found a job in a factory for a time. After that, he contacted his brothers, Napoleon and Claude as well as his sisters Marie and Josephine and joined them in Connecticut where he found employment in the cotton mills in Moosup and Putnam. Alfred's brother Joseph was living near Plattsburgh, New York and working in the mines.

It was common knowledge that work in the cotton mills and the factories was dangerous as well as harmful to a person's health. The mills were frequently called "sweatshops" or "graveyards of the poor." The dust in the stifling and airless mills was a constant health hazard and could lead to debilitating respiratory problems as well as tuberculosis. Shifts in the mills were from six o'clock in the morning until six o'clock in the evening. Two to three times a week, two hours of overtime was required. The pay was so low that Alfred had barely enough money to pay for his room and board.

In order to protect his health, Alfred would never work in one of the mills or factories for more than several months at a time. He would change to outdoor work as a farm laborer and even though the pay was much less, he felt that his health was safeguarded.

On one occasion, Alfred was working in a hayfield and was exhausted after what seemed like an endless day of labor. He began to daydream and he prayed to St. Joseph, "Where will I die, St. Joseph?" He then experienced what he called a "waking dream." He saw a large stone building with many windows and a tall spire with a cross on it. Actually, the building that he saw had not been built yet. Many years later when he saw Notre Dame School for the first time, he instantly recognized it as the building in his dream. He did not die there but he lived and worked there for forty years. It was also at Notre Dame School that he discovered his life's work, the building of the Oratory of St. Joseph.

Alfred sang hymns while he worked and used his spare moments to pray. With his long work week, he had very little free time. He spent whatever free time he had, as well as all of Sunday, in church. He was well-liked and made many good friends while living in the United States. His sister Léocadie said of him, "He was so sweet. He was loved by everyone." His new friends often expressed surprise at how religious he was.

The three years that Alfred spent in the United States brought him nothing he had hoped for. In 1867, twenty-two-year-old Alfred decided to go back to Canada. His health was so compromised that he could not work in the mills any longer. As an unskilled, itinerant laborer, he had only been able to find jobs that were low paying or seasonal. Financially, he was no better off than he was before he left Canada.

Throughout his life, Alfred rarely spoke about his time working in the United States. In addition, he said little or nothing about his childhood and youth. Almost all of the information that is known about his early life was supplied by various family members.

Alfred decided to move to Sutton, Quebec where his brother Claude and his sister Léocadie had settled. In Sutton, Alfred found a job as a gardener and handyman for the parish priest. When the parish priest was transferred, the new priest decided that a gardener was not a necessity and Alfred had to once again search for work.

Alfred found employment as a stable boy and farm worker in St. Césaire for Louis Ouimet who had given him a job some years before. By the time Alfred had reached the age of twenty-five, he had worked at ten different trades in nine different towns.

When Alfred was not working on the farm or taking care of the horses for Mr. Ouimet, he was spending any free time he had at the church. He volunteered to do chores and odd jobs on the church grounds and at the rectory.

In St. Césaire, Father André Provencal served as the parish priest. He was loved and admired by his parishioners for his kindness and his deep spirituality. Alfred began to visit the rectory regularly in order to speak to Father Provencal and the two had many heart to heart conversations together. Facing the uncertainties of his future, Alfred asked Father Provencal for advice.

Father Provencal had recently built a boarding school for boys and asked members of the Holy Cross Congregation to act as administrators of the school. Eighty students who ranged in age from eight to fourteen years old were enrolled and six members of the Holy Cross Congregation lived and worked at the school. Some of the brothers and priests served as the teachers and others did the maintenance work and the gardening. The school was flourishing and enrollment was continually increasing.

Father Provencal asked Alfred if he would be interested in becoming a religious brother of the Holy Cross Congregation. Alfred would benefit from having the support and friendship of a community that had the same spiritual ideals that he had. He would be able to assist at Mass and receive Holy Communion daily.

Alfred told Father Provencal that he had always wanted to be a religious brother and that no other vocation really appealed to him. But he felt that his lack of education and the fact that he could barely read or write would prove to be an obstacle to his admission into the Holy Cross Congregation. Father Provencal assured Alfred that it would not be a problem. He could be admitted as a working brother. He would help with maintaining the grounds and buildings and take care of the manual work at the school. His lack of education would certainly not be an issue.

Alfred had been thinking a lot about his future. Even though he was knowledgeable and experienced in farming, he knew that he did not want to be a farmer or a landowner. He was definitely not interested in making a lot of money. As one person observed, "Alfred did not seem to be made to live in the secular world." He felt the greatest happiness when he was in church or in the company of priests or other members of the clergy.

The Holy Cross Congregation maintained a high school in St. Laurent, a primary school in St. Césaire, and an elementary school in Côte-des-Neiges. The congregation was consecrated to St. Joseph, the Protector of Canada. That fact was very appealing to Alfred who had grown up with a strong love for St. Joseph and had been taught from his childhood to revere him.

When Alfred applied for admission to the Holy Cross Congregation, Father Provencal wrote a letter of recommendation for him to the Director of Novices, Father Julien Gastineau. He wrote, "I am sending you a saint for your community."

In the autumn of 1870, twenty-five-year-old Alfred Bessette traveled to Montreal where he was received warmly by Father Gastineau and began his novitiate. As a novice, he was given a new name. He would be known as Brother André after his saintly mentor, Father André Provencal. He also received the black habit of the Holy Cross Congregation. That same year, Pope Pius IX proclaimed St. Joseph the patron of the Universal Church.

The brothers got up at five o'clock in the morning and remained extremely busy until they recited the final evening prayers together and retired at 7:30 p.m. During his novitiate, Brother André scrubbed the floors and did the general cleaning. Father Gastineau observed what a hard and dedicated worker he was. Halfway through his novitiate, Brother André was transferred to the St. Laurent School and was assigned to be linen keeper, attendant in the infirmary, and general house cleaner.

An outbreak of smallpox occurred in the summer of 1871 at St. Laurent School and a number of the students as well as members of the staff contracted the disease. The infirmary was completely full. One of the teaching brothers and one of the novices died. Father Beaudet, the superior of the school, asked the members of the Holy Cross Congregation at the Notre Dame School for help in caring for the sick who were in quarantine.

Brother André, who was working at the Notre Dame School, was transferred temporarily to St. Laurent to help take care of the sick in the infirmary. When he got to St. Laurent, he organized a procession and a statue of St. Joseph was carried through the infirmary as well as through all of the rooms of the school. Everyone prayed for St. Joseph's intercession. From the day that Brother André arrived at St. Laurent School to help, there were no new cases of smallpox and no more deaths. Within two days, everyone who was sick had recovered.

André's health in the novitiate was very poor. He suffered from severe stomach pains, digestive problems and debilitating headaches. On occasion, he coughed up blood. He ate very sparingly, usually just a bit of dry bread dipped in milk. He never weighed more than 110 lbs. and stood just a little over five feet tall. As he grew older his weight dropped down to 100 lbs. He was so short that he was sometimes described as dwarfish.

When the Provincial Council of the Congregation of the Holy Cross met on January 8, 1872, they decided that Brother André would not be allowed to make his temporary vows because of his numerous health problems. They felt sure that he would not be strong enough to do the heavy manual labor that would be required of him as a working brother. He was completely crushed by the news. He asked his superiors to allow him to stay on just a little longer and they agreed to it.

Father Pierre Guy, who had recently replaced Father Gastineau as Novice Master, was impressed by Brother André's many virtues and by his unique spiritual gifts. He wanted him to be allowed to continue in the novitiate. He wrote a letter to the new Provincial Superior, Father Camille Lefebvre and told him of the piety of Brother André. He said, "If this young man is unable to carry out his duties because of his health, at least he will be able to pray for us."

One day, the bishop of Montreal, Ignace Bourget, made an official visit to St. Laurent School. André gathered up all the courage he could muster and approached the bishop at a moment when the bishop was alone. He told him that he was deeply disappointed that he was going to be dismissed from the novitiate because of his poor health. The bishop spoke to him in a loving and fatherly way and told him not to worry. He assured him that he would indeed be allowed to continue on as a novice in the Congregation of the Holy Cross.

In August of 1872, the Provincial Council met again and had a change of heart regarding the dismissal of Brother André. Taking into account his great zeal and piety, the Council decided unanimously to allow him to make his temporary vows. Brother André felt that this new development was due to Bishop Bourget's direct intervention.

On February 2, 1874, the Council permitted Brother André to make his final vows, promising his commitment to his religious vocation for the rest of his life. A formal photograph was taken of him for the occasion. He was wearing the black habit of the Holy Cross Congregation with the traditional black cord around his waist, a plain wooden cross around his neck and a medal of St. Joseph pinned on his habit. He looked much younger than his twenty-eight years.

After Brother André made his final vows, his superiors assigned him to be the doorkeeper at Notre Dame School. They believed that his cheerful disposition and friendly demeanor made him the perfect choice to greet the visitors who came to the school daily. He was polite, helpful, even-tempered, discreet, and patient, and he had a good deal of common sense. Those were all qualities that would serve him well as doorkeeper. He would spend the next forty years of his life working in that capacity.

As doorkeeper, Brother André's room, called the "porter's lodge," was segregated from the rest of the Holy Cross community. It was located near the entry door to the school so that anyone who called would receive prompt service. Brother André took all of his meals alone in the porter's lodge so that he could remain close to the door. His bed was actually a hard bench that was only sixteen inches wide. Many of the fathers of the students at Notre Dame School liked to go to the porter's lodge to converse with Brother André.

Brother André, with his sensitive stomach, had a hard time digesting the food that was served to the community so he usually just had milk and dry bread. One of the brothers encouraged him to tell the cook about his problem and to ask her to prepare something else for him to eat. "I could never do that," Brother André replied. "I would be afraid that she would think I did not like her cooking and it might hurt her feelings."

Shortly after Brother André was assigned to Notre Dame School, he wrote a letter to his Aunt Rosalie and Uncle Timothée. He told them that he was very happy as a Holy Cross brother and he proudly stated that if they were ever able to visit him, as the doorkeeper, he would be there to open the door and to greet them upon their arrival. He dictated the letter since he had never learned to write.

Every morning at five o'clock, Brother André rang the bell and then knocked on the door of every member of the Holy Cross Congregation, making sure they were all awake. After that, he awakened all the students. When necessary, he helped the youngest children get ready for school.

As doorkeeper, throughout the day, Brother André greeted the many visitors who came to the door of Notre Dame School. It was his job to enforce the visitation hours and to keep track of the sign-in log for all the students. He cleaned the corridors, washed the windows, swept the rooms, the chapel, the staircases and the hallways. He did the landscaping, maintained the grounds, worked in the wine cellar and did general handyman duties. When one of the priests or brothers returned from a trip, it was Brother André's responsibility to fix him a meal.

Father Louage, who became the superior in 1880, was hot-tempered. Brother André often got on Father Louage's nerves and was scolded by him on a regular basis. It seemed that Father Louage was always unleashing his anger on Brother André. The other brothers called Brother André the "lightning rod of the school" because he was so often on the receiving end of Father Louage's wrath.

On Wednesdays, Brother André went by horse and buggy through the streets of Montreal, dropping off the students' dirty laundry to their homes and picking up their clean laundry. The nuns who worked at the school had originally been responsible for picking up the laundry but they had such a heavy work load that the task was given to Brother André.

Brother André also ran errands in town and took the outgoing mail to the post office, bringing back letters and packages to distribute. In addition, he was the official barber for an ever-increasing number of boys enrolled at Notre Dame School. He also cut the hair of the Holy Cross priests and brothers. In the evenings, he repaired the vestments and sewed for various members of the religious community. He also made the twisted and tasseled waist cords of their habits. Even though his workload was excessive, he felt it was a great honor to be a member of the Holy Cross Congregation and he was very happy in his religious vocation. All the priests and brothers in the congregation had numerous responsibilities and like Brother André, had to work extremely hard.

Brother André was also the appointed undertaker for the congregation. When a Holy Cross priest or brother died, it was Brother André's job to wash and dress the body in order to prepare it for burial. In Montreal, there were a number of poor people who were not able to afford the services of an undertaker. Brother André assisted them as well.

On one occasion Brother André collapsed, spitting up blood. The doctor was sent for and said that he was suffering from pneumonia as well as exhaustion. He would need two months of complete rest in order to get well. Those were hard words for Brother André to hear. He could not bear to be idle and took no pleasure at all in rest. He wanted to be active and working nearly all the time.

After the doctor left, Brother André's superior, Father Louage, came to his room to check on him. Brother André asked his superior, "Would it bother you if I died here at the school while scrubbing the floors or cleaning the windows?" His superior made no reply. Brother André then said, "If it does not make a difference to you, it does not make a difference to me." André went back to work almost immediately, ignoring the doctor's orders.

Brother André, even in his youth, lead a penitential life. He restricted his sleep, claiming that there was too much work to do to sleep. He slept six hours or less and often worked eighteen hours a day. He liked to get up very early and throughout his life, he never rose later than five o'clock in the morning. He ate little and he ate poorly. He was always extremely thin. He believed that it was advantageous to a person's physical as well as spiritual health to "eat as little as possible and work as much as possible."

Brother André's breakfast generally consisted of coffee and a piece of bread with no butter. He ate very little meat. When he was invited to a friend's house for dinner, he would eat whatever was set before him. He often made himself little balls of flour cooked in boiling water with bouillon added. Because of his chronic stomachaches and intestinal cramps, he could not tolerate very much food. He never went to a doctor to find out about his stomach trouble and he never prayed to be healed.

Some believed that the dietary restrictions he imposed upon himself as a young man had damaged his health and had given him lifelong digestive problems.

Brother André practiced frugality to a degree that many considered extreme. From the poverty of his childhood and youth, he had learned to live sparingly. In the evening, he always checked to make sure that no extra lights were left on. He did not want the congregation to waste money on unnecessary lighting. It was observed that he wore the same black habit every day for ten years.

On one occasion, Brother André approached the mother of one of the students at Notre Dame school who was a seamstress. He told her that his habit was so old that he could not wear it anymore. He showed her two of the habits that he had used in the past and asked her if she could sew them together to make one new habit for him. When she saw the condition of the two habits, she said it would be impossible. They were too old and too threadbare to be of any use.

Brother André did not keep up with the news or read newspapers or magazines and he refused to listen to the radio. He had no interest in politics and would not discuss the subject with anyone. He did not smoke or drink and had no hobbies or amusements.

The Congregation of the Holy Cross had a tradition of anointing the sick with oil from a lamp that had burned before a statue of St. Joseph. It was often referred to as "oil from St. Joseph's lamp." They would then rub the affected area with a medal of St. Joseph that was wrapped in cloth and placed on the outside of the person's clothing. Whenever Brother André was ill, he asked to be anointed with the oil and medal of St. Joseph and he recommended this practice to others as well. He also kept a good supply of St. Joseph medals and would give them to anyone who was in need.

Often if people were ill, Brother André would anoint them with the oil of St. Joseph and would also rub the affected area with a medal. He would then pray for healing through the intercession of St. Joseph. He would do this for the men who came to him and asked for his prayers. For the women, he gave each one a medal of St. Joseph and asked them to use it themselves along with the oil of St. Joseph. Brother André always stressed that the medal and the oil had no mysterious or supernatural properties. The inexpensive medals were made out of tin and the oil was simple olive oil.

If a student at Notre Dame School had a headache, Brother André would often touch a medal of St. Joseph to his head and pray for him. Many times, it happened that the headache would disappear. Likewise, if a student was under the weather for any reason, Brother André would pray and use the medal and the results were often amazing.

Brother André was never too busy to lend a listening ear to any of the students who wanted to talk to him and he would encourage them by saying, "What the Holy Spirit did for the apostles, he will do for you!" He taught them special prayers to recite and spoke to them frequently about St. Joseph.

The students at the school loved Brother André and felt his genuine care and concern for them. One student wrote, "For us, Brother André was perfection. We respected him. When we greeted him, he always had a beautiful smile."

At Notre Dame School, word began to spread about the saintly doorkeeper. There was talk about the reported healings of the students who came to him with stomachaches and headaches. But there were also more dramatic cures reported by adults who claimed healings from terminal illnesses and life-threatening diseases when Brother André prayed for them. More and more people began seeking out Brother André, asking for his prayers. Complete strangers began to knock on the door at Notre Dame School, wanting to speak to the doorkeeper they had heard so much about.

The first documented cure of an individual who was healed as a result of Brother André's prayers took place on February 5,

1877. Brother Aldéric Manceau, a teaching brother who worked at Notre Dame School, cut his leg on a piece of iron. A serious infection set in and although the doctor tried many remedies, nothing seemed to work.

After a month of suffering from pain and swelling in his leg, Brother Aldéric was told by his doctor that his leg might have to be amputated. Knowing the great faith that Brother André had in the devotional oil, Brother Aldéric asked Brother André to obtain oil for him from St. Joseph's lamp. The oil was put on Brother Aldéric's leg and many prayers were offered up to St. Joseph for healing.

When Brother Aldéric woke up the next morning, the pain and swelling in his leg was gone. Several days later, he took off the bandage and saw that the wound had healed. Free of all symptoms, he was able to go back to his teaching job at the school.

Another remarkable healing took place when a woman on crutches came to see Brother André. At the time, Brother André was busy on his hands and knees scrubbing the floor at Notre Dame School. When he was told that the woman was there to see him, he did not get up to go and speak to her. He did not even look up. He simply said, "Let her walk," as he continued to scrub the floor. When the woman was told what Brother André had said, she was cured on the spot. From that time forward she was able to walk without the help of crutches. She told many of her friends about her miraculous healing.

When Brother André was thirty-two-years-old, five well documented cures that were attributed to his prayerful intercession were published. However, Brother André made it quite clear that he had no power to heal anyone. He would say to those who came to him asking for his prayers, "Personally, I cannot do anything to help you. Only St. Joseph can. Pray to him and ask him to intercede for you and he will do so."

When Father Louis Geoffrion became the director of the Notre Dame School and superior of the community, he gave Brother André his full support. But the school doctor, Dr.

Joseph Albini Charette did not share his sentiments. Although Dr. Charette was a devout Catholic, he was opposed to Brother André's habit of anointing the sick with St. Joseph oil. He began to call Brother André a "quack doctor."

On one occasion, one of the students from Notre Dame School came to Dr. Charette's office with a high fever. Dr. Charette sent him to the infirmary and put him on complete bed rest. Brother André visited the boy and prayed for him as he touched him with the medal and oil of St. Joseph. "You are not sick," he said to the boy. "You can get up and go to the playground now."

When word got back to Dr. Charette, he was furious. Even though the doctor admitted that the boy's fever was gone and that he had regained all of his strength, he felt that Brother André had overstepped his bounds by going against his orders. He felt that Brother André was endangering the lives of the students and had to be stopped.

Dr. Charette complained to the superior and said that sick people who were seeking to talk to Brother André should not have free access to the school. Some of the parents of the students complained as well. They felt it was unhealthy to have the sick near their children. Some had contagious diseases and could pose a health risk to the students as well as to the staff.

As time passed, the visitors who came to Notre Dame School continued to increase. Often, people wandered unsupervised through the halls looking for Brother André. The constant stream of visitors to the school became an annoyance and a distraction to the staff.

It was decided that it would be best for all concerned if Brother André met with the sick across the street from the school in the outdoor tramway station shelter on Queen Mary Road. The shelter was unheated and open on the side facing the tracks. The new arrangement worked out well but proved to be a hardship in the winter when people had to wait in the frigid, bone-chilling weather.

Mr. and Mrs. Sauvage owned a religious articles store that was located right beside the tramway shelter. They let Brother André use two rooms in their store, one as his office and one as a waiting room where he received the sick. The overflow had to wait outside in the open air in the tramway shelter. Brother André was very grateful to Mr. and Mrs. Sauvage for their generosity. Nevertheless, he felt very sorry for those who had to wait outside during the winter months.

Just behind the tramway shelter was a heavily wooded area on the mountainside of Mount Royal that was owned by a man named Michael Guerin. He was an obstinate and bad-tempered man who would turn his vicious dogs on anyone who stepped on his property. The Holy Cross Congregation learned that Mr. Guerin had decided to sell his land. They wanted to purchase it but Mr. Guerin, who had a strong dislike for the Holy Cross Congregation as well as the Notre Dame School, refused to sell it to them.

Father Louis Geoffrion, the director of the school and superior of the community, was concerned that developers would come in and purchase Mr. Guerin's land. He had already heard talk that there were plans to do so. If the land was used to build commercial establishments such as restaurants or bars, the peaceful and private surroundings that the staff and the students enjoyed would be gone. The Holy Cross Congregation wanted at all costs to safeguard the spiritual atmosphere of Notre Dame School.

One day, Father Geoffrion and Brother Alderic walked to Mr. Guerin's property and placed a medal of St. Joseph in the hollow of a tree, praying that the Holy Cross Congregation would be able to purchase the land. Remarkably, in only a matter of days, Mr. Guerin had a complete change of heart and decided to sell his land to the Holy Cross Congregation.

After the twenty-five acres on Mount Royal was purchased, a portion of the land was cleared and a pathway up the slope was constructed which was named St. Joseph Boulevard. Later a stage for school pageants was built and a picnic area was also constructed. Other than that, there were no specific plans for the land.

In 1900, Brother André asked the new superior, Father Benjamin Lecavalier, if he would be willing build a small chapel on a portion of the recently purchased land. It would be a shrine in honor of St. Joseph, a sacred place where people could come to pray. Father Lecavalier was not at all interested in the proposition. Frequently Brother André would bury a medal of St. Joseph on the land where he hoped the future chapel would one day be erected and he continued to pray and to hope.

One day, Brother Alderic said to Brother André, "Something very strange has been happening. I have a statue of St. Joseph in my office and every time I come back to the office, the statue has been turned so that it is facing the window." "It is not strange at all," Brother André replied. "St. Joseph wants his chapel on the mountain. I am the one who turns the statue and I place him where he can look at the mountain all day long."

Almost one year later, Brother André became ill and was sent to the infirmary. It happened that Father Lecavalier was also ill and in the infirmary in a bed close to Brother André. Brother André spoke a lot about the shrine that he hoped would be built on the mountainside of Mount Royal, going into great detail regarding what he had in mind. It would be very small and thus it would not be expensive to build.

Father Lecavalier had no recourse but to listen to Brother André as he spelled out all of the specifics, over and over again. He was able to sway Father Lecavalier to his side and he convinced him to give his permission for the construction of a chapel dedicated to St. Joseph.

In order to provide money for the building of the chapel, Brother André asked Father Lecavalier for permission to save the five cents he received for every haircut he gave the boys at Notre Dame School and permission was granted. Four years after his initial conversation with Father Lecavalier, Brother André had a total of $200.00 which he had saved from the haircuts.

Brother André also placed a statue of St. Joseph on the land where he hoped the chapel would one day stand and put a small dish at the base of the statue for donations. He spread the word to everyone he met and encouraged people to walk up the hill to where the statue of St. Joseph had been placed and to say a prayer and to consider giving a small donation. Almost every day Brother André went up to see if anyone had put any coins in the dish.

Father Lecavalier determined the exact spot on the mountain that would be best to build the shrine. In all humility, Brother André told him that he had another idea. He explained to his superior that he had already seen the chapel in its finished form and in all of its beauty, but he had seen it in another spot, which he then pointed to. Father Lecavalier agreed to build it in the place that Brother André wanted. The father of one of the students at Notre Dame School told Brother André that he would like to donate all of the lumber for the project.

The land had to be built up and leveled on the mountainside in preparation for the chapel. Brother André hired workmen to do the job and before long all of his savings was depleted. At the beginning of each week, Brother André hoped for the best but had no idea where he was going to get the money to pay the workmen at the week's end. He had to pray constantly that more funds would come in.

After receiving their wages at the end of the day on Saturday, the workers would always ask Brother André if he wanted them to return the following Monday. He would explain that he wanted them to come back but he was not sure how he was going to get the money to pay them. The workmen said they would be willing to wait for the payment if necessary and they always returned on Monday morning. Often in mysterious ways, the money would come just when needed most and the workers never once had to wait for their wages.

Brother Abundius Piche, the carpenter for the Holy Cross community, built the St. Joseph chapel. It measured sixteen feet by twelve feet and took Brother Abundius seven days to complete. The Oratory could seat approximately ten people comfortably. Brother André was sure that it would eventually need to be enlarged but he was still very happy with the modest beginnings.

Brother Abundius also constructed a beautiful pine altar for the chapel. The chapel was named the "Oratory" which means "place of prayer." It was built high on the mountain in a wooded area of great natural beauty. In October 1904, a special Mass was held to celebrate the opening of the Oratory.

Brother André had a statue of St. Joseph that he wanted to place in the Oratory and asked one of the residents at the nearby Home for the Elderly to paint the statue blue and white. The back of the Oratory had big double doors that opened outward so that people seated outside on benches could view the services. The Oratory had no windows and because it was unheated, it was not open to the public during the winter months. Brother André made sure that a candle was always burning before the statue of St. Joseph and he went there every day to pray.

In 1906, Father Georges Dion became the superior of the Holy Cross community that served at the Notre Dame School. One of his goals was to stay in the good graces of Archbishop Bruchési. When Father Dion visited the Oratory and saw all of the crutches, canes and braces that were displayed there, he asked for an explanation. He was told that many people who had asked Brother André to pray for them had been healed. From time to time, people placed the canes and crutches they no longer needed in the Oratory as a testimony of the grace they had received.

Father Dion said that he did not want to encourage fanaticism so he had all the crutches removed from the Oratory. Brother André spoke to Father Dion at length about the matter and pleaded with him to put the crutches back. He felt that it strengthened people's faith in the power of prayer. He also said that it was a testimony to the powerful intercession of St. Joseph.

Father Dion finally agreed to put the crutches back in the chapel. As Father Dion got to know Brother André better, he grew to revere him and eventually became one of his biggest supporters.

Dr. Charette continued to spread his hateful rhetoric even though Brother André was no longer seeing the sick at the school but at the tramway shelter instead. He mocked Brother André openly about his use of the St. Joseph oil, calling him the "old greaser." A group of doctors made a public statement that Brother André was endangering the health of the citizens of Montreal. The Catholic doctors showed much more hostility toward him than the Protestant doctors.

Brother André endured the persecution without retaliating in any way. He suffered in silence when hearing the cruel comments and continued to use the medal and the oil of St. Joseph with the sick and the infirm. Newspaper reporters wrote defamatory articles about him, ridiculing him and calling him the "old polisher." With all the trouble swirling about, Brother André's superiors were considering transferring him to their congregation in New Brunswick.

Although he did not respond to the insults or defend himself in any way, Brother André was very hurt by the words of Dr. Charette as well as others. He was called a fake healer and a charlatan. Some called him "the old meddler." A local priest wrote an article that was very hostile saying that Brother André had created "a religion of massage." When Brother André read the article, he burst into tears.

Dr. Charette filed a formal complaint against Brother André and submitted it to the Montreal Board of Health. A doctor was sent by the Board of Health to interview Brother André and to determine whether any of his actions were illegal in regard to his ministry to the sick. The doctor asked Brother André a number of questions including the methods he used when trying to help the sick. Brother André showed the doctor a medal of St. Joseph and some of the devotional oil he used when he prayed for the sick. He offered the medal and the oil to the doctor, telling him that it might be useful to him.

The doctor could sense Brother André's sincerity and his goodness and felt certain that nothing harmful could ever result from his dealings with the sick. He had complete trust in the humble brother and was sure that anyone who met him would benefit from the encounter, just as he had benefitted. The doctor assured Brother André that he was doing nothing wrong and he had nothing at all to worry about.

One day Dr. Charette's wife had a severe nosebleed and no matter what remedy was tried, the bleeding would not stop. Mrs. Charette wanted to see Brother André but her husband would not allow it. However, the loss of blood was so great that Dr. Charette became afraid that his wife might go into shock. In his desperation, Dr. Charette considered asking Brother André to come to his home to pray for his wife. But after making so many public statements against Brother André, he felt that he could not invite him to his house.

Dr. Charette went to Notre Dame School and told Brother André about his wife's condition. It was a very short conversation. Brother André said only, "Your wife will not die," and with that he walked away. When Dr. Charette returned home he found that his wife's nosebleed had stopped. When he made some calculations, he discovered that the bleeding stopped at the approximate time that he was talking to Brother André. His wife never suffered from a nosebleed again.

After witnessing the healing of his wife, Dr. Charette had a complete change of heart and never mocked or ridiculed Brother André again. Instead, he became one of Brother André's biggest supporters. He asked Brother André to accompany him on his sick calls and Brother André was more than willing to do so. Dr. Charette grew to have so much faith in Brother André that he frequently advised his patients to go to the Oratory and ask Brother André to pray for them.

After several large donations came in, Brother André asked Father Dion for permission to use the money to enlarge the St. Joseph's Oratory. It could only seat twelve people for Mass while the overflow had to sit on benches outside in the open air. With the crowds getting larger and larger, it was obvious that something had to be done.

Father Dion had to get formal permission from Archbishop Bruchési for the enlargement. Brother André told Father Dion to hold a medal of St. Joseph tightly in his hand and to silently pray when he made the request. All went well and Archbishop Bruchési agreed to the enlargement.

Brother André on occasion would tell people who were ill that they, in fact, were not ill. He did so with Calixte Richard, a carpenter. Calixte visited Brother André and asked him to pray for his healing. Calixte, who had a stomach tumor, was so ill and weak that he was incapacitated. "You are not sick!" Brother André said to Calixte.

Brother André invited Calixte to go over to the school kitchen with him for a bowl of soup but Calixte told him he was not able to eat. Brother André asked him, "If you were to be healed by St. Joseph, would you come here and work on the enlargement of the Oratory?" "Of course, I would," Calixte replied. Calixte decided to go to the school with Brother André and have a bowl of soup. After they shared the meal together, Brother André told him to report for work the following day. Calixte returned at 6:15 a.m. the next morning, completely cured.

Soon walls were constructed to enclose the Oratory and a wooden canopy was built over the area where people had previously sat in the open air. Several years later, a charcoal stove was installed so that people could enjoy services year-round. In addition, electric lights were added as well as a reed organ.

In 1909, Brother André was named the official guardian of the Oratory. As guardian, he would devote all of his time and his energy to the sick and the afflicted. He moved from his porter's cell at Notre Dame School where he had lived for forty years to a cell that had been built for him beside the Oratory. In the past, he slept on a narrow wooden bench only sixteen inches wide. Now he had a folding bed of his own. He also had a small office that he could use to receive the sick. He was sixty-four years old. As gifts and donations came in, improvements were made to the Oratory. Soon an impressive tower was built for the purpose of housing a bronze bell. On the Feast of the Ascension in 1910 more than 3,000 people followed in procession as a brand-new statue of St. Joseph which had been blessed by Pope Pius X was placed in the Oratory. That same year, there were numerous cures that were written up in the major newspapers and because of the publicity, Brother André gained national fame.

Louis Cayer of New Bedford, Massachusetts, Brother André's nephew, was astonished on one occasion to see a newspaper article titled, "The Miracle Man of Montreal" about Brother André's healing ministry. Louis put two and two together and realized that the "miracle man" that was mentioned in the newspaper was none other than his "Uncle Fred." Louis could not have been more surprised.

By now, Brother André was also receiving hundreds of letters each day. Father Dion assigned Brother Marie Auguste to serve as Brother André's secretary and to answer the letters. Later, Brother André would have four secretaries helping to answer the 80,000 letters that came in each year.

Brother André was happy to have Brother Marie Auguste helping with the mail, but he also wanted a priest to be assigned to the Oratory to serve as chaplain and to celebrate Mass and hear confessions. Father Dion said that he did not have any priests to spare.

Brother André suggested that Father Adolphe Clément would make an excellent chaplain but Father Dion explained that he would be of no use because of his failing eyesight. If Father Clément was interested in being the chaplain, Brother André wanted to at least give him a chance to see if it might work out.

One of the Holy Cross brothers took Father Clément's arm and guided him up the steep incline to the Oratory to see Brother André. Father Clément told Brother André that it would be impossible for him to assist as chaplain since he was no longer able to read the prayers out of the Mass book. For eight years he had been suffering from an eye disease that caused progressive blindness. He was thirty-three years old. It was very painful to his eyes to be in the light and because of that he had to stay in semi-darkness almost all of the time.

Brother André told Father Clément not to worry because his sight would be restored. The next day, Father Clément was still unable to read the Mass prayers. However, the following day there was a dramatic improvement in his eyesight. He was able to read without any trouble at all. From that day forward, he served as the chaplain of the Oratory, working alongside Brother André and helping him in any way he could.

Not only did Father Clément witness remarkable healings at the Oratory, he saw numerous spiritual healings and conversions as well. Father Clément said that once, during a period of thirty days, he read ninety-four letters that had been sent to the Oratory reporting physical healings. A visiting priest came to the Oratory and referred to it as the "Lourdes of Canada."

Father Clément served as chaplain of the Oratory until 1926. At that time, he became the superior of the community and served in that position until 1934. For more than twenty years he was able to read without glasses and only used them when he was nearing the end of his life.

In 1910, Mrs. Armand Grothe's eight-month-old baby boy had been hospitalized for meningitis compounded by pneumonia. The right side of his body was paralyzed and his head jerked constantly. Doctors said that the infant would not last through the night. One of the nurses at the hospital went to the Oratory after her shift was over to tell Brother André about the baby's serious condition and to ask for his prayers. He told the nurse to rub the baby with a medal of St. Joseph. She did what he recommended and noticed an immediate improvement. Almost at once, the baby's head stopped its incessant jerking and by the next day the paralysis was completely gone.

Another amazing healing took place in 1911 when Antonio LeRoux of Montreal visited the Oratory. Antonio had lost 90 percent of his vision in both eyes. When he visited the Oratory, Brother André made little crosses on his eyelids with St. Joseph oil. He told Antonio to return to the Oratory every day for the next two months and he would apply the oil to his eyelids. At the end of two months, Mr. LeRoux could see perfectly. Although his vision was now perfect, he began to experience a terrible pain in his back. "Before your eyes were healed, you were accustomed to wearing glasses. Begin to wear your glasses again and you will notice that the pain in your back will subside," Brother André said to him. Although it did not make sense, Mr. LeRoux did not question Brother André but did what he told him to do. He received instant and permanent relief from the debilitating back pain.

Just as Dr. Charette had done in the past, a number of physicians got together and filed a formal complaint against Brother André. This time the doctors claimed he was practicing medicine without a license and that he was endangering the lives of the citizens of Montreal. They said that he was an ignorant man, uneducated and almost illiterate. When Brother André was told about the unkind remarks he said, "It is true that I am an ignorant man. Everyone knows it. But that is why God can use me."

Archbishop Bruchési decided to organize a commission to make an inquiry and investigation into the complaints and claims against Brother André and his work at the Oratory. All of the interviews were conducted under oath.

The commission interviewed the brothers and priests of the Holy Cross Congregation as well as Brother André's superior, Father Georges Dion. Father Dion was one of Brother André's strongest defenders and spoke very highly of him, saying that he was an exemplary religious and a model to all of the others in the congregation. Father Dion described Brother André as "innocent, artless, humble and without guile."

The commission also interviewed some of the people who claimed they were healed after asking Brother André to pray for them. One was a woman who said that she had been suffering from a serious internal infection as well as a tumor. Her father visited Brother André and told him about his daughter's life-threatening illness. He begged Brother André to pray that she be healed. Brother André told him that he was very busy and he would not be able to talk to him until the following day. "But my daughter might be dead by tomorrow," the man exclaimed. "Your daughter is no longer suffering," Brother André said. That very day, Brother André began a novena with the man for the healing of his daughter. Upon returning home, much to the man's surprise, he found that his daughter felt much better. By the end of the novena, she had completely recovered.

The members of the commission interviewed Brother André and talked to him at length about his work as a member of the Holy Cross Congregation. They asked him why he did not simply leave the sick people in God's hands and stop ministering to them. At least that way the doctors would stop complaining about him. His simple answer was, "I do what I feel I must." When the commission asked him if he had anything to do with the healings that had been reported, he said that he did not. He was absolutely certain of it.

On March 20, 1911 the commission completed their report, which was then put on the desk of Archbishop Paul Bruchési. They stated that they were impressed by Brother André's outstanding character and that his work reflected the highest spiritual ideals. They concluded that the extraordinary happenings and healings that had been reported at the Oratory were a result of supernatural intervention. After reading the report of the commission, Archbishop Bruchési gave his stamp of approval, just like the superior, Father Dion had, and said that

Brother André could continue with his work and his ministry to the sick.

Brother André's family by now had left Canada and were all living in the United States. His sister, Léocadie lived in West Warwick, Rhode Island and his sister Alphonsine lived in Natick, Rhode Island. His brothers Napoleon and Claude lived in Sterling, Connecticut. His sisters Marie and Josephine lived in Connecticut as well. Isaïe lived in Richford, Vermont. His brother Joseph had settled in Centerville, Minnesota but had passed away in 1905.

In 1911, Mrs. Eugenie Miville visited Brother André's sister Alphonsine in Natick, Rhode Island. Eugenie and Alphonsine were the best of friends. Léocadie, the sister of Alphonsine and Brother André, was there as well. Eugenie shared with the two women that Brother André had been instrumental in healing her husband. The doctors had pronounced him incurable, but he recovered after visiting Brother André.

Eugenie was surprised that Léocadie and Alphonsine were both skeptical about Brother André's reputation as a healer. They made light of it, believing it to be nonsense. Nothing that Eugenie said could convince them otherwise. Léocadie told Eugenie that she would only believe in Brother André's gift of healing if the pain in her legs left her. Alphonsine evidently had the same attitude because she said that the only way she would believe would be if the pain in her back went away.

When Eugenie Miville returned to Montreal, she told Brother André what his two sisters had said. "Tell them to write to me," Brother André replied. A few months later Brother André received a letter saying that both of his sisters had been relieved of their pain.

In 1912, Brother André made a trip to West Warwick, Rhode Island to visit Léocadie whom he had not seen for many years. News that Brother André was in West Warwick traveled fast and soon it seemed that everyone in the town was knocking on Léocadie's door hoping to greet Brother André. Each night of his stay, numerous sick people crowded into Léocadie's home in order to see him and to ask for his prayers. Léocadie took Brother André to see many members of their family who lived in different parts of New England. Newspapers published articles about his visit as well as the miraculous cures that were being reported.

Brother André began to make two trips a year. In the spring, he traveled through Canada and to New York and New Jersey. He often stayed in parish rectories with priests whom he had known when they were students at Notre Dame School. He would stay a night or two at the parish, holding prayer services and visiting the sick in hospitals and then move on.

On one occasion, Brother André visited Father Frank Cornish at his parish in Keeseville, New York. He asked Father Frank what time the evening devotions were held in the parish. Father Frank said that they did not have any evening devotions due to lack of interest. They did have a Holy Hour but it was only scheduled once a month.

Brother André told Father Frank he was happy that they had a Holy Hour once a month but said that it would be much better if they had the Holy Hour every week. "I have a very difficult time just getting the parishioners to attend Mass on Sundays," Father Frank said. "I know they would not be interested in a weekly Holy Hour," he added. "But every house in the neighborhood has the lights on in the evening," Brother André replied. "I think God's house should be lighted too. I think your parishioners would come to a weekly Holy Hour if you make it available. I want you to promise me that you will have a Holy Hour once a week," Brother André said.

Father Frank agreed to it and made the announcement during Brother André's visit to the parish. There was a huge turnout for the first Holy Hour. Father Frank attributed it to the fact that everyone knew that Brother André was going to be there and so they wanted to be there as well. He was certain that the enthusiasm would not last.

A year later, when Brother André returned to Keeseville and visited Father Frank's parish, Father Frank told him that the Holy Hour was still being held every week and was very well-attended. People even came from other cities in order to attend. Father Frank was amazed at the success of the Holy Hour and grateful to Brother André for insisting that it be held at his parish. Father Frank said later that he had learned more from Brother André than from all the priests he had ever known. Several years after Brother André's death, Father Frank traveled to Montreal to visit the Oratory. He said that there was a tremendous improvement in his health after that very short visit.

Every autumn, Brother André went to New England and stayed with various family members. Each day of his visit he would attend the early morning Mass at the local parish. He knelt for the entire Mass. After the Mass ended, he would stay for a long time in the church to pray. Later in the morning, he would visit friends and relatives in the area. Usually in the afternoon, he visited the sick in the hospitals. In the evening he would receive the sick who came to his family's home to see him. All of the vacations he took were "working vacations" and he never traveled simply for pleasure.

Mr. Michel Trudel, an accountant, was one of the volunteers who often drove Brother André on his trips through Canada and the United States. He always made sure to keep the tank full of gas because he knew that Brother André did not want to stop for any reason. He kept a thermos of coffee as well as some biscuits in the car which they would have for lunch. Brother André never wanted to stop at a restaurant for meals because he said it took too much time.

In 1912, the Oratory was enlarged once again. It now had stained glass windows as well as seating for two hundred people. Brother André moved to a room inside the Oratory which was directly above the newly renovated sanctuary. A staircase in the back of the Oratory led up to his room. He was happy to have

a two-burner stove on which he cooked his meals. He also had
a small lamp which always burned before a statue of St. Joseph.

That same year, Archbishop Bruchési came to bless the
chapel enlargement of the Oratory. On the day of his visit,
Brother André was working in the kitchen. One of the members
of the Holy Cross community went to the kitchen to tell Brother
André some important news. "The Archbishop would like you
to join him for lunch today. Fix yourself up a bit and make sure
your habit is clean!" the brother told him excitedly. Brother
André was happy to accept the Archbishop's invitation for lunch
but could not understand what the fuss was all about.

During their lunch together, Archbishop Bruchési asked
Brother André about his devotion to St. Joseph. "Have you ever
had a vision of St. Joseph?" he asked. Brother André said that he
had not. "Did St. Joseph ask you to build the Oratory on Mount
Royal?" the Archbishop inquired. Brother André told him that
he did not. He explained that all of his desires to have St. Joseph
known and loved came from his personal devotion to him. On at
least one occasion, Archbishop Bruchési asked Brother André to
pray for him and to touch him with the medal of St. Joseph.

That afternoon, when Archbishop Bruchési pronounced the
solemn blessing on the new enlargement of the Oratory he said:

> I see here a movement of piety which heartens me.
> This Oratory could be justly compared to the mustard
> seed, so little in itself, which nevertheless produces a
> great tree. In the beginning a hand, pious and simple,
> placed a statue here. Each day people came to pray.
> Soon a little chapel rose on this spot. But the devotees
> of St. Joseph became more and more numerous and
> it was necessary to enlarge the chapel many times.
> Today this is the last addition which I shall come to
> bless. But this work is only beginning and I foresee in
> the future, perhaps not far distant, a church, a basilica
> worthy of St. Joseph rising on Mount Royal and

facing that most magnificent horizon. What shall I say of the miracles which take place here? If I deny them, these crutches and braces, witnesses of all the donors, will speak in my place. . .It is certain that extraordinary things have taken place here, and even greater prodigies than physical cures. . .The greater things are the spiritual healings. . . .I beg you to come here often to pray.

The Oratory continued to draw more and more people who came on pilgrimage to pray and to see Brother André. Even though the Oratory had been enlarged, it was obvious that a much larger church was needed. The Congregation of the Holy Cross established a Council of the Oratory in 1912 in order to plan for the future. Brother André was a Council member and he was deeply respected by the others appointed to the Council. For the most part, when he voiced his wishes, they were implemented.

The Council moved forward with plans to construct a huge basilica on the slope of Mount Royal, dedicated to St. Joseph, protector of Canada. The building of St. Joseph's Basilica, would be accomplished step by step. First the Crypt Church or Lower Church had to be built which would be the foundation for the basilica that would rise over it. The basilica would be an immense shrine with a dome that would overlook all of Montreal. Finding the money for the project would be a challenge and Brother André was willing to do whatever was needed in order to make St. Joseph's Basilica a reality.

The architectural plans called for an escalator that would carry people up to the main body of the church. Brother André was completely against the installation of an escalator. He said that people would grow in faith much more if they climbed the stairs and they would obtain more graces as well.

When the work was begun on the Crypt Church, Brother André spent as much time as he could at the construction site. He was there early each morning, long before the workers arrived. He also visited the site on his lunch break each day.

Joseph Malenfant, a well-to-do sixty-year-old widower learned about the plans for the future St. Joseph's Basilica in a very unusual way. Joseph lived a peaceful life on his farm at St. Hubert de Temiscouta, about three hundred miles east of Montreal. When he took stock of his life, he felt that something was missing. He wanted to live his life in service to others and he wondered how he could accomplish it.

Joseph Malenfant had been having recurring dreams in which he saw an elderly man making an attempt to build a church and calling to him for help. The dreams were uplifting in a way that Mr. Malenfant could not explain and although he did not know the meaning, he felt the message was of a spiritual nature.

With all his heart, Mr. Malenfant wanted to find the man he had seen in his dreams. He learned that there was an elderly man living in Montreal who was trying to build a basilica, so he headed to Montreal to see if he could find him. When he entered the Crypt Church at the Oratory, he saw Brother André and recognized him at once as the man in his dream. When Brother André saw Mr. Malenfant in the church, he said to him, "I am in great need of your help."

Visiting the Oratory and meeting Brother André made a profound impression on Mr. Malenfant. He was so drawn to the life of the Holy Cross priests and brothers that he asked the superior, Father Dion, if he could enter the community as a lay brother. Father Dion told him that unfortunately, he was past the maximum age for admission.

Even though Mr. Malenfant would not be allowed to enter the Holy Cross Congregation, he still had a great desire to do something to help Brother André. He decided to travel through Canada asking for donations to support the works of the Oratory.

He traveled from town to town, sleeping in barns at night and walking the highways in the day. He knocked on the doors of both the rich and the poor, telling each one about the wonderful works of the Oratory in Montreal and asking for a donation. Many of the local people hurled insults at him and ridiculed him but he continued in his work. When Mr. Malenfant had collected $1,400.00 in donations, he returned to Montreal and gave it to Father Dion.

When the *Annals of St. Joseph,* a magazine highlighting the work of the Oratory was first published in 1912, Mr. Malenfant decided to try to obtain subscriptions to the magazine. He traveled through Canada during the summers, going door-to-door asking for subscriptions, and during the winters, he stayed at the Oratory. In ten years, Mr. Malenfant obtained 35,000 subscriptions to the *Annals of St. Joseph* magazine. For the rest of his life, until his death in 1924, he sought subscriptions for the magazine. Through his great effort, information about the work of St. Joseph's Oratory spread throughout Canada.

On one occasion, Brother André learned that his picture was going to be put in an upcoming issue of the *Annals of St. Joseph* magazine. He went to the superior and told him that he did not want to be featured in the magazine. "Please don't put a photograph of me in the *Annals,*" Brother André pleaded. "But it is not a problem. It is a group photograph of seven people and you happen to be in the photograph," his superior said. Try as he might, he could not change the superior's mind. Brother André was not happy about it but he had to accept it.

There were many sick people who wanted to see Brother André but they were too ill to travel from their homes to the Oratory. In order to accommodate those people, Brother André walked or took the trolley to visit them after his work day was over. However, the number of sick people who wanted to see him was continually increasing. They often contacted his superior, Father Dion, with their requests. Father Dion decided it would be best to have a volunteer driver take Brother André on the evening sick calls. He would be able to visit many more people that way. Brother André at this time was seventy years old.

Father Dion determined who he wanted Brother André to visit each evening and gave him the names on a list. Many of the people were suffering with very serious and life-threatening illnesses. Brother André always said that even if a person had a contagious disease, he was not afraid to visit them. He had no fear of germs. However, in order to protect his driver, he would not allow him to enter the sick room with him when he went on his nightly calls.

Brother André insisted that his driver maintain a fast speed, often much faster than the speed limit allowed, so that they could visit as many of the sick as possible. Brother André was acquainted with all of the policemen in Montreal and their esteem for him was so great that they would never issue a speeding ticket to his driver. Frequently, the policemen would ask Brother André for his autograph.

Brother André prayed the Rosary enroute to his sick calls each evening. He would dedicate each decade for the intentions of a person who was ill and in need of prayer. His volunteer drivers estimated that he prayed about thirty rosaries a day.

Brother André and his volunteer driver usually finished their sick calls around ten o'clock in the evening and then went back to the Oratory together to make a Holy Hour. Brother André would light a one-hour candle and they would kneel together and pray before the Blessed Sacrament.

Brother André visited the sick every evening except Friday. On Friday evenings he conducted a Holy Hour followed by Stations of the Cross, which was open to the public. The Friday evening devotions were very popular and very well attended.

Leopold Lussier, an employee of the Montreal Fire Department, was one of Brother André's volunteer drivers who took him on his evening sick calls. Leopold was aware that Brother André suffered from a heart condition and that his doctor forbid him to climb stairs because of it. Leopold, who was strong and robust, had no problem carrying Brother André up several flights of stairs. He would simply sling him over his shoulder and walk up the stairs with ease.

Arthur Ganz, a successful insurance agent, like Leopold Lussier also drove Brother André on his sick calls. Once, Arthur drove Brother André on a call to visit a very poor woman who had four children. The table and chairs in the house were nothing more than wooden boxes that had been turned upside down. The mother was greatly comforted by Brother André's visit and by the encouraging words he spoke to her. All four of her children were sick at the time. "Your children are all going to feel better tomorrow. I am certain of it," Brother André said. As he was leaving, the woman tried to slip fifty cents into his hand. "I cannot accept this," Brother André said to her. "You need to keep it for yourself and your children."

When they were returning home, Brother André told Arthur Ganz that he was very concerned about the woman and her children. He said they would need to make sure that the family received the help they needed. That very day, Brother André arranged for a friend to take food and other needed items to the woman's house. When Brother André returned two days later, the children were all well and playing in the yard.

Once a woman named Mrs. Bruhlmann told Arthur Ganz of a miracle she had received the first time she visited Brother André. She had been suffering from cancer for three years when she met the famous doorkeeper. She was only able to eat one beaten egg a day and her body was wasting away. Brother André advised her to pray and to use the blessed oil and the St. Joseph medal. The very day she did so, she was able to eat three eggs instead of one. Two weeks later Mrs. Bruhlmann could eat anything she pleased and her health was completely restored.

On one occasion, when Brother André and his volunteer driver were on their way to the evening sick calls, their car stopped at a red light and someone recognized Brother André. Before the light turned green, a sick woman was brought to the car. The driver pulled the car over to the side of the road and Brother André got out and prayed for the woman. In a very short period of time, the sick and elderly who lived in the nearby apartment house learned that Brother André was just outside their door. Numerous people came out to the street and asked him for his prayers. He talked to each person individually and anointed some with St. Joseph oil. The number of people on the street waiting to greet him kept increasing. Finally, he was able to get back in his car and continue on to his destination.

Dominic Cormier was a close friend of Brother André's as well as one of his volunteer drivers. Dominic often had Brother André over for dinner and he made his house available to him whenever he needed rest. On weekdays after Dominic got off work, he would pick Brother André up at five o'clock in the afternoon and drive him to the homes of the sick. They were usually able to visit ten or more sick people on a given evening.

Dominic worked as an auto mechanic for a Cadillac dealer in Montreal. The owner, Mr. Walsh, who had the highest esteem for Brother André, allowed Dominic time off from work in order to drive Brother André on his sick calls. He also let Dominic use, free of charge, the finest Cadillac on the lot for the trips. Dominic noticed that Brother André hardly took notice of the beautiful car. It made absolutely no difference to him what kind of car he rode in.

Dominic was convinced that Brother André was a saint and because of it, he had a great desire to have a relic. Knowing that Brother André often cooked his own meals, he decided to buy him a brand-new kettle. Brother André was delighted with it and couldn't wait to use it. Dominic felt very lucky that he was able to keep Brother André's old kettle as a relic.

Joseph Pichette, the brother-in-law of Dominic Cormier, was the owner of a shoe store in Montreal. He was twenty-five years old when he met Brother André for the first time. Joseph was suffering from a severe heart condition as well as kidney and intestinal trouble and was under the care of Dr. George Aubry.

One day a woman named Mrs. Lucas came into Joseph Pichette's shoe store and told him about her experience with Brother André. She went to see him because of an ulcerated arm. Brother André told her to put a drop of St. Joseph oil on her arm, rub it with a medal and drink a tiny bit of the oil. When she did so, she was healed.

Shortly after Joseph met Mrs. Lucas, he met a man named Louis Bertrand who told him that Brother André had cured his father who was suffering from cancer of the arm. Louis showed Joseph a photograph of his father's cancerous arm and then another photograph showing his perfectly normal arm taken after the healing. Dr. Campeau of Montreal confirmed the cure. After hearing the testimonies of Mrs. Lucas as well as Louis Bertrand, Joseph had a great desire to meet Brother André and to ask him to pray for his own serious health problems.

When Joseph told Dr. Aubry that he intended to visit Brother André, Dr. Aubry warned him not to do so. According to Dr. Aubry, Brother André was "crazy." He explained that Brother André was a man with no education and had no ability to help the sick.

Dr. Aubry told Joseph that climbing the steep path up to the Oratory could be dangerous, taking into consideration Joseph's heart condition. He said that it was the worst heart condition he had seen in all of his years of practicing medicine. As of late, Joseph had been coughing up blood and seemed to be growing worse by the day. Dr. Aubry told him to set his affairs in order because he was dying and nothing else could be done for him.

Joseph was very sick when he finally went to see Brother André. He was also in a state of despair. He told Brother André the complete story of his deteriorating health. "If you cannot help me, then there is no hope for me at all," he said to Brother André. Brother André advised him to get a St. Joseph medal and drink a small amount of the St. Joseph oil and return in one week. Joseph came back in a week's time but his health had not improved. Joseph went to see him many more times after that, but there was no improvement.

Father Dion, the superior, had given Brother André permission to allow sick men to spend the night in his living quarters above the chapel from time to time. On the occasions when the sick stayed with him overnight, he would dedicate more time to deep prayer for their healing. Brother André told Joseph he could spend the night in his apartment above the chapel if he wished. Brother André also advised him to begin a nine-day novena to St. Joseph for healing.

The night that Joseph Pichette came to Brother André's room as a guest, there was another man staying there who had a diseased leg. They slept on little cots that were separated by a curtain for privacy. Brother André slept apart from the two men on a thin mattress on the floor without a pillow.

For the first nine days that Joseph stayed at the Oratory, André rubbed him two or three times a day with the medal of St. Joseph. However, there was no improvement in his condition. On the ninth day, Joseph told Brother André that unfortunately, he was not feeling any better. Brother André then began to intensify his prayers for Joseph.

Every morning Brother André's alarm clock went off at four-thirty a.m. He boiled some potatoes and pieces of pork and veal on the stove and told Joseph to put them in the stew later in the morning. Brother André left early to go to the chapel and then to work. In the afternoon, he came back to his apartment for lunch. He served a big dish of meat, potatoes, noodles and vegetables to Joseph but Joseph said that he would not be able to eat it. Brother André insisted that he eat, even though he did not want to. He told Joseph that he would feel much better after the meal. Brother André also gave him three big pieces of bread.

After sharing the meal with Brother André, Joseph realized that he was completely free of pain. Brother André told Joseph that it would be a good idea if he went out for a long walk and he did so. That evening, they had the rest of the vegetables and pork for dinner. Joseph told Brother André that there had been a big improvement his health. He felt better than he had felt in ages. When he went to bed that night, he had a deep and restful sleep. It was the first night he had been able to sleep well in the nine days he stayed at Brother André's apartment.

The next morning Brother André told Joseph that since he was feeling so good, there was no longer any reason for him to stay at his apartment. It was time for him to go back home. When Joseph returned home, he learned that Albertine, his wife, was visiting a relative in St. Esprit. He rode his bicycle two miles to the station and boarded a train to St. Esprit. From there, he rode his bicycle five miles to the house where his wife was staying. She was shocked to see her husband looking so well. She was beside herself with joy and began to cry.

Joseph rested at home for eight weeks and gained twenty pounds in the process. When he finally returned to the Oratory, he saw the man who had been his roommate in Brother André's apartment. The man was delighted to see how healthy Joseph looked and said that he hardly recognized him.

Brother André advised Joseph not to tell his doctor about the cure and explained that for the most part, the doctors were very hostile toward him. Joseph decided not to go back to see Dr. Aubry. However, Joseph's wife told Dr. Aubry the news regarding his healing. Dr. Aubry said that the cure would not last more than a month. Twenty-five years later, Joseph was still in good health and working regularly.

As a shoe store owner, Joseph, from time to time, would give Brother André a brand-new pair of shoes, keeping his old ones as a relic. Joseph noticed that Brother André wore his shoes until they were almost useless. He always preferred to get his shoes repaired rather than to get a new pair. Joseph would try to explain to Brother André that his shoes were beyond repair but he could never convince him.

One man who came to see Brother André had been injured in a hunting accident. The lead pellet had remained in his hand and caused blood poisoning. His doctors said that amputation of his hand was the only remedy. Brother André rubbed the infected area with a medal of St. Joseph and prayed. Almost immediately, the wound in the man's hand began to drain and he went away cured.

When Brother André was certain that a person was going to be healed, he sometimes advised that person to take a course of action that could be considered reckless. One of the Holy Cross brothers, Brother Osée Coderre, recalled the case of a workman from St. Laurent who had a tragic accident. His leg was crushed under a very large boulder and when gangrene set in, the doctors said they had no choice but to amputate.

On his way to the hospital for the surgery, the man decided to stop at the Oratory and speak to Brother André about it. Brother André told him not to go to the hospital for the surgery but instead to go back home and start a novena to St. Joseph for the cure of his leg. He would join him from the Oratory in making the novena. When the novena ended, the man was cured. In order to show his profound gratitude, the man and his two sons often came to volunteer their services by making improvements to the road leading to the Oratory.

There was no denying that Brother André possessed the gift of healing. He also had the gift of prophecy. On one occasion, when Brother André was having dinner with his good friend Joseph Pichette, he asked about the health of all the members of Joseph's family. Joseph said that everyone in the family was in good health except his sister who happened to be ill at the time. "But your brother will be passing away soon," Brother André said. Joseph was shocked by the words and was certain that Brother André was wrong. His brother, who was a physician, was in good health. Two months later, Joseph's brother died suddenly and unexpectedly.

Dr. Henri Dufresne called Brother André on the telephone on one occasion to say that he was very worried. His wife was suffering from insomnia and had not slept for a very long time. "But your wife is asleep right now," Brother André said. Although

Dr. Dufresne doubted it, he went to check on his wife and was very surprised to find that she was sleeping soundly.

Brother André sometimes exhibited knowledge of who was going to be healed and who was not going to be healed. Several of the priests of the Holy Cross Congregation asked Brother André how he was able to have such knowledge. "There are times when it is easy for me to see that someone is going to be healed," Brother André said. On another occasion, in reply to the same question he said, "In some cases, it is evident that St. Joseph wants to heal the person." His answers to such questions were always elusive and noncommittal.

In 1936, Monsignor George Gauthier, the acting archbishop of Montreal, had a massive heart attack and was lying in the hospital in critical condition. Brother André told his friend, Arthur Ganz, that the archbishop would survive. "It is the next heart attack that will kill him," Brother André said. Four years later, Archbishop Gauthier had a second heart attack which proved to be fatal.

In addition to the gift of prophecy, Brother André also possessed the gift of reading hearts. On occasion, when people came into the office to see Brother André for the first time, they were surprised to find that he knew certain information about them that they had disclosed to no one. Sometimes when his visitors were talking to him, they would bring up things that happened in their past "No, it did not happen that way," Brother André would sometimes say and then he would go on to describe what actually happened. His visitors had to admit that he was right.

One young woman went to the Oratory to talk to Brother André about a personal matter. She wanted her brother to support her after their parents' death but was certain that Brother André would not approve. She said to Brother André, "I would like to ask you to pray for my special intention." "But your special intention is not good," he replied and the conversation ended at that.

Brother André's gift of reading hearts was also evident on one occasion when he encountered a woman who owned a boarding house. She was extremely worried because all of her boarders had recently moved out. She visited Brother André on the advice of a friend. She had never thought highly of him but was desperate for a solution to her problem. She had an urgent need to rent out the rooms in her boarding house since it was her livelihood. Brother André said to her, "When you stop making derogatory comments about the Oratory and when you stop making fun of me in public, your boarders will return." The woman felt deeply embarrassed but had to admit that Brother André had told the truth and that she deserved the correction.

In addition to his gifts of healing, prophecy and reading of hearts, Brother André possessed other mystical gifts. One evening Brother André was kneeling in prayer at the foot of the altar rail in the chapel. His friend, Adélard Farbe was with him. As Brother André was praying, he became enveloped in a beautiful light. Rays of light were also coming from the statue of St. Joseph which was on the altar. There was no other light in the chapel except the dim sanctuary lamp.

Adélard became frightened. He went over to Brother André and touched his arm but he did not move or even seem to be aware that Adélard was there beside him. Adélard ran to get the sacristan, Brother Ludger. When they went back to the chapel together, the light had disappeared and Brother André was leaving to go to his room. Adélard and Brother Ludger went outside to see if perhaps the moon had caused the light in the chapel to shine on Brother André but there was no moon that night.

Paul Corbeil, another friend of Brother André's, had a similar experience. One evening he was praying with Brother André in the Oratory chapel when he saw "beautiful rays of light" shining on Brother André. The experience lasted for only a few seconds but Paul remembered it for the rest of his life. Many years later, Paul was able to testify to it when he was interviewed by clergy members who were gathering information for Brother André's Cause for Canonization.

Raoul Gauthier, a captain in the Montreal Fire Department, became a close friend of Brother André's. He was a kind and loving family man, greatly devoted to his wife and six children. Even with so many virtues, Captain Gauthier still had some bad habits to overcome. For one, he had the habit of swearing. Brother André talked to him about it and helped him. He was able to stop swearing completely.

Captain Gauthier had a deep sense of loyalty to the other firemen in his department. If any became sick or injured, he made a personal visit to them either at the hospital or in their homes. He invited Brother André to accompany him on the visits and Brother André was happy to do so. As time passed, Raoul and Brother André became very close friends.

After he met Brother André, Raoul decided to place a statue of St. Joseph on his desk at the Fire Department. He introduced the firemen to Brother André and in a short time Brother André became a very special friend to the many firemen of Montreal. Raoul also encouraged the firemen to volunteer at the Oratory by greeting the visitors and assisting the sick. The firemen had a retreat house in the country on the outskirts of Montreal. Raoul made it available to Brother André and told him he could spend time there whenever he needed rest from his many duties.

On occasion, Brother André would accompany Raoul and his family to their summer home on the shores of the St. Lawrence River. He had a great love for Raoul's six children and became like a grandfather to them.

Raoul Gauthier was promoted to Fire Chief of the Montreal Fire Department. He was killed in the line of duty when an oil tanker that he was on, the *Cymbeline,* caught fire at Vicker's Dry Dock in Montreal. Chief Gauthier and his men were on the deck trying to put out the fire when the ship was rocked by a tremendous explosion. It catapulted Raoul and three of his men into the air and then down into the fiery water. Four days later, the bodies of three of the firemen were recovered but the remains of Chief Gauthier could not be found. The water had been dragged twenty times in search of him.

Brother André was informed about what had happened and was taken to the site of the accident. One of the firemen told Brother André that Chief Gauthier's body must have been carried downstream with the current but Brother André said that he did not think so. He stood on the edge of the dock and gazed silently at the water. He then said a prayer and threw two St. Joseph medals into the water. The next morning, at the spot where the two medals had fallen, Chief Gauthier's body floated to the top of the water.

On one occasion, a man came to see Brother André and introduced himself by saying, "I am the chaplain of the King of England. His Majesty, the King has read a book about you and he asked me to visit you during my travels in Canada." Brother André seemed to listen to the man without interest. Titles, wealth and worldly acclaim made no impression on him. After a few minutes, he cut the conversation short and took leave of the visitor by saying, "Excuse me. There are some sick people who are waiting to see me at my office today."

Azarias Claude was a nominal Catholic who had heard of Brother André's healing gifts but was skeptical. Nevertheless, he decided to accompany his wife one day, when she had an appointment to talk to Brother André at the Oratory.

During the visit, which lasted no more than five minutes, Brother André invited Azarias to come back again at a future date. "You know, it is not necessary to be sick in order to see me," Brother André said to him. The five-minute visit with Brother André made a big impression on Azarias and took away his skepticism completely. He had a great desire to visit Brother André again. He would have returned that very evening or the next day but he was afraid of what people might think of him.

Azarias began to think about Brother André constantly and his desire to visit him again became overwhelming. He had a hard time concentrating on anything else. He even lost all interest in his work and his business affairs. All he could think about was Brother André.

One week later, Azarias made a return trip to see Brother André and they were able to converse together for over an hour. Brother André talked about his devotion to St. Joseph. Azarias noticed that he talked about St. Joseph in intimate terms, as though St. Joseph was a member of his family or his personal friend. After that, Azarias began visiting Brother André once each week and the two became close friends.

Azarias had a serious drinking problem but after he began visiting Brother André, he lost all desire to drink. It was surprisingly easy for him to give up what had been a serious addiction. Azarias said, "Brother André totally changed the course of my life. He taught me how to practice renunciation and how to do penance. I became a fervent disciple of St. Joseph and began to receive Holy Communion daily." Among the thousands of people who met Brother André, Azarias is probably the one who was the most radically changed by the encounter.

Azarias Claude retired from his business in order to be the full-time volunteer receptionist at Brother André's office. He worked there for fifteen years. He managed the waiting room and because of his exceptional organizational skills, the office ran smoothly.

People sometimes asked Brother André for his opinion regarding an operation that their doctor was urging them to have. Azarias observed that if Brother André encouraged the person to have the operation, the operation proved to be successful. On occasion, Brother André would say to a sick person emphatically, "You are not sick!" Azarias observed that when Brother André voiced those words, the person made an immediate recovery.

While volunteering at Brother André's office, Azarias once witnessed an amazing healing. A wealthy and arrogant woman came to the Oratory in a limousine driven by her personal chauffeur. She had another attendant at her side. She walked into the office on crutches. Brother André spoke to her for a short time and then rang the bell to mark the end of their visit. The woman became angry because she felt that she did not have adequate time to tell Brother André the full story of her health complaints. She was also angry because she felt that he was rude to her by dismissing her in such an abrupt way. The woman did not realize that she had left Brother André's office without using her crutches. Someone in the crowd told her, "Do not be angry. You are walking unassisted. You have been healed!" When the lady and her two companions realized what had happened, they all began to cry.

Brother André asked Azarias to keep a supply of women's coats in the closet of the office and if a woman came into the office dressed immodestly, she would be told to put one on. Once, a lady who was dressed in an inappropriate way came to Brother André for counseling. He told her that she would never be able to receive the favor she wanted from St. Joseph dressed in such an immodest manner. "Go home and come back dressed appropriately and then I will talk to you," he said.

Brother André was described by his friends as being reserved and it was noted that in his dealings with women, he was especially reserved. While he was generally sparing in his speech, with women he was extremely brief. He would not sit next to a woman on a train and he refused to ride in a car alone with a woman. If a woman came to talk to him at the office, he opened the window that looked right into the waiting room.

Brother André was a person of great modesty. Even in his old age, he would not allow anyone to help him get dressed. He would never laugh at an off-color joke and if someone had the audacity to tell such a joke in front of him, he would glare at the person. People learned very quickly never to repeat such a joke in his presence again. Once, one of the brothers found Brother André in tears. He explained that he had looked out the window and had seen a beautiful woman and had a temptation.

On one occasion, Azarias found himself in grave financial trouble and asked Brother André for advice. He explained that he was not able to keep up with his mortgage payments and was on the verge of losing his house. Brother André prayed with him and for him and encouraged him to trust in God. However, Azarias' situation did not improve and he continued to be plagued with financial troubles.

One evening, Brother André was having dinner at Azarias' home before the two made their customary sick calls. Azarias was talking to Brother André about his financial woes when there was a knock on the door. It happened to be snowing heavily that night. Brother André opened the door to a stranger who handed him a package and said, "This is for the man with the financial problems." Then he walked out the door and was soon lost sight of in the snowstorm. When Azarias opened the package, it turned out to be the exact amount of money that he needed to pay his debts.

Azarias observed that Brother André's only winter coat was in terrible condition. Because of that, when Brother André was traveling, he was in the habit of borrowing a black overcoat from a friend. Azarias wanted to buy Brother André a new overcoat but he said that he did not want one. However, Azarias kept bringing the subject up, claiming that a new coat was a necessity. Brother André finally said that he would agree to it but he only wanted a second-hand coat or a very inexpensive one.

Azarias took Brother André to a tailor shop and chose a good quality material for the coat but Brother André said that the material was too expensive. He explained that he would not feel comfortable wearing such a fine piece of clothing. He would only accept it if Azarias called his superior and received permission. Azarias received the permission and Brother André wore the coat for the next fifteen years. Azarias kept Brother André's old coat as a relic.

Like Azarias Claude, Ludger Boisvert was another individual whose life was radically changed by his meeting with Brother André. In 1918, Ludger was admitted to Montreal's Hotel Dieu Hospital for painful growths in his bladder. After receiving a thorough examination and taking numerous tests, the doctor told him the sad news, that his condition was terminal. With surgery, he would be able to live for a year or two at the most, but without the surgery, he would die. Ludger decided not to have the surgery. The doctor told him frankly that he would probably not live more than three weeks.

Ludger went to talk to Brother André about his diagnosis. Brother André told him to get a medal of St. Joseph along with the consecrated oil and to rub the affected area. The entire conversation took about two minutes. Ludger did not have any confidence in the advice Brother André had given him and felt that he needed to have a longer conversation with him. He went to the rear of the line and waited for a chance to speak to Brother André once again.

When Ludger's turn came, Brother André was annoyed with him since they had already spoken together that day. He told Ludger to leave. Ludger got right back in line and waited once again. When his turn came, Brother André was out of patience with him and would not speak to him. Ludger told Brother André that he would keep getting in line until he was given the time he needed to talk about his illness.

Brother André's heart finally softened and he told Ludger to sit in a chair by his office and he would call him when he could see him. Ludger sat on the bench all afternoon and when Brother André finished speaking to all of his visitors for the day, he called Ludger to come into his office.

Ludger spoke to Brother André at length and told him that he had been suffering for a long time. As the father of eleven children, he loved his family very much and wanted very much to live. But if, because of his illness, he could no longer be of any use to his family, he wanted to die as soon as possible. Brother André asked him if he was afraid of dying and he said that he was not. Brother André asked all of the priests and brothers in the Holy Cross Congregation to make a novena to St. Joseph for the healing of Ludger. He asked Ludger to join in the novena.

Ludger received a complete healing and enjoyed good health for another twenty-seven years.

On December 16, 1917, the Crypt Church opened its doors to the public. It was designed in the solemn and beautiful renaissance architectural style and built to hold two thousand people. Inside the church was a magnificent nine-foot statue of St. Joseph, carved from white Carrara marble by a prominent sculptor in Italy. Stained glass windows of the finest quality were added while beautiful candelabras of gold were placed on either side of the altar. In addition, exquisite chandeliers hung from the ceiling.

Once the Crypt Church opened to the public, a huge influx of people began to visit. High schools, colleges, sodalities, as well as parishes with their parish priests all came on pilgrimage to the Crypt Church. Thousands of young people affiliated with the Catholic Association of French-Canadian Youth came for prayerful gatherings at the Crypt Church.

On August 31, 1924, the three hundredth anniversary of the naming of St. Joseph as the patron saint of Canada, thirty-five thousand people gathered at the Oratory in order to celebrate the auspicious occasion. It was by far the largest crowd ever to assemble at the Oratory. On that day, Monsignor Pietro di Maria, the apostolic delegate to Canada, blessed the cornerstone of the future St. Joseph's Basilica.

The following summer, Brother André would celebrate his 80th birthday. Long before the day arrived, members of the Holy Cross community were busy with preparations for the big celebration. Father Roy and Father Clément would also be honored. Father Alfred Roy was celebrating his 50th anniversary in the priesthood and Father Clément was celebrating his 25th anniversary in the priesthood.

People began climbing the stairs to the Oratory on their knees as early as six o'clock in the morning on the big day. By eight-thirty in the morning, 25,000 people had arrived. The bishop of London, Ontario, his excellency Bishop Michael

Francis Fallon, O.M.I. presided at the Mass. Brother André almost always declined to have his picture taken but, on this occasion, he gladly stood next to his two good friends, Father Roy and Father Clément for a photograph. By 1926, more than one million people were visiting the Oratory each year. One year later, construction work began in earnest on St. Joseph's Basilica.

When Brother André was in his eighties, he admitted that he was never well and that he was always in pain. He suffered from angina pectoris, which caused severe chest pains. In addition, he had frequent stomachaches and nausea due to chronic digestive problems. Nevertheless, he refused to take the medicine that Dr. Lamy prescribed for stomach spasms. He continued to push himself to the limit and refused to slow down. Dr. Lamy observed that Brother André did not seem to be the least bit worried about his health.

Leone Valente, a foreman by trade, was a friend of Brother André's. Leone said:

> I was aware that Brother André was in poor health. On several occasions, friends came to my house with the Brother and they would say to my wife, "Brother André is exhausted. He just can't go on." My wife used to ask him to rest on a makeshift bed in the living room. She would give him a warm blanket and a hot water bottle for his feet. . .I never heard Brother André complain about his poor health or even say, "I'm tired." I do not know if his sickliness was a means of purification for him, or if it stood in the way of his sanctification. I always remember Brother André with a smile on his face.

Brother André did not let his poor health interfere with his work or his ministry to the sick. He traveled by car and by train on his numerous trips throughout Canada and the United States. Because of their esteem for him, railroad officials let him travel free of charge and went to great lengths to accommodate him.

Once, on the way back home from Toronto, he accidentally boarded the wrong train. When the conductor realized that Brother André was on his train by mistake, he immediately notified the stationmaster at the next stop. The stationmaster was waiting for Brother André when he got off. He had already arranged for him to be transferred to an express train to Montreal, which made an unscheduled stop in order to pick him up. Not realizing the lengths people would go to help him because of their esteem for him, Brother André was under the impression that anyone who boarded the wrong train received such assistance.

On overnight train trips, Conrad Laporte used to travel with Brother André and assist him on the trip. He encouraged Brother André to sign up for first class train travel so that he could have private accommodations and sleep in a comfortable stateroom, but Brother André refused. Due to his austere and ascetic ways, he would not consider first class travel.

On Conrad's first overnight train trip with Brother André, at the end of the day, they went to their compartment where they knelt for Evening Prayer. After praying for a while, Conrad said that he was tired and wanted to go to sleep. He climbed up into the upper bunk and Brother André said he would retire soon. When Conrad woke up in the middle of the night, Brother André was still kneeling in prayer. Conrad said that whenever their train pulled into the designated stop, there were hundreds of people gathered, waiting to speak to Brother André.

Once, Brother André was returning home to Montreal by train. He almost always wore his black clerical robe distinguishing him as a brother of the Holy Cross Congregation, but on this occasion, he was dressed in civilian clothing and was wearing a black hat. He was sitting next to the window and had some crutches propped up in the seat next to him. The crutches belonged to those who were healed during his recent trip and he was bringing them back to place in the Oratory.

On the train trip, some of the crutches accidentally fell to the floor making a loud noise, which caused the conductor to come over and investigate. When he saw Brother André sitting next to all the crutches, he asked him if he was a salesman for orthopedic devices.

When Brother André told the conductor his name and that he was a brother of the Holy Cross Congregation, the conductor suddenly recognized him. He got down on his knees and with great emotion he said, "Brother André, I wrote a letter to you some time ago asking for your prayers and I was healed." Tears were falling from the conductor's eyes. Other passengers on the train noticed and rushed over to talk to Brother André. Soon there was a crowd around him. Brother André was gracious to everyone and spoke to each person who greeted him. He preferred traveling by car rather than by train because on the train, his presence caused too much of a commotion when he was recognized.

Once, Brother André visited his cousin, Dr. Homer Bessette in Holyoke, Massachusetts. While there, he accepted an invitation to speak at a reception for one thousand people at the Nonotuck Hotel in Holyoke. Because of his timidity, he usually could not be persuaded to give a public speech. Only a very good reason, like promoting devotion to St. Joseph, could convince him to do so and for this special occasion, he agreed to speak.

During his stay at Homer's house, Brother André felt lightheaded and complained that he was exhausted. Homer grew worried and advised him to cancel his speech at the hotel. Brother André said that he had no choice but to keep his commitment since he did not want to disappoint so many people.

When Brother André walked into the crowded ballroom of the hotel, he began to feel worse. When it came time for him to give his speech, he stood up, but feeling weak, he immediately had to sit back down. After resting for a few moments, he got up again and tried to continue his speech. Suddenly, he fainted and fell to the floor. He was taken to Mercy Hospital for observation and after he was released, he immediately went back to his cousin's house and to visiting and receiving the sick.

Brother André's reputation as a person of holiness continued to grow. He was considered a celebrity in the city of Montreal, a fact that was hard for him to grasp. His popularity increased with the passage of time. One of the members of the Holy Cross Congregation noted that the more his fame increased, the more humble he became. During his lifetime, millions of dollars passed through his hands, all used to build the shrine in honor of St. Joseph, but he himself lived as a poor man. He called himself "St. Joseph's little dog."

Brother André never took credit for the Oratory or spoke of it as "his work" but always said that it was the work of St. Joseph. He never promoted himself. He would not agree to interviews and he would not talk with the media. He chose an obscure and hidden place in the last choir stall behind the altar as his assigned seat where he sat each morning for Mass and for his daily prayers. He preferred to stay in the background and never wanted to draw attention to himself.

The Oratory was robbed on two separate occasions. The first time, thieves broke in and stole one hundred dollars in donations. In the second theft, two altar vases were taken. It was a terrible shock to Brother André. He said that the money as well as the vases belonged to St. Joseph and he was devastated that someone would do such a terrible thing.

Adélard Fabre was the custodian at the Oratory. Often, in the evening after a long day of work, he and Brother André would go to the chapel and pray together. Frequently, Brother André would speak to Adélard about the Passion of Jesus. Brother André's eyes would fill with tears as he went into great detail regarding the sacrifices Jesus made by offering his life on the cross. He could easily talk for several hours on the subject.

On one occasion, Adélard saw two men carry a woman who was unable to walk into Brother André's office. The woman's driver followed them. The woman had come from her home in Lac Nominingue and stayed about a half-hour in Brother

André's office. Adélard saw her walk out of his office without any assistance to the car that was waiting for her on the street.

The driver was stunned at the miracle the woman had received and told Adélard that she had not walked in four years. He was so overwhelmed that he had to regain his composure before he could start up the car and drive her the one hundred miles back to her home. The driver said that he felt guilty because for about three months she had been asking him to take her to see Brother André and he had refused. Brother Ludger witnessed the miracle as well and said to Brother André, "You certainly have done a lot of good this morning," Brother André said to him, "No, I have not done anything. It is God who does it all."

In 1926, Brother André visited his nephew John Boulet, in Arctic, Rhode Island. During his stay, he received the sick in his nephew's home and prayed for each one of them. One particular day, over one hundred people were crowded into John Boulet's home. Lionel Maynard was among the many sick who were there that day. A friend of Lionel's encouraged him to visit Brother André and he was finally able to do so.

Lionel Maynard had been diagnosed with Pott's Disease, a type of tuberculosis of the spine. He suffered with chronic and intense pain and partial paralysis. His doctor, Dr. Fulgence Archambaulter sent him to a specialist, Dr. Maria Danfoth of Providence, Rhode Island who admitted him to the hospital for four weeks. However, he did not improve. Upon release, he wore a plaster corset reinforced by an iron corset and had to walk with crutches.

When Brother André saw Lionel sitting in a chair in the living room, he walked over to him and asked him to stand. As Lionel slowly rose to his feet, he was in excruciating pain. André told him to walk around the room without his crutches. With a great effort, Lionel forced himself to walk around the room but he was only able to walk very slowly.

Brother André told Lionel to walk faster and he found that he was able to do so. "I want you to walk even faster than that," Brother André said. Lionel realized that not only was he able to walk faster but he was also suddenly free of the chronic, debilitating pain. He was walking so fast that he was almost running. Many of the people present had seen the pitiful condition Lionel was in when he entered the house and they were astonished to witness such a miracle.

Lionel gave his corset brace and his crutches to Brother André who took them back to Montreal with him and placed them in the Oratory. Lionel then visited Dr. Archambaulter who was shocked to see that he was walking normally. Lionel told him that all of his pain had vanished. He examined Lionel and found a large depression in his back caused by the deteriorating vertebrae. Dr. Archambaulter informed him that even though he was pain-free and had regained his ability to walk, he still had Pott's Disease and it was important for him to continue with the treatment plan that had been prescribed.

Against Dr. Archambaulter's advice, Lionel traveled to Montreal in order to see Brother André again. Brother André placed a St. Joseph medal over Lionel's clothing and rubbed his back with it. He then gave the medal to Lionel and advised him to use it every day, just like he had demonstrated. Brother André also asked Lionel to stay in his apartment over the chapel for two days. They would be able to pray together there for Lionel's complete healing. As it turned out, Lionel stayed with Brother André for six weeks. Lionel said that for those six weeks, when Brother André was not working or ministering to the sick, he was in his room in prayer.

At the beginning of his stay, Lionel told Brother André that the dressing on his back needed to be changed by a doctor. It was a procedure that was both painful and time-consuming. Brother André said that he would like to change the dressing himself. With a simple movement of his hand, he removed the dressing very quickly, causing no pain at all to Lionel.

During the six weeks that Lionel stayed in Brother André's apartment, the depression in his back gradually became smaller and smaller. Finally, all that remained was a small mark. When he went back to Rhode Island and saw his doctor, the doctor was amazed. After an examination, his doctor concluded that he no longer had Pott's Disease.

The Little Sisters of the Holy Family assisted the priests and brothers of the Holy Cross Congregation in Montreal. Among other things, they did the laundry for the Holy Cross Congregation. On one occasion, two of the Little Sisters came to speak to Brother André in his office. They were both anxious to have a relic of Brother André. While in his office, they spotted one of the tassels that he wore on the cord of his habit. When he looked away from them for a brief time, they quickly took the tassel. He was very upset when he learned what they had done and took steps to get his property back. He also learned that some of the Little Sisters were keeping his old clothing as relics. From that time forward, he began to count every piece of his laundry to make sure it was all there. To be on the safe side, he began to burn his worn-out clothing in the fireplace.

In the spring of 1927, Brother André made his customary trip to New York and New Jersey. During the trip, he visited Father Roger McGinely, who had been a former student at Notre Dame School and who was now the pastor of St. Aedan parish in Jersey City, New Jersey. When Brother André arrived, practically the whole town turned out to welcome him. Father McGinely organized a solemn procession and a reception in his honor. There were colorful decorations everywhere as well as flags flying. The city was sparkling as never before.

When Brother André returned home to Montreal, he told his superior about the festivities and said, "I had a wonderful visit in Jersey City and it was decorated beautifully in honor of someone, I know not who." Brother André did not realize that he was the "someone" the city was honoring. He could never really comprehend his fame or his immense popularity.

On one occasion, Brother André visited his friend, Joseph Dieudonne-Hebert in Granby, Quebec. He arrived at Joseph's house at five-thirty in the morning and proposed that they go to early Mass. Joseph told Brother André that he would take him to the church but that he would not attend Mass with him. "But I wanted us both to receive Holy Communion together this morning. Why is it that you do not want to go to Mass?" Brother André asked. Joseph seemed to have one excuse after another. "I cannot receive Communion before making my confession and my parish priest is away on vacation," Joseph said. "No, he is not away on vacation. He is at the church," Brother André replied.

When Brother André and Joseph arrived at the church, they found that the pastor had returned unexpectedly from vacation. Joseph attended the Mass and afterward introduced Brother André to his pastor who greeted him in a cold and unfriendly manner. Joseph was very angry at the priest's conduct. When Joseph and Brother André left the church, Joseph spoke in a disparaging way about the priest's bad manners. Brother André said to him, "Every priest represents Jesus Christ. It is not for us to criticize them." However, Joseph was so upset that he continued to make angry comments about the priest. Brother André said to him, "Joseph, I love you very much and I am so happy to be able to visit you in your home. But if you continue to criticize the priest, I will not come to visit you again."

Brother André welcomed people of different faiths or no faith at all. He never took the hardline approach with people and he never tried to pressure anyone to become a Catholic. He was not judgmental and he condemned no one. He simply wanted to help people.

When visitors who were ill came to see Brother André, he might spend five minutes or less praying with them and for them. But if the visitor was an unbeliever or had lost his way in life, he would often spend an hour or more talking with the person. People often said that he treated unbelievers with more attention and sympathy than he did the people of faith. Sometimes he would take a small statue of Jesus out of his desk drawer and then talk about the Passion of Jesus, his eyes filling with tears while he spoke.

Brother André encouraged people to read the Gospels, the *Imitation of Christ* by Thomas à Kempis and the lives of the saints. Those were his favorite sources of inspiration along with *The Herald of God's Loving Kindness* by St Gertrude of Helfta and a book of meditations on the holy wounds of Christ by Visitation Sister Marie Marthé Chambon. He did not apologize for the fact that he was barely able to read and write and would sometimes say, "It is not necessary to be well-educated or to have spent many years in college, in order to love God. It is sufficient to want to do so generously."

On one occasion, Brother André visited a family and said to them, "Your house is beautifully furnished but there is something that makes me very sad. The crucifix is over in the corner where no one can see it. I do not think Jesus holds the first place in your hearts." Brother André wanted everyone to have a crucifix in their home and to put it in a prominent place.

It was noted that many Protestants held Brother André in the highest esteem and a number of them had a framed picture of him on display in their homes. Many had received graces and physical healings through their encounters with him. Protestant physicians had an especially high regard for him.

In the Protestant hospital in Montreal, there were strict visiting hours. The doctor in charge told his staff that the enforcement of the visiting hours applied to everyone, with the exception of Brother André. Brother André had the doctor's permission to come to the hospital and visit the patients at any time of the day or night. In the Catholic hospitals, that was not the case. The visiting hours were over each evening at 8:30 p.m. and just like everyone else, Brother André was required to follow the rules and to leave at that time.

Mrs. A. H. Anthony, a member of the Methodist church, visited Brother André on one occasion and asked him to pray that she might be healed of cancer. Brother André asked her if she had a devotion to St. Joseph and she said she did not. He told her that he would not be able to help her unless she was willing to pray to St. Joseph. Just as he had advised many others before her, he asked Mrs. Anthony to wear a medal of St. Joseph around her neck. Next, he explained to her how to use the devotional oil of St. Joseph with the medal. He asked her to go into the church and to kneel before a statue of St. Joseph and to pray for healing. As a Methodist, Mrs. Anthony felt that medals, blessed oil, statues and the like were superstitious nonsense.

A friend of Mrs. Anthony's encouraged her to do what Brother André had asked her to do. They went into the church together and she knelt before a statue of St. Joseph. Mrs. Anthony prayed with all the sincerity of her heart and asked St. Joseph to heal her. She promised him that she would honor him and would follow him wherever he wanted to lead her.

Mrs. Anthony was suddenly filled with a profound happiness. She began to cry. Her friend thought she was crying because of the pain of her illness but she told him she was not in any pain. They were tears of joy. She felt a sense of lightness and well-being and had the desire to sing and to praise God.

Mrs. Anthony was miraculously healed of cancer. She remained a member of the Methodist church but continued to follow Brother André's advice by practicing the devotions that he had suggested to her. Brother André never advised her to become a Catholic.

Another amazing healing that occurred involved Mr. Desjardins, from Garson, Ontario, Canada. In 1929, Mr. Desjardins was in a serious accident that left him paralyzed. He was in physical therapy for over a year. During that time, he regained the ability to sit up in a wheelchair but not much more. He went to see Brother André in 1931 and had to borrow money from a friend in order to do so.

When Mr. Desjardins arrived at the Oratory, he was told that Brother André was sick and was not able to have visitors. He waited one month for a chance to see Brother André. When they finally met, Mr. Desjardins told Brother André that his doctors had said that nothing could be done to help him. Brother André observed Mr. Desjardins' condition and said to him, "Your legs are lifeless and dead, but if you have faith, I ask you to get up and walk."

With great determination, Mr. Desjardins slowly got up out of his wheelchair. He took one step, then another step. He was able to walk all the way across Brother André's office and then exhausted and perspiring, he walked back to his wheelchair and sat down. Brother André asked him to get up and to try to walk again. This time, it was much easier for him to do so. Brother André then told him to go into the chapel and pray to St. Joseph. From that time forward, he was on the road to recovery.

Many of the people who came to Brother André did not receive a physical healing. However, most of those who were not healed physically, were healed mentally and spiritually and left Brother André's presence feeling uplifted and consoled. Some died shortly after their meeting with Brother André but they died at peace with God. There were also numerous conversions.

One of the conversions involved a former student of Notre Dame School who became seriously ill. He had completely abandoned his faith and had not been inside a church in over twenty years. As his condition worsened, his family wanted him to see a priest, but he refused. They asked Brother André for advice. Brother André told them to talk to the man about his old classmates, teachers and friends at Notre Dame School and to see if he might like a visit from Brother André, the former doorkeeper. The man said that he remembered Brother André and he would indeed like a visit.

Brother André spoke to the man lovingly and gave him a medal of St. Joseph. "You must prepare yourself for death," Brother André said to him. "You must not be afraid of Jesus." Brother André then spoke to him of the mercy of God and urged him to talk to a priest and to make his confession. "I will do so," the man replied. "I will speak to any priest you send to me," he added. Before the priest went in to talk to the man, Brother André said to him, "Do not scold him. Make it easy for him to make his confession."

Once Brother André visited a man in the hospital who was dying. He told Brother André that his children were young and he could not bear the thought of leaving them. "Do not worry about your children. St. Joseph is going to look after them," Brother André said to the man. "You will have a peaceful death," he added. The man had been in a state of despair when Brother André came to visit him. However, Brother André's presence had a transforming effect on the sick man. He died peacefully on the day after Brother André's visit.

Brother André sometimes dreaded the long and weary days at the office. Listening to human miseries for hours on end could be monotonous. He grew impatient with the people that came to him for counseling when they talked on and on with a complete disregard for the many others who were waiting in line. Occasionally he would become irritable and lose his temper with his visitors. He always regretted it.

One day a woman came into Brother André's office and said to him, "I am here because I am in need of prayer. I am so very tired." Brother André said to her, "I will pray for you but I ask you to pray for me as well because I too am very tired."

Brother André's superior would sometimes make arrangements for him to stay at a retreat house so that he could get away from the endless lines of people and rest for a few days. On one occasion, Brother André was sent for a few days of rest to the Holy Cross Seminary in Quebec City. The priests and brothers were ordered to keep the information a strict secret. Unfortunately, the details were leaked out and his whereabouts was printed in the newspaper. Soon, throngs of people showed up at the seminary door pleading to speak with Brother André.

Brother André looked forward to his yearly trip to New England because he loved to visit his family. He also looked forward to getting some extra rest, as he was usually exhausted when he arrived. Sometimes his upcoming visit was announced in the newspapers and on the radio. At those times, the crowds that came to see him were so large that it caused traffic jams in the city.

Aurore Lawrence of West Warwick was the grandniece of Brother André. She said that when Brother André visited her family, he never gave them advance notice. He would simply show up at the door. Nevertheless, the family was always delighted to see him. Aurore described him as "very jolly and down to earth." People from the neighborhood would come over as soon as they learned Brother André was there. In a short period of time, over one hundred people would be inside the house.

Brother André's niece, Attaria Lafleur, who lived in Moosup, Connecticut said that when Brother André visited, he made the Stations of the Cross with her family every Friday evening. If he had any free time, he often liked to spend it alone in his room. Attaria said that Brother André was always happy and that his presence uplifted others. He was never known to gossip or to talk about the faults of others.

When he visited his family, he would ask each one if they had attended Mass and received Holy Communion on the previous Sunday. He often spoke to them about heaven and the beauty of heaven. Once a woman told him that heaven was very far away. He then repeated the "Our Father" in a whisper. "I know that God heard my prayer, even though I was whispering. That shows that we are very close to heaven," he said to her. He used to say that we are only separated from God by a thin veil.

Once when Brother André was visiting his sister, Léocadie, he looked out the window and saw over 200 people standing in front of the house. It was disappointing to him because it interfered with the time he had hoped to spend with his family. Nevertheless, he did not want to turn anyone away. He said to Léocadie, "Line the people up and I will see each one of them." On that particular day, the task kept him busy until midnight.

Brother André's niece, Suzanne Paine of Natick, Rhode Island described Brother André as a quiet, dignified man who never spoke of worldly affairs and spent most of his time praying or ministering to the sick. When Brother André traveled to Moosup to visit his nephew, Henry Bessette, he loved to get updates on all the family members. Brother André would sit beside Henry in the living room and hold his hand. The other family members were touched by the innocence and childlike spirit of Brother André.

Brother André was described by relatives and friends as a truly happy man who loved to laugh and to tell jokes. He used to say that happiness comes from God while sadness comes from the devil. He believed that joy was the hallmark of the Christian life and he used to repeat, "Let us never give way to sadness. Let us always be cheerful and avoid giving pain to anyone."

Dr. Lionel Lamy, Brother André's physician, described him as shy and reserved. He did not talk about himself and never spoke about his personal difficulties or innermost feelings, not even with his closest friends. During recreation, when the Holy Cross priests and brothers were all together, Brother André preferred to listen rather than to talk. Dr. Lamy said, "Brother André did not talk much, and when he did, it was only of God."

Eighteen-year-old Holy Cross Brother Placide Vermadère, the organist for the Holy Cross Congregation in Montreal, became a close friend of Brother André's. On occasion, Brother André took Brother Placide to his room to show him some of the letters he had received. Brother Placide said that many of them were very tragic. He described Brother André's room as "a sanctuary."

When Brother André returned from his sick calls late in the evening, he would ask Brother Placide to help him shut the windows in the Crypt Church. He liked to have Brother Placide nearby because he was somewhat afraid of the dark. After closing all of the windows, the two made the Stations of the Cross together. Brother André liked to make the Stations very slowly so that he could meditate deeply on each Station. Brother Placide often grew sleepy and would sit down in one of the pews, waiting for Brother André to finish his prayers.

Brother Placide said that he would have paid much closer attention to the things that Brother André said and did if he had known the tremendous recognition and honor he would one day receive. He said that knowing Brother André and spending time with him had been the greatest privilege in his life.

In his old age, Brother André began to have fainting spells several times a day. Sometimes, his legs would give way and he would fall on the ground. One evening when his good friend Joseph Pichette came to take him on his sick calls, his breathing was labored and he was very weak. Joseph asked Father Clément for permission to take Brother André to his home so that he could rest and regain his strength and the permission was granted. After a few days at Joseph's house, Brother André had not improved, so Dr. Lamy had him admitted to the hospital.

Brother André was diagnosed with double pneumonia as well as stomach and liver trouble and spent three weeks in the hospital. Due to his celebrity status, complete strangers would sometimes peek into his room just to get a glimpse of the famous man. This was upsetting to him and he asked the hospital staff to try to put a stop to it.

Sister Leroyer, who was assigned to be his nurse, was deeply impressed by his piety as well as the patience he exhibited in his sufferings. She said that she benefitted greatly by the spiritual conversations she had with him while he was in her care. When she confided some of her personal problems to him, he told her that it would be to her greatest advantage to write them down on a piece of paper and place them at the bottom of the statue of St. Joseph at the Oratory.

When Brother André was released from the hospital, he went back to the Oratory but he no longer had the energy to greet large numbers of people as he had done in the past. He was frail and barely able to work. His superior wanted to protect his health and felt it was beneficial for him to spend time away from the Oratory in order to escape the crowds. For that reason, he began to spend more and more time at the home of Joseph and Albertine Pichette. Joseph Pichette was Brother André's best friend in the world and they enjoyed a friendship that lasted for more than thirty years. Joseph estimated that as Brother André's volunteer driver and as his friend for many years, he had personally witnessed at least one thousand miracles of healing through Brother André's prayerful intercession.

In 1936, Father Albert Cousineau, the superior, called a meeting of the Council of the Oratory. Canada was going through a severe economic depression and donations for the building of St. Joseph's Basilica had dried up. It had been several years since any work had been done on the basilica.

The most immediate problem was that the Council of the Oratory did not have enough money to pay their creditors. The Council needed a loan of 1.2 million dollars in order to pay their bills and they knew it was not possible to get it. Without the loan, they would be forced to declare bankruptcy. In addition, if the basilica remained without a roof for much longer, the resulting weather damage would be such that it would have to be torn down and rebuilt again from scratch. The obvious conclusion was that financially, it was impossible to continue the work on the basilica and the whole project would have to be abandoned.

When another meeting of the Council of the Oratory was called in November, Mr. Viau, the architect of the basilica was present. Mr. Viau warned that the freezing rain and heavy snow that was bound to fall that winter would probably cause irreparable damage to the structure. No one had a single idea regarding how to solve the financial crisis and save the basilica. A feeling of deep sadness and pessimism pervaded the meeting.

Brother André was the only exception. During the meeting, he did not seem sad or worried in the least. Rather, he seemed upbeat and enthusiastic as he voiced his suggestion. He wanted the members of the Holy Cross Congregation and those on the Council to go in procession to the unfinished basilica carrying a statue of St. Joseph. They would then leave the statue inside the unfinished building in the open air. "If St. Joseph wants a roof over his head, he will surely make a way for us to complete the work," Brother André said.

Father Cousineau, the new superior, agreed to Brother André's suggestion. Praying the Rosary, Father Cousineau led the procession up the steep mountain path to the basilica on Mount Royal. Leaning on Brother Placide's arm, Brother André walked in procession with the others, but due to his age and infirmities, was unable to make it to the top. Father Charron, the superior provincial, placed a statue of St. Joseph inside the basilica.

At 90 years of age and in very poor health, Brother André decided to make a trip to New York City to seek donations in order to save the basilica. On the same trip, he made a visit to his family in New England. As he did on all his trips, he brought his battered old briefcase filled with a large supply of St. Joseph medals to pass out. In New Bedford, Massachusetts, he visited his grandnephew, Jules Cayer. Jules noticed that Brother André had great difficulty getting up the stairs in the house and was extremely feeble.

Brother André also visited with his grandniece, Aurore Lawrence, in West Warwick, Rhode Island. She observed that for a man who was 90 years old, Brother André's mind was very sharp. He then stopped in Woonsocket, Rhode Island where he stayed with friends. In Woonsocket, he received three to four hundred visitors a day and passed out St. Joseph medals to everyone he met. Knowing that his end was near, Brother André said that they were the last medals he would ever give out. He became ill and was forced to return to Montreal.

When Brother André returned home, he was thrilled to report to the Council of the Oratory that he had received a very generous check from Mr. John Burke, the secretary of the Rockefeller Foundation. In addition, Father Cousineau was successful in obtaining several large loans for the basilica. The loans received totaled 1.2 million dollars, the amount that was needed to keep the work going.

Through the loans that had been secured by Father Cousineau, Brother André was convinced beyond any doubt that St. Joseph's Basilica would indeed be built, even though he knew he would not live to see it. St. Joseph's Basilica, the largest shrine in the world dedicated to St. Joseph would open its doors in 1967, thirty years after Brother André's death.

At 90 years of age and in failing health, Brother André still held office hours. He saw pilgrims for a few hours every Wednesday and Sunday. He would have liked to spend more time with the visitors but he did not have the physical strength to do so. Just getting through the Wednesday and Sunday visits was difficult for him. He suffered from chronic dizziness and weakness.

On Christmas Eve, 1936, Brother André visited some patients at the hospital and then attended the three Christmas Eve services at the Oratory. He became so dizzy during the Mass that he had to be taken to his room. He told Father Clément that it would be his last Christmas.

On December 26, Brother André visited Joseph and Albertine Pichette in their home. Even though he was feeling ill, after his visit with the Pichettes, he went to the hospital to visit Father Cousineau's stepfather as well as several others who were ill. When he returned to the rectory, he began to feel worse.

Father Cousineau assigned Brother Placide to attend to Brother André in his illness and to stay at his side night and day. Brother André was suffering and spoke very little. He did not complain about his condition but appeared to be praying. Several times he asked Brother Placide to rub his chest with a medal of St. Joseph.

Brother André was well-prepared for death. He told some of his closest friends that his earthly work was done. He was ready to go home to his Father in Heaven and he was at peace.

As the days passed, Brother André grew weaker. Father Cousineau the superior, and Father Charron the provincial, spoke to Dr. Lamy about the state of Brother André's health.

Dr. Lamy thought that Brother André might have had a mild heart attack and recommended hospitalization.

Dr. Lamy told Brother André it would be to his benefit to check into the St. Laurent Hospital where he would be able to rest and to be under the care of competent health professionals. Brother André agreed to it. Father Cousineau had a tremendous devotion to Brother André and was terribly worried about him. He was well aware that his condition was grave. He could not bear the thought that anything might happen to him.

Brother André was bundled up in many layers of heavy blankets in order to protect him from getting a chill in the harsh winter weather. He was then taken by ambulance to St. Laurent Hospital. Brother Placide rode in the ambulance with him.

Brother André's nurse was Sister Marie Camille Fortin of the Sisters of Hope. She was told to allow no visitors to come in to Brother André's room. Brother André was suffering intensely and vomited almost continually. Nevertheless, he did not complain and he did not seem to be worried in the least about his condition. He told Sister Marie Camille that he did not want any morphine or other pain killing drugs. He said that he had more faith in prayer than in medicine.

On January 2, Brother André suffered a stroke which caused excruciating pain on the left side of his body. Nevertheless, his mind was alert and he was still able to joke with Sister Marie Camille and make her laugh. Father Cousineau and other members of the Holy Cross Congregation were constantly at his side. By January 4, his pain worsened. Father Charron, in the presence of other Holy Cross priests, gave the Last Rites to Brother André who by now had become comatose. Hundreds of people stood on the street outside the hospital, keeping vigil and praying for Brother André in the frigid winter air.

Because Brother André was an internationally renowned religious figure, newspapers worldwide reported on his condition. Even though Brother André was 91 years old, people were shocked to hear the reports of his health crisis. The Crypt

Church was filled with people who were praying for his recovery. People throughout Canada had their radios on, waiting to hear updates.

While Brother André was in a coma, the St. Laurent hospital administrators allowed friends, admirers and even some of the patients in the hospital to go to his room and to touch their rosaries, medals and religious articles to his body and to pay their last respects. Cures were reported as people prayed at his bedside.

At 11:30 in the evening, only the priests and brothers of the Holy Cross Congregation remained in Brother André's room where they recited the Litany of the Dying. At 12:50 a.m. on January 6, 1937, on the Feast of the Epiphany, Brother André passed away.

Brother André's body was taken back to St. Joseph's Oratory as church bells all over Montreal tolled, announcing his passing. Thousands came by automobile, bus, and railway trains from all parts of the United States and Canada enduring snow, sleet, and freezing rain. The trolley cars in Montreal were running constantly but were not sufficient for the demand. The tramway company was forced to bring very old trolley cars out of retirement and back into service in order to provide transportation for the multitudes.

Five hundred police officers and firemen were on duty to maintain order during the days that Brother André's body lay in state. In order to allow the greatest number of visitors to see him, 110 people per minute passed by his casket to pause for a few seconds and gaze at him one last time. The church remained open throughout the day and night. Brother Placide said that all through the night, the sound of automobile traffic on the street was so loud that it was almost deafening. It was estimated that one million people had come to Mount Royal to pay their final respects to Brother André and to attend his funeral.

Brother André's funeral was held on Tuesday January 12, in the Crypt Church of the Oratory and was attended by the Secretary of State of Canada, the Prime Minister of Quebec, the mayor of

Montreal, members of Parliament and other dignitaries. Bishop
Eugene Limoges presided at the funeral Mass and Cardinal Jean
Villeneuve preached the sermon. Noting the vast numbers of
people who were in attendance, the Cardinal said, "Look to the
life beyond and think of the seal that the Lord puts on the life of
the humble. No prince of the Church or of the State could have
a funeral such as this."

In his homily, Cardinal Villeneuve also said:

> On the tomb which houses the revered remains
> of the apostle of St. Joseph, three words are inscribed:
> *Pauper, Servus, et Humilis – Pauper:* Poor he was, the
> brother you came to see on so many occasions. *Servus,*
> Servant: the brother, who held the lowest rank in his
> community. *Humilis:* And he was assuredly humble,
> so much so that he never realized the breadth of his
> work or imagined that he could attract crowds.

After Brother André's death, many miracles through his
intercession were reported. A medical office was set up at the
Oratory in order to examine the cures. It was estimated that
between 1937 and 1977 approximately 125,000 healings through
the intercession of Brother André had been reported. Brother
André was canonized in Rome on October 17, 2010 by Pope
Benedict XVI. His liturgical feast day is January 7.

*The best preparation I can make for death is to live the reality
of the Paschal mystery as fully and as deeply as possible in union
with Christ, because Christ will re-live that mystery in me at the
hour of my death. If I am following the spirituality of the Paschal
mystery, I expect to die and rise again many times in the course of my
monastic life, in my daily tasks and duties, in unexpected events and
circumstances, and in my life of interior prayer. . .I expect to have to
let go and give up again and again, discovering a new richness of
life each time. . .I will learn to trust more and more this Father into*

whose hands I shall one day, freely and gladly, hand over my life. On that day my final act of dying will be inserted irrevocably into the saving death and resurrection of Christ my Lord.

-Father Charles Cummings, O.C.S.O.

Chapter 5

Blessed Solanus Casey

Bernard Francis (Barney) Casey was born in a three-room log cabin in Oak Grove, Wisconsin on November 25, 1870. He was the sixth child in a family of six girls and ten boys. His parents, Bernard Casey Sr. and Ellen Murphy, both Irish immigrants, had met at a Fourth of July picnic in Biddeford, Maine.

Bernard Casey Sr. made shoes for the Union Army during the Civil War and later owned his own shoe store. After he and Ellen married and moved to Newcastle, Pennsylvania, his shoe business took a downward spiral. As he weighed his possibilities, he concluded that farming would be a much better prospect. Barney and Ellen bought 80 acres of government land in Oak Grove, Wisconsin and planted wheat. Later they moved to a larger farm in Big River, Wisconsin.

Church was a six-mile journey by horse and wagon and the Caseys left two hours early on Sunday mornings in order to get to Mass on time. Since the wagon only had enough room to carry half of the family, on a given Sunday, half the children would go to church with one parent and the next Sunday the other half of the children would go with the other parent. Those staying home had their own church service, reading the Sunday scriptures and talking about the Gospel of the day.

Barney's earliest memories were of his mother and father as they gathered the family together for evening prayers. Barney often said that one of the greatest gifts God gave him was his loving and devout parents who taught him about his Christian faith. At seven o'clock each evening, Bernard Casey rang a little bell to signal time for evening devotions which always included the recitation of the Rosary. Prayers for a good harvest, protection from prairie fires and protection of their animals were included every evening. Often children from the neighboring farms would join them. Barney later recalled that all through the years, even when he and his brothers became teenagers, his father would encourage them to pray by repeating to them, "Prayer, boys, prayer!"

Bernard Casey also gathered his children together regularly and read classical literature and poetry to them. Charles Dickens, James Fenimore Cooper, John Greenleaf Whittier and Henry Wadsworth Longfellow were favorites. Bernard and Ellen also taught their children popular Irish ballads and songs from their homeland. Barney played the violin and harmonica in accompaniment.

In 1878, black diphtheria struck the area where the Casey family lived and two of the children, twelve-year-old Mary Ann and three-year-old Martha died. Several of the boys also contracted the disease. Young Barney caught it as well and it damaged his vocal cords and affected his voice, making it high-pitched and wispy for the remainder of his life.

Life in the wild and rugged countryside could be harsh and dangerous at times for the Casey clan. On one occasion, a prairie fire destroyed the Casey family's barn but fortunately the house was not touched. Barney and his brothers once had a frightening encounter with a bear that chased them as well as a close call with a wildcat. Luckily, no one was harmed. There was also the threat of rattlesnakes that were prevalent in the area.

In 1882, the family moved to a 345-acre farm in Burkhardt, Wisconsin. Close by was Dry Dam Lake where the children enjoyed swimming and fishing in the summertime. When the lake froze over in the winter, it became their ice-skating rink. Horseshoes was another favorite pastime. On the farm, Barney and his brothers helped chop wood and cut down trees. They fed the horses and pigs, worked in the fields, tended the large vegetable garden and took the cows to pasture. Barney and his brothers often studied their catechism while watching over the cattle. Years later when Barney reflected on the happy and idyllic days of his childhood, he loved to recall the great beauty of the natural surroundings - the wildflowers, the vines laden with berries, and the gentle deer. He referred to the land as an "earthly paradise."

When Barney was twelve years old, he spent two weeks at St. Patrick's Church in Hudson, Wisconsin preparing for his first Holy Communion. Barney and the other First Communicants stayed in the homes of the parishioners of St. Patrick's parish. They attended morning and afternoon class taught by Father Thomas Kelly, the pastor. About the same time, Barney's brother Maurice entered the St. Francis Seminary in Milwaukee to begin his studies for the priesthood. He returned home after three years due to psychological problems.

The Casey brothers formed their own baseball team and named it "The Casey Nine." Barney usually played catcher, his favorite position. His brothers pooled their money and bought a set of boxing gloves. They set up a boxing ring next to the barn. They all enjoyed boxing matches, except Barney, who refused to participate. He never gave an explanation but his brothers were sure it was because he did not want to hurt anyone. Along with the youth who lived on nearby farms, the Casey boys participated in high jumping and pole vaulting. Barney always showed good sportsmanship. Winning or losing did not make much difference to him. He was just happy to play.

In his youth, Barney developed a strong devotion to the Rosary through the influence of his mother. When he was a teenager, he made a commitment to himself to pray a second Rosary every evening in addition to the Rosary he recited with his family. One night, Barney was extremely tired after a long day of work on the farm and felt he had no choice but to skip his nightly Rosary. However, with determination, he forced himself to pray it and he managed to finish.

That night, Barney had a vivid dream, one that he would remember for the rest of his life. He was in a large pit and flames were surrounding him on all sides. He tried to find an escape route and suddenly looked up and saw a huge Rosary just above his head. He grabbed onto it and was pulled out of the fiery pit. Many years later, on the occasion of his parents' fiftieth wedding anniversary, he was asked to give a talk. Among many memories and reflections that he shared for that special occasion, he told the story of this vivid dream to all who were gathered.

At fifteen years of age, Barney was almost finished with elementary school. For the pioneer families, schools in the rural areas were closed during the harvest season. All members of the Casey family helped with the farm work as their survival depended on it.

In the mid 1880's, when it became increasingly hard for farmers to make ends meet, Barney and his older brothers looked for outside jobs in order to help the financial needs of the family. Barney was sixteen years old when he left school temporarily and traveled the twenty miles to Stillwater, Minnesota to look for employment. He found a temporary job at the lumber mill. He worked as a river driver and guided the logs that made their way down the St. Croix river toward the mill. In Stillwater, Barney lived with his uncle, Father Maurice Murphy in the rectory at St. Michael's parish. In winter, when the river froze, Barney went back home to continue his schooling.

In many ways, Barney was a typical teenager. He enjoyed socializing with his school friends as well as playing his violin at barn dances. A lifelong lover of music, he was able to play the popular songs of the day and was in demand as a violin player at the weekend parties and social gatherings. Barney met a girl named Rebecca Tobin at school and the two enjoyed spending time together. Rebecca was as kind and sweet as she was beautiful. As time passed, their friendship deepened and they began dating. Soon, the two fell deeply in love.

When Barney was seventeen years old, after finishing the eighth grade, he returned to Stillwater to look for work. The money he sent home to his parents was very necessary for the family's survival. He was happy to find work at a brick kiln.

One day at the job, a worker accidentally fell into a deep pit filled with water. Realizing that the man could not swim, Barney immediately jumped into the water with all his clothes on to try to save him. The man was panic-stricken and began struggling with Barney and pulling him under the water among the weeds. Barney was not able to free himself from the man's grip. Suddenly, Barney grabbed his brown scapular of Our Lady of Mt. Carmel that he always wore around his neck. At that moment, he felt himself being pulled up to safety. Strangely enough he felt like it was the scapular that was pulling him upward. Barney believed that Our Lady of Mt. Carmel had saved his life. Tragically, the man that he was trying to save, drowned.

After working at the brick kiln, Barney got a job at the State Penitentiary as a prison guard. It was while working at the prison that seventeen-year-old Barney's uncanny ability to help people became evident. Many of the prisoners found that they could open their hearts to Barney and tell him their innermost thoughts and feelings. He took a genuine interest in them which they responded to. Many felt their burdens were somehow lifted when talking with Barney. While working at the prison, he lived with his Uncle Pat and Aunt Mary Murphy.

The following summer, Barney found a job as a part-time streetcar conductor on Stillwater's brand-new electric trolley line and became one of the first streetcar conductors in the Midwest. The job had much better possibilities for future advancement and Barney enjoyed the work.

While working in Stillwater, Barney kept in touch with Rebecca Tobin through letters. At seventeen years of age, he proposed marriage to her. He felt sure that he would be able to make a good living as a conductor for the streetcar and would be able to provide for her. When Rebecca told her mother, her mother refused to give approval to the engagement. She felt that Rebecca was too young, being only sixteen-years-old. To distance Rebecca from Barney, her mother sent her away to boarding school in St. Paul. While in Stillwater, Barney received a letter from Rebecca telling him the news. He was never to see her again.

From Stillwater, Barney moved to Appleton, Wisconsin, where he got a full-time position as a street car conductor. A year later, a better opportunity opened up for him on the streetcar line in the city of Superior. He wrote to his family and encouraged them to move to Superior. It was a booming town in 1891 and showed no signs of slowing down. For one thing, jobs were plentiful. For the last three years, the crops had failed on the Casey farm due to drought and cinch bugs. Barney was convinced that his parents and the entire family would be much better off moving to Superior.

Due to his urging, Barney's three older brothers, Jim, Maurice and John moved to Superior and the four brothers rented a house together. Their sister Nell moved in to keep house and cook for them. Not long after, Barney's parents sold their farm in Burkhardt and the entire family moved to Superior.

One afternoon while Barney was working as a conductor on the trolley car in Superior, a tragic incident occurred. He stopped the trolley when he saw a crowd of people gathered around a woman who had been stabbed and was lying across the trolley tracks in a pool of blood. A drunken sailor with a knife in his hand was standing over her. Soon two policemen arrived and arrested the man. Seeing the lifeless body of the woman on the tracks shocked Barney to his core. The experience proved to be a turning point in his life. He felt that he could not simply pray to God to end the violence in the world. He realized that he had to do something about it.

Two days later, Barney visited his pastor, Father Edmund Sturm, at Sacred Heart parish in Superior and told him that he wanted to be a priest. Barney was twenty-one years old. Father Sturm suggested that he apply to the diocesan seminary of St. Francis de Sales in Milwaukee. It was known as the "German Seminary." Barney did not delay but applied at once and was accepted. Since he had only completed the eighth grade, he would be attending the St. Francis seminary high school for the first four years with boys much younger than himself.

At the St. Francis de Sales seminary, the rigid daily schedule was regulated by bells. Summoned by the bell, the students rose at 5:30 a.m. for Morning Prayer followed by meditation and then Mass. Throughout the day there were academic classes and periods set aside for study. The Rosary was recited together at five o'clock in the afternoon. The busy day ended with Night Prayer at nine o'clock p.m.

Life at the minor seminary was disciplined, ordered and austere. Barney applied himself and studied hard. There was ample time for recreation as well. In the winter, the seminarians had a chance to enjoy ice skating and during the spring they played baseball. In order to make money to pay for his tuition, Barney became the seminary barber. During the summer vacation, he would return home to spend time with his family in Superior as well as reconnect with the friends he had gone to school with.

Barney studied very hard and got good grades during the first year at St. Francis de Sales. The other students looked up to him as a big brother. He was optimistic, cheerful and very likeable. The fact that he was much older did not prove to be an obstacle. After several semesters, Barney's grades began to slip. He had trouble with algebra, geometry and Latin classes. He worked hard and raised his grades so that he could enter the first year of the college classes but his grades began slipping again. Although he was not getting failing marks, in some of the classes he was just barely passing. German was especially difficult for him.

After much thought and deliberation, the seminary administrators called Barney into the office and told him that he would not be able to continue in his studies for the diocesan priesthood. They explained that they did not think he would be able to master the upcoming college level courses with the academic excellence expected of a seminarian. He had studied at St. Francis de Sales for four and a half years and was now twenty-five years old.

Barney's superiors felt that he had a vocation and suggested that he apply to a religious Order if he wanted to continue to study for the priesthood. The religious Orders were more flexible regarding academic studies and Barney would have a better chance of succeeding. His superiors encouraged him to visit the St. Francis Capuchin seminary in Milwaukee, just five miles away.

Barney paid a visit to the Capuchin seminary in Milwaukee but was not impressed by what he saw there. He did not go into detail except to say that he did not care for the long beards that the Capuchins customarily wore. Nothing about the monastic life of the Capuchins seemed appealing to him. He went back home to his family in Superior, Wisconsin, feeling discouraged and not sure what to do next.

Barney made an appointment to talk about his concerns to the saintly priest, Father Eustace Vollmer, a Franciscan of the St. Louis province. Because of Father Vollmer's reputation for holiness, many people in the Superior area sought him out and profited by his spiritual counsel. Barney had visited him in the past for spiritual direction. Father Vollmer told Barney he felt sure that he had a vocation to the priesthood and encouraged him to seek admittance to his own religious Order, the Franciscans. He also encouraged him to keep his options open and to apply to the Capuchins as well as the Jesuits. Barney followed Father Vollmer's advice and sent out letters of application to the various religious congregations.

In a short time, Barney received a reply back from Father Bonaventure Frey telling him that the Capuchin religious congregation would be happy to receive him in their novitiate. Barney was not at all enthusiastic. He preferred any other religious Order to the Capuchins and was not sure what to do. He continued to pray to God, asking for guidance.

Barney decided to make a novena to the Blessed Mother on the Feast of the Immaculate Conception on December 8, praying to be guided to the right religious congregation. He told his mother and his sister Ellen that he would like them to join him in the novena and they agreed to do so. He was confused about the next step he should take and was still considering the Franciscan Order as a possibility.

During the Feast Day Mass on December 8 at Sacred Heart parish in Superior, Barney felt the presence of the Virgin Mary and heard the distinct words - "Go to Detroit." Barney knew instantly what that meant. The Capuchins were the only religious Order at that time who had their novitiate in Detroit.

As far as Barney was concerned, the words that he had heard, "Go to Detroit" were an unmistakable sign, an answer to his prayers. Barney had already been accepted by the Capuchins in Detroit. Father Bonaventure's letter confirmed it. Barney did not want to delay but to leave right away. For the first time, he felt a sense of excitement, even enthusiasm. He took the night train from Superior, Wisconsin on the three-day journey to Detroit. It was snowing heavily when he arrived at St. Bonaventure Monastery on Christmas Eve.

Barney was greeted at the door by the Father Guardian and the Novice Master. They offered him dinner but he said that he was too exhausted to eat. They showed him to his small cell and bid him goodnight. Suddenly Barney's mind became filled with doubts. Everything at the monastery seemed strange and unfamiliar to him. He wondered if he would truly be able to make the commitment to monastic life.

At midnight, Barney awakened to the sound of church bells and the singing of Christmas Carols in German. When he opened his cell door, a number of brown-robed Capuchins were standing there, each holding a lighted candle and summoning him to follow them as they walked in procession through the halls and corridors of the monastery to the chapel. Barney quickly joined them and was deeply edified by the beautiful and solemn Christmas Eve midnight Mass celebrated by the entire community.

All of Barney's doubts about joining the Capuchins faded away on Christmas Eve but they returned the very next day. He had a terrible feeling of dread about the new life he was embarking on and began to wonder if he could be happy in it. Already, he had a strong temptation to quit and go back to his family in Wisconsin and to everything that was near and dear to him. His apprehension and trepidation lasted for three weeks. The day before his investiture into the Capuchin Order, he was filled with doubts and anxiety.

At the moment he entered the chapel to receive his brown habit and white cord at his investiture on January 14, 1897, the doubts ceased and never bothered him again. He would wear the Capuchin habit for the next sixty years. Barney was given a new name, Francis Solanus after St. Francis Solano, the Spanish missionary to Peru. Since another one of the Capuchins was named Francis, Barney would be known simply as "Solanus." His family and extended family were very proud of him. Two of Solanus' brothers became priests, one of his uncles was a priest, and one of his cousins was named the cardinal archbishop of New York.

Life in the novitiate was austere and rigorous but not greatly different from the schedule Barney kept at St. Francis de Sales minor seminary where he had studied for four years. The community got up at 4:45 a.m. in order to assemble in the chapel for Morning Prayer at 5:10 a.m. Mass was at six o'clock in the morning followed by a simple breakfast eaten together in silence. The novices then went to morning classes. During lunch, one of the Capuchins read aloud from the lives of the saints. In the afternoon, the novices spent several hours in manual labor. After supper, all assembled in the chapel for Night Prayer followed by bedtime which was at 9:30 p.m.

On July 21, 1898, Brother Solanus made his first profession of vows. In August, along with the other recently professed, Brother Solanus took a train to Milwaukee to continue his academic studies for the priesthood at St. Francis major seminary.

At the major seminary, life revolved around prayer, work and study. As a general rule, no visitors were allowed. The classes at the seminary were taught in German and the class discussions were in German as well. Brother Solanus' imperfect grasp of German proved to be a great obstacle to him. The textbooks were in Latin, a subject that had been difficult for him in the minor seminary. Latin continued to be a problem for him. Philosophy also proved to be difficult for him. During the first three semesters, his grades were passing but below average. His instructors became concerned when they realized his academic weaknesses but they were not severe with him in any way and they supported him and hoped for his success.

In addition to his studies, Brother Solanus was assigned work as the sacristan of the chapel as well as the head of the altar servers. He enjoyed the work very much. He was painstaking and meticulous in his duties as sacristan, taking care of every detail with the greatest attention.

At the major seminary, the director in charge of all of the students was Father Anthony Rottensteiner. He was known for his austerity, his brilliant intellect and his demand for excellence. Many of the students felt intimidated by his powerful position as director and by his military-like strictness.

Father Anthony, who made it a habit to become well-acquainted with all of the seminarians, recognized something extraordinary in Brother Solanus. For one thing, he interacted with the other seminarians in such a loving and generous way. He was always thinking about the needs of the community rather than his own needs. His heart was open to everyone. Father Anthony also noticed that he performed his duties as sacristan with perfection. It was hard to imagine how anyone could perform them better. But whether Brother Solanus would succeed in his academic classes on dogma, moral theology, canon law, scripture, liturgy and church history was yet to be determined. With all of his heart, Father Anthony wanted Brother Solanus to be ordained.

During the fourth semester at the major seminary, Father Anthony began to privately tutor Brother Solanus in his studies. He was willing to go to any length to help him improve his grades. In class, Father Anthony phrased the questions to Solanus in such a way as to help him give the correct answer. He was never severe with him. The students were happy that Father Anthony was giving Brother Solanus extra help in his academic studies. Like Father Anthony, the students loved and admired Brother Solanus for his goodness, humility, and deep spirituality. Some of the instructors were not sure if Brother Solanus would be able to pass all of the required classes. Father Anthony said, "We shall ordain Brother Solanus. Do not doubt it. He will be another Curé of Ars."

Father Boniface Goldhausen was a classmate of Brother Solanus. Father Boniface said:

> As far as his work was concerned, he was always on time. I do not remember that he ever came late for religious exercises or for the work to be done. It was always perfect. . .He was very exact and painstaking. . .At times I would go down to the choir when he was busy there. I would observe him. I was highly edified. On feast days, he would put perhaps three candles and three bouquets out. Then he would put the candles, one on each side and he would go way back and look at it. If it wasn't exactly perfect he would go back and move one candle until they were just where he wanted them. It was the same thing with the bouquets. . .It took him at least a half hour to trim that simple choir altar. But at the

same time, he seemed so recollected. When he was finished, he made his adoration. One would notice that he was deeply absorbed spiritually. That's the one thing I cannot forget.

Father Boniface also remembered that Brother Solanus enjoyed playing checkers during recreation. Oddly enough, he always preferred that his opponent win the game. His generosity and regard for others was apparent even in simple games.

Brother Solanus' superiors wanted him to understand that his ordination to the priesthood was not guaranteed. They asked him to put in writing that he was aware that he might not be ordained or that if he was, he might not receive full faculties. Father Solanus wrote:

> I, Brother Solanus Casey, having entered the Order with a pure intention and of my own free choice, wish to remain in the Order, and I therefore humbly ask for admission to solemn profession. However, since I do not know whether as a result of my meager talents and defective studies, I am fit to assume the many-sided duties and serious responsibilities of the priesthood, I hereby declare that I do not want to become a priest if my legitimate superiors consider me unqualified; (2) that I still wish to be able to receive one or other of the orders, but will be satisfied if they exclude me entirely from the higher orders. I have offered myself to God without reservation; for that reason I leave it without anxiety to the superiors to decide about me as they may judge best before God. I do not want to become a priest if my superiors consider me unqualified. . .I will be satisfied if they exclude me entirely from the higher orders. I have offered myself to God without reservation. For that reason I leave it without anxiety

to the superiors to decide about me as they may judge best before God.

Brother Solanus had been a seminarian at the major seminary from 1898 to 1904. During his final year in the major seminary, he was concerned about his grades and wondering about his future. He wrote a letter to his sister Ellen saying that in all likelihood he would be ordained and that he hoped the Holy Spirit would guide the decision of his superiors. Instead of signing his name to the letter, he wrote the word "Resignation" with a small cross at the end. His great desire was to be completely resigned to the will of God.

Besides Brother Solanus, there were five others in the class who were preparing for ordination. Brother Solanus' grades for the most part were average and, in some cases, just a little below average. Of the six men in the class, three had received mostly good and very good grades. Brother Solanus, Brother John O'Donovan, and Brother Damasus Wickland received almost all average grades. The superiors decided that Brother Solanus, Brother John and Brother Damasus would be ordained *sacerdos simplex* or simplex priests. They would be able to celebrate Mass and perform all other priestly functions but would not have faculties to hear confessions or to preach doctrinal sermons.

John O'Donovan later spoke to his superiors, asking them to give him full priestly faculties and he received them. It was thought that Solanus too could have received full faculties if he had pressed for them, but he never did. He never complained about the decision of his superiors but accepted it with grace and humility. He never showed the slightest bit of resentment or disappointment. He never discussed his feelings about having limited priestly faculties with anyone.

On July 24, 1904, Father Solanus Casey was ordained in Saint Francis of Assisi church in Milwaukee by Archbishop Sebastian Messmer. He was thirty-three years old and had been in formation for the priesthood for twelve years. He celebrated his first Mass at St. Joseph church in Appleton, Wisconsin one week later. His family traveled the three hundred miles from Superior to Appleton for the occasion. They could not have been prouder. It was the first time he had seen his mother since leaving for the Capuchin novitiate in Detroit eight years before. His brothers, Jim, Maurice and Edward were present. All through the Mass, his father wept tears of joy.

A short time after ordination, Father Solanus was sent to his first assignment at the Sacred Heart friary and parish in Yonkers, New York. At Sacred Heart, Father Bonaventure Frey, the pastor, assigned Father Solanus to be the sacristan as well as director of the altar servers. As sacristan, it was his job to care for the priestly vestments, always making sure that they were clean, mended and pressed. He also had to take care of the altar linens and the sacred vessels. In addition, it was his responsibility to see that ample hosts and wine were on hand for every Mass. He was also in charge of scheduling the altar servers at the various Masses and he trained them in their duties at the altar.

Usually it was a Capuchin brother rather than a priest who was assigned to the tasks that were given to Father Solanus at Sacred Heart parish. Father Solanus had studied for the priesthood for more than a decade. Some might have concluded that the duties he was given at Sacred Heart parish were demeaning and belittling for an ordained priest. Father Solanus did not feel that way. He took great pride in his work and considered it a joy and a special privilege. He once confided to a friend that of all the different duties a Capuchin was assigned to, he considered the job of sacristan to be the most desirable. There a person could spend so much of his time in the presence of Jesus in the Blessed Sacrament.

Father Solanus was conscientious in his training of the altar boys and held high standards regarding the performance of their duties. He was very strict with them. He felt anxious and upset on many occasions when the altar boys failed to serve at the Mass in a dignified way. One time their inattentiveness to their duties became so troubling to him that he made a Novena to Our Lady of Perpetual Help. Shortly after the Novena was completed, he noticed a great improvement in the conduct of the altar boys.

In order to encourage the altar boys as well as to reward them for their service, Father Solanus gave them either a gold or silver medal as well as a pearl knife according to the length of time of their service at the altar. He also took them on outings from time to time, outings that everyone enjoyed. They visited St. Patrick's Cathedral in New York City and took subway rides to Manhattan. They also went swimming at Rockaway Beach and attended baseball games. Toward the end of the day, Father Solanus always treated the boys to an ice cream soda. Finally, they would visit a church and pray together before going home.

One of the altar boys, James Lawless, later in life recalled, "Father Solanus was the personification of patience when it came to teaching us our Latin for serving Mass. He was a patient, dedicated, and devoted servant of God."

Many of the children who attended the parish elementary school at Sacred Heart remembered the kindness of Father Solanus. One was seven-year-old Loretta Brogan. Loretta had attended the morning Mass at Sacred Heart one day when the school was on a special schedule for a Field Day. Morning classes were replaced by outdoor activities. After the Mass, Father Solanus saw Loretta walking past the monastery and asked her where she was going. She told him that since classes would not begin until later that morning, she was going home to have breakfast and then would come right back to school. Father Solanus would not allow her to walk the long distance home. He took her to the rectory and fixed breakfast for her. Loretta felt awed and more than a little shy, sitting at the large table in the priests' dining room. When she finished her breakfast, Father Solanus walked her over to the school to join her classmates.

Father Solanus fully engaged himself in the parish activities at Sacred Heart, enjoying the parish picnics and special celebrations. He looked forward to the Labor Day Festival and always enjoyed the food as well as the carnival games, especially pinning the Wheel of Fortune. At the parish elementary school, he joined the boys in their games of *fungo*, a game similar to baseball.

One of the nuns who belonged to the Sisters of St. Agnes Congregation once approached Father Solanus at one of the Sacred Heart parish festivals. He was eating a hot dog with mustard and sauerkraut when she walked up to him. She told him that she was worried because her father had remarried outside the Church and had stopped going to Mass. She asked Father Solanus to pray for him. Father Solanus told her that he would indeed pray for her father. He assured her that everything was going to be fine and told her not to worry about it anymore. With his customary simplicity, he kept eating his hot dog as they conversed. The nun had no idea that her family was about to receive a wonderful grace. Shortly after her conversation with Father Solanus, the nun received a letter from her brother. He said that their father had just had his marriage convalidated and had started going to Mass again.

When Father Aloysius Blonigen succeeded Father Bonaventure at Sacred Heart parish, he decided to appoint Father Solanus as the friary doorkeeper/porter. He was to serve as a kind of receptionist and greet the people who knocked on the office door at the monastery and to see to their needs. His new job suddenly brought him in contact with a lot more people than ever before. Many of those who came to the door wanted advice or counseling regarding various personal problems. Some sought his advice concerning marital problems. Others asked for help with an addiction. Young people often came to discuss their vocation in life with him. Many had serious illnesses and asked for his prayers. During Father Solanus' many years of counseling, ministers from sixteen different Protestant denominations visited him, seeking his help.

Father Solanus had a great gift of empathy and insight when counseling people and before long, numerous individuals were calling Sacred Heart parish asking to speak to him. He made himself available to everyone. He spoke very quietly and calmly and was always ready and willing to listen to anyone at any time of the day or night. One person described him by saying, "He accepted people wherever they were. If you were sick, he hurt with you. He was very compassionate. He could say a few words to you and you would feel perfectly at ease." He was extremely patient with people's failings. Many said that after talking to him, they felt as if a great weight had been lifted from their shoulders. It was observed that even crying babies seemed to relax when Father Solanus held them in his arms.

People coming to Father Solanus for counseling could easily spend two hours talking to him. When they shared their personal problems, he tried to give them his best fatherly advice. After an initial visit with him or a telephone conversation with him, a number of people would write to him. He felt that it was very important to answer every letter received and to let each person know that he cared about them. It was not uncommon for the correspondence to continue for many years.

Carmella Petrosino, an eight-year-old Italian girl, used to knock on the door at Sacred Heart regularly asking for Father Solanus. When problems arose in her neighborhood, Carmella was told to "Go and get the holy priest." Father Solanus and Carmella would then walk together to the home of the person in need, and once they were there, Carmella would translate from Italian to English, relaying the message to Father Solanus. There were many Italian families in Yonkers at the time who did not speak a word of English. Father Solanus showed great concern for the Italian immigrants in the neighborhood and went out of his way to help them.

On one occasion, Father Solanus asked Carmella what she wanted to be when she grew up. She replied that she wanted to be a nun, a Sister of St. Agnes. "You will be a nun!" he said to her with confidence and his words proved true. Later in life, Carmella recalled that Father Solanus took a great interest in her and they had many wonderful conversations together while walking through the neighborhood on the way to visiting the sick.

Many years later, when the Tribunal of judges was considering Father Solanus' Cause for canonization, Carmella was called as a witness to testify. She told the Tribunal that the sick people of Sacred Heart parish received Father Solanus' special care and that his presence brought them great comfort. He was available at a moment's notice to visit someone in their home. He was also extremely kind to the poor and the downtrodden. Carmella said that many miracles and healings occurred when Father Solanus prayed for the sick.

As time went by, more duties were given to Father Solanus at Sacred Heart parish. He served as chaplain to the Sacred Heart League and with painstaking care, he prepared the devotional talks which he gave at the meetings. He was also put in charge of the Children of Mary, a sodality for young women. He always made sure a large plate of cookies was available at the end of each meeting for the girls who belonged to the Children of Mary.

After serving for fourteen years in Yonkers, Father Solanus was transferred to the Capuchin parish of Our Lady of Sorrows on the Lower East Side of Manhattan. Once again, he was assigned as sacristan and director of the altar servers as well as head of the Young Ladies Sodality. His new assignment allowed him much more free time and he used the extra time to study scripture as well as read the lives of the saints and the writings of the Church Fathers. One of his favorite saints was St. Therese of Lisieux. He had read her autobiography, *The Story of a Soul*, nine times. He also had a devotion to St. Francis of Assisi, St. Gerard Magella, St. Anthony of Padua and a special devotion to St. Joseph.

Father Solanus loved to pray the Angelus as well as the Little Office of the Blessed Virgin Mary. He prayed to the Virgin Mary under the titles of Our Lady of Perpetual Help and Our Lady of Lourdes. He always had a Rosary in his hand, even when he was counseling people in the church office. He had a devotion to the

Sacred Heart of Jesus and enjoyed giving Sacred Heart badges to his visitors. He would frequently sign his letters, "Yours in the Sacred Heart, Father Solanus."

At Our Lady of Sorrows, Father Solanus was able to spend a lot of time in the chapel in adoration before the Blessed Sacrament. His time at the parish proved to be very fruitful spiritually. Three years later, Father Solanus was transferred to Our Lady of the Angels in Harlem, New York. He was fifty years old.

Father Solanus' main job at Our Lady of the Angels was as doorkeeper/porter. He would answer the door for all who came to the front office and try to meet their needs. Knowing his natural gifts and abilities in counseling people, his superiors wanted him to concentrate exclusively on pastoral work. They were aware that he had done a great deal of good and had helped many people in his previous assignments as doorkeeper.

At Our Lady of the Angels, Father Solanus encouraged people to enroll in the Seraphic Mass Association. People enrolled with a specific intention in mind, like healing of an illness, help in financial matters, direction regarding a career change, harmony in the family and the like. Those who enrolled enjoyed the benefit of being remembered in the prayers and Masses of the Capuchin Friars around the world and the small donation that was given supported the Capuchin foreign missionaries. At Sacred Heart parish in Yonkers, Father Solanus had taken enrollments as well. The cost of enrollment was a minimal fifty cents per year and the charge was waived if a person could not afford it. Father Solanus would fill out an enrollment card for each person and then enter their name in a book. He would then give each person a blessing.

When people came to Father Solanus with a prayer request or with a desire to enroll in the Seraphic Mass Society, he generally asked the person to do something more in their spiritual life than they were in the habit of doing. He did not want them to remain passive in their relationship with God, simply asking God for this favor or that. If they went to Mass on Sunday only, he might encourage them to go to Mass once during the week in addition to Sunday. If they went to Confession once every six months, he might ask them to go once every three months. If they were not in the habit of donating to help the needy, he might ask them to begin to do so or to volunteer in the soup kitchen.

Before long, a number of people began to report that healings, immediate resolutions to problems, profound graces and miracles had occurred after Father Solanus took their enrollment in the Seraphic Mass Association and prayed for them. Although enrollments were available at all of the other Capuchin friaries, the cures were only being reported by those who were enrolled at Our Lady of the Angels by Father Solanus.

Word spread quickly and soon more and more people were knocking on the door at Our Lady of the Angels, wanting to speak to Father Solanus and to enroll in the Seraphic Mass Association. The miraculous cures, graces, healings and conversions would continue for the next thirty-six years. Many years before, Father Anthony, the director of the Capuchin seminary, predicted that Father Solanus would someday be another Curé of Ars. At Our Lady of the Angels, the truth of Father Anthony's words began to unfold.

In November 1923, when the Capuchin Provincial, the Very Reverend Benno Aichinger made his yearly visitation to Our Lady of the Angels friary and parish, he had already heard talk of the favors people were receiving who had been enrolled by Father Solanus in the Seraphic Mass Association. He asked Father Solanus about it. Father Solanus explained that people were indeed receiving healings and graces but emphasized that he had nothing to do with it. He never attributed any of the healings to himself but gave all of the credit to God.

Father Benno was edified by Father Solanus' humility and piety and told him that he wanted him to keep a journal and to record the special graces that people were receiving who had enrolled in the Seraphic Mass Association. That very day, Father

Solanus began to write down the special favors in a notebook. Between November 8, 1923 and July 28, 1924, he wrote ninety-six entries in his notebook which included physical healings, problems resolved and graces received.

One entry Father Solanus made in his notebook regarded a man from Freehold, New Jersey who was in a mental institution in Philadelphia. His family enrolled him in the Seraphic Mass Association on December 1 and before Christmas they reported that there was a remarkable improvement in his condition. He wrote a letter to his family and the content demonstrated that he was thinking clearly and logically. By March, he was out of the institution and back at work. His family considered it a miracle.

Another entry Father Solanus made in his notebook concerned Jean Dorothy Ward. Her six-year-old daughter had suffered from convulsions from the time she was three months old. At times, she had as many as twenty convulsions a day. After she was enrolled in the Seraphic Mass Association, she never had another convulsion.

One woman enrolled her brother Michael, who had been away from the Church for nine years and had left his wife four years previously. Almost one month after enrolling him, she came back to Father Solanus to say that Michael had been to confession and had already attended Mass three times. This occurred right after his enrollment. When Michael was asked why he had suddenly returned to the practice of his faith, he replied that he did not know.

While at Our Lady of the Angels, Father Solanus also found time to minister to the prisoners in the Harlem jail. He regularly led the Rosary, said Mass and counseled the prisoners. Throughout the year, he brought them newspapers to read and during the Christmas season, he sent a personal Christmas card to each one of the prisoners. He also celebrated Mass at the Juvenile Detention Facility for incarcerated youth.

In the summer of 1924, Father Solanus was transferred from Our Lady of the Angels in Harlem to St. Bonaventure Capuchin monastery in Detroit, the headquarters of the Capuchin Order. It took almost no time for him to pack his few belongings in preparation for the move to Detroit.

At St. Bonaventure, the day began early. The Capuchins woke at 4:45 a.m. and gathered in the chapel for community prayers at 5:15 a.m. Mass was celebrated at 6:15 a.m. followed by breakfast which was eaten in silence. The Capuchins then set about their work until noon when they gathered in the chapel for midmorning prayer. Lunch and a short period of recreation followed. They then resumed their work until Evening Prayer at 5:30 p.m. followed by dinner. The Litany of the Blessed Virgin Mary and Night Prayers were recited as a community before bed. Father Solanus' designated seat in the chapel was next to a window in which the cold regularly came through. He never asked that his place be changed and it never was.

At St. Bonaventure's monastery, Father Solanus was assigned to be the assistant doorkeeper/porter to Brother Francis Spruck. Brother Francis was also the tailor for the Capuchin province and he made and repaired all of the brown habits. At the friary's main entrance, the tailor shop and the front office were next to each other.

For the most part, the front office at St. Bonaventure's was relatively quiet. Brother Francis was able to handle the visitors to the monastery as well as his sewing work quite easily. However, the office began to get busy shortly after Father Solanus arrived. Either Brother Francis or Father Solanus would answer the door when someone rang the bell. When the bell began ringing constantly, they placed a sign on the door that read, "Walk In."

As always, Father Solanus would let people take as much time as they needed to talk to him. Whoever had a problem and wanted to speak to Father Solanus about it would receive his complete attention for as long as they wanted. He seemed to be completely oblivious of the time. But Brother Francis was not oblivious of the time. Brother Francis was organized, practical, detail-oriented and efficient. After Father Solanus' arrival, Brother Francis felt that the order and efficiency of the office was quickly unraveling. He was also annoyed by Father Solanus' slow and easy-going personality.

As far as Brother Francis was concerned, allowing people to talk for two hours in a private counseling session was excessive. Brother Francis also became irritated that the people in the office were waiting hours on end to speak to Father Solanus. All of the chairs in the waiting area were full and they remained full throughout the day.

Brother Francis thought it was very odd that none of the people who were waiting to see Father Solanus grew impatient but seemed content to wait as long as necessary. He would frequently remind Father Solanus to finish up his visit because more and more people were coming into the office to wait. But it seemed that Father Solanus was not able to cut the visits short. He would never hurry anyone who came to him for help. When Brother Francis got upset about the office situation and lost his temper, he would shout at Father Solanus calling him "Casey" but it didn't seem to faze him a bit.

At St. Bonaventure's, there was only one telephone line which came through the front office where Father Solanus worked. Even when he was in the middle of counseling someone, if the phone rang, he was required to answer it. While Father Solanus was at St. Bonaventure's, the number of telephone calls increased to such an extent that more phone lines had to be put in. In time, the office had to be enlarged to accommodate the crowds.

It is estimated that Father Solanus saw between one hundred and fifty to two hundred people every day at St. Bonaventure's. Most of the people made a relatively short visit, asking Father Solanus for a simple blessing or a prayer. But about fifty of those two hundred people came for counseling and usually wanted to talk at length about their problems.

Father Solanus continued to record the graces that were being reported by those who had enrolled in the Seraphic Mass Association. He would eventually fill seven notebooks with over 6,000 entries of graces received. As far as he was concerned, recording the information in the notebooks was a matter of obedience.

The number of people who went to St. Bonaventure monastery to see Father Solanus continually increased with the passage of time. Father Solanus often got to the front office at seven o'clock in the morning and frequently stayed until ten o'clock at night. After the last person left, he would mop the floor and then go over to the chapel to pray before going to bed.

Clare Ryan of Detroit had been diagnosed with cancer of the stomach by Dr. Reiger at Harper Hospital in Detroit. Dr. Reiger told Clare that her condition was terminal and that nothing could be done for her. She then went to see Father Solanus. Father Solanus blessed her with a relic of the True Cross, a small piece of wood from the Cross that Jesus was crucified on. When he did so, she was cured.

After that, Clare visited Father Solanus at the monastery every two weeks for a year. Her visits were curtailed when she came down with severe arthritis and was in bed for nine months. Finally, her husband took her to see Father Solanus at St. Bonaventure's but she was not able to get out of the car. Solanus put his priestly stole on and went out to the car and blessed Clare with holy water. He then prayed over her for about fifteen minutes. When she went home, she was able to walk up the stairs in her home for the first time in nine months. Father Solanus assured her before she left that she would be all right.

Another impressive healing involved Sister Mary Joseph who worked at St. Joseph Mercy Hospital in Detroit. Sister Mary Joseph contracted a severe strep infection in her throat. Her temperature soared to a dangerous 105 degrees as she drifted in and out of consciousness.

The doctor told the hospital supervisor, Sister Mary Philippa, that Sister Mary Joseph's condition was deteriorating and that the infection was spreading. By now, her neck was completely rigid and she was suffering from uncontrollable choking spells. She was being constantly monitored and the doctor was prepared to perform an immediate tracheotomy if necessary.

Sister Mary Philippa became alarmed and called Father Solanus who came to the hospital at once. When he arrived, he went to Sister Mary Joseph's bedside and began to read slowly and deliberately from a small book of prayers. Sister Mary Joseph was in the midst of a choking spell when Father Solanus walked in the room but the choking stopped as soon as he began the prayers. He blessed the Sister with the relic of the True Cross. For two hours, he prayed for her and read aloud from the Gospel account of the Passion. Sister Mary Philippa and two other nuns remained in Sister Mary Joseph's room for the duration of the time that Father Solanus was there. Finally, before he left, he said to Sister Mary Philippa, "I will not need to return. Sister Mary Joseph is going to be well very soon."

A hospital driver was provided to take Father Solanus back to the monastery. As they were leaving the hospital, an acquaintance of Father Solanus approached him in the hall and asked him if he would stop at his wife's room and give her a blessing before he left the hospital. Father Solanus was happy to do so.

Afterward, the man walked Father Solanus to the elevator. "I want you to prepare yourself because your wife is not going to live," Father Solanus told the man. The man thought Father Solanus must be mistaken. "My wife is not that ill. She had a simple operation which is certainly nothing to worry about," he said. "Put your wife in the hands of God and let us both pray for her," Father Solanus said to him.

The hospital driver noticed that Father Solanus was very quiet on the way back to the monastery and seemed to be praying. When the driver got back to the hospital, he told Sister

Mary Philippa about the conversation Father Solanus had with the man who had asked him to come to his wife's hospital room. Sister Mary Philippa told the driver that the man's wife had just passed away.

Father Rupert Dorn, who later became the Capuchin provincial, wrote his impressions of Father Solanus and said:

> He was very kind, simple, and straightforward. One of the things that impressed me was the fact that Father Solanus never tried to impress anybody else by his actions or words or any other thing. He merely said what had to be said. . . When he talked with people, they received the impression that, at that moment, they were the most important people in the world to Solanus.

The Great Depression began with the U.S. stock market crash of 1929 and lasted for ten years. It was considered the worst economic crisis of the 20th century. By 1933, nearly half of America's banks had failed, and unemployment was approaching 30 percent of the workforce. Industrial cities like Detroit were hit especially hard by the depression. As unemployment increased throughout the city of Detroit, so too did the hungry and destitute people who knocked on the door of St. Bonaventure's asking for food. In the beginning, Father Solanus and Brother Francis answered the door and gave food to the needy.

Father Solanus would go into the monastery kitchen and take whatever food was available to give to the person standing at the door. Brother Daniel Brady, when he was a novice, was the cook at St. Bonaventure's. He would often protest, telling Father Solanus that he was taking the food that was to be served to the Capuchins for dinner that evening. Father Solanus would say to Brother Daniel, "As long as there is one hungry person, this food does not belong to us."

Times were hard and continued to get harder. After the stock market crash in 1929, the situation became desperate. Father Solanus and Brother Francis still had their work in the office to do and could no longer manage the crowds who were coming to the door for food. Finally, it was decided that the Third Order hall that was attached to St. Bonaventure Church would be used to feed the hungry. Father Herman Buss who was the Spiritual Director of the Third Order of St. Francis became the soup kitchen supervisor. Many members of the Third Order volunteered to help prepare and serve the food. Before long, between fifteen hundred to three thousand people came to the soup kitchen every day for a meal of homemade soup, bread and coffee. Food was also regularly taken to the homebound.

When Father Solanus was able to, he would leave the front office and go over to the soup kitchen to help serve the meals. He enjoyed mingling with the people and especially liked to talk to the men waiting in the food line. Many of the men had lost their jobs. Father Solanus asked them about the kind of work they had done before they were laid off and since he had numerous contacts in the Detroit area, he put the word out, trying to help the men find work.

Once, one of the volunteers came to the front office and complained to Father Solanus about a destitute woman who had a meal at the soup kitchen that day. Doughnuts with sugar topping had been set out that day for dessert while the jelly doughnuts remained in the kitchen. The woman asked for a jelly doughnut. "They should eat what is set out for them and not ask for anything else," the man said to Father Solanus. "I do not understand that," Father Solanus replied. "If the lady wanted a jelly doughnut, why couldn't you go to the kitchen and get one for her?"

Arthur Rutledge, a fireman, was a regular volunteer in the soup kitchen. He had a great admiration for Father Solanus and felt blessed to be his friend. Once, when Father Solanus was at the hospital visiting the sick, he was surprised to see Arthur there in a wheelchair. He told Father Solanus that he had a tumor in his stomach and was going to be operated on. Father Solanus put his hand on Arthur's stomach and prayed. He told Arthur to be sure to have one more examination before the operation. The doctors did a final examination and discovered that the tumor had disappeared. Arthur was discharged the next day and was soon back at his volunteer position in the kitchen as well as his job at the Fire Department.

Father Herman Buss often had many anxious moments as the supervisor of the soup kitchen. One of those moments occurred when the soup kitchen ran out of food while two hundred people were still waiting in line for something to eat. Father Herman rushed over to the front office and told Father Solanus the situation, thinking that he would be able to call one of his wealthy friends and ask for assistance. But he did not do so.

Instead, Father Solanus went over to the hall with Father Herman and told the men who were waiting in line to be patient and to wait just a little bit longer. He explained that they had run out of food but assured them that God would provide. He asked all the men to join him in praying the *Our Father*. At the conclusion of the prayer, Father Herman opened the door and there stood a bakery man with a big basket full of bread. His whole truck was full of food. When the men in line saw the bakery man, many of them began to cry. Father Solanus said, "See, God provides. Nobody will starve as long as we put our confidence in God."

Because of his duties as doorkeeper in the front office, Father Solanus could not help at the soup kitchen as much as he would have liked to. Nevertheless, Father Herman said that he often felt the spiritual presence of Father Solanus in the soup kitchen. "Through his holiness, I believe that Father Solanus was the one who assisted us in getting help from Divine Providence. God was blessing the operation because we had a holy man right there," Father Herman said. Father Solanus' constant prayer was that the soup kitchen would be able to meet the needs of the many,

many hungry people in Detroit. He once said, "The definition of religion is charity."

Father Solanus tried to find donors who would be willing to help with the many expenses of the soup kitchen. He knew a number of influential and wealthy people in Detroit from businessmen to politicians and he called on them for financial help. One who was numbered among the "rich and powerful" was Frank Murphy, the mayor of Detroit. Frank Murphy had come to the monastery on numerous occasions asking Father Solanus for advice. Even after he became the governor of Michigan, he still visited Father Solanus. Father Solanus asked Frank to support the soup kitchen financially and he was more than happy to do so. Frank Murphy later became a Justice of the U.S. Supreme Court. Father Solanus also asked another friend, Tom Bresnahan, the mayor of River Rouge, Michigan for financial help. He too was happy to donate to the soup kitchen.

Father Solanus took every opportunity to talk to farmers about the good works of the soup kitchen and he tried to persuade them to donate food from their farms. He contacted grocery stores, asking the butchers to donate meat bones for the soup and visited bakeries, asking for day-old baked goods. He also asked the wealthy people he knew to supply cars that were needed to regularly pick up donated food from the local grocery stores.

Noting the large number of destitute people the Capuchins were feeding on a daily basis, the city of Detroit organized a benefit party to honor them and thank them for their work at the soup kitchen. The day of the big celebration, Father Solanus was asked to speak on the radio, on Station CKLW, to talk about the Capuchins' ministry to the poor and the hungry. During the radio broadcast, Father Solanus thanked the people of Detroit as well as the people of the neighboring city of Windsor, Ontario for their help in sustaining the soup kitchen. He said, "We have tried to be of service to the poorest of the poor. I must add that it is our simple duty."

During the depression years, when Father Solanus enrolled people in the Seraphic Mass Association, he often asked them to give a monetary donation to the soup kitchen. One time, Clare Ryan went to the monastery to speak to Father Solanus. He told her that if she had any spare change in her purse, he would like her to put it in the Poor Box for donations for the needy. As it turned out, Clare had 78 cents in her purse and that was all the money she had to her name until her husband received his next paycheck. Father Solanus walked over to the Poor Box and pointed it out to Clare. She put the money in. Later, when Clare looked back on the experience, she said that since that time, she never lacked for anything but always had the resources to meet all of her financial obligations.

Mr. and Mrs. Nardi of Detroit were on the brink of financial ruin during the depression years and were about to lose their business as well as their home. Mrs. Nardi had the idea that perhaps having their home blessed might improve their situation. She asked her pastor to come and bless her home but he said he was too busy to do so. When she asked Father Solanus, he agreed to it. Father Solanus walked through her home and blessed each room. The door to one of the rooms was closed. Mrs. Nardi explained that her husband was in the room but he was ill. Father Solanus went inside and blessed him.

After Father Solanus left, Mr. Nardi began to feel strong and energized. His 104-degree fever left him almost immediately. The next morning, he was able to resume all of his normal activities. At the same time, Mr. and Mrs. Nardi's financial situation improved significantly and they were able to pay all of their bills.

Whenever Father Solanus could get away, he would ride with some of his friends to out-of-the-way farms to make pickups of donated food for the soup kitchen. The Rosary was always prayed on the way. It was a real treat for him to get away from the telephone calls as well as the endless stream of visitors who came to see him at the front office. He told a friend that the long hours in the office speaking to troubled people day in and day out could be monotonous and exhausting. He looked forward to being out in the fresh air in the countryside and enjoyed putting the bags of beans, bushels of potatoes, fruit and fresh vegetables on the truck. At times, he got on a ladder, helping to pick the fruit off the trees.

One time, Father Solanus and a friend took a one-hundred-mile trip north of Detroit to pick up food donations for the soup kitchen. Father Solanus had never learned how to drive so a companion always took him wherever he needed to go. It happened to be a very cold day and the temperature continued to drop throughout the afternoon. Among other things, they were given a very large rooster. For the journey home, the rooster was put in a chicken crate that was far too small. Father Solanus could not bear to see the rooster cramped in such a small crate. He took it out of the crate and put it under his arm in order to protect it from the cold until they got back to the monastery.

In 1935, Father Michael Cefai, the pastor of St. Paul's Maltese Catholic Church in Detroit wanted to find a priest to assist him every week with two Sunday Masses in his parish. He visited Father Marion Reossler, the superior at St. Bonaventure monastery, to see if one of the Capuchins might be able to help out. Father Marion told him that all of his priests were already assigned to Masses on Sundays and none of them would be available. He added that he did not think Father Solanus would be of much use to him since he was not allowed to hear confessions and could not speak Maltese. Father Solanus happened to come into the office when the two priests were discussing the matter. He said that he would really like to help out at St. Paul's and asked Father Marion if he could do so. Since Father Michael seemed happy about it, Father Marion agreed to it.

Arrangements were made for one of the ushers from St. Paul's parish to drive over to the monastery and pick Father Solanus up for the weekend Masses. At St. Paul's parish, it wasn't long before the youth, the middle-aged, the elderly, and the very elderly all sought Father Solanus out. Father Michael was delighted that Father Solanus was so popular with his parishioners.

Father Michael's parents as well as his sisters, lived with him in the rectory at St. Paul's parish. His sister Evelyn worked as his housekeeper and was also a wonderful cook. They usually asked Father Solanus to stay for a home-cooked dinner after the Sunday Mass. Father Michael noticed that the parishioners at St. Paul's would always walk with Father Solanus and talk to him as he went from the church to the rectory for Sunday dinner.

Once, Father Michael was getting ready to go on a sick call. He walked over to the church with his father to get the keys to the Tabernacle and to the cabinet that contained the Holy Oils, but the keys were missing. He turned his pockets inside out and showed his father that the keys were not anywhere to be seen. Father Michael told his father to go back to the house and check on the desk and table. Father Solanus happened to be visiting at the house that day. Father Michael's sister Evelyn was there as well.

When Mr. Cefai told Father Solanus that the keys were lost, Father Solanus asked everyone in the house to kneel down and say a prayer to St. Anthony, the finder of lost objects. When they finished the prayer, Father Solanus said to Mr. Cefai, "Go back over to the church and tell Father Mike that the keys are in his pocket." When Mr. Cefai relayed the message, Father Michael reminded him that he had turned both of his pockets inside out in front of him and there were no keys. However, he looked inside his pockets once again and found the keys.

Father Michael and Father Solanus got along very well. They talked together frequently and enjoyed sharing funny stories and jokes with each other. Father Michael felt indebted to Father Solanus because his own father had been healed by him. Father Michael's father had been suffering from chronic pain. Father Solanus prayed for him and told him to offer all of his sufferings to God for the conversion of lost souls. Right after that, his pain disappeared completely.

A young girl who was a parishioner at St. Paul's parish once told Father Michael that she was suffering intensely from a severe case of eczema on her hands. She had tried countless remedies but none gave her any relief. Father Solanus too had suffered from painful eczema for many years. Father Michael took the girl to see Father Solanus who gave her a blessing and touched her hands. She never had trouble with eczema again.

In addition to Father Michael Cefai, another priest who would send his sick parishioners to Father Solanus was Father William Murphy, the pastor of Saint David's parish in Detroit. Father William, who later became the Bishop of Saginaw, Michigan told the sick to ask Father Solanus for his blessing and his prayers. He had such confidence in Father Solanus that he would advise his parishioners, "Do whatever he tells you to do." Brother André Bessette, now St. André Bessette visited Father Solanus on one occasion and asked for his blessing. Father Solanus, who had the highest esteem for Brother André then asked him for a blessing as well.

In later years, when Father Solanus was transferred out of the Detroit area, he would call Father Michael Cefai's sister Evelyn and tell her when he was coming back in town for a visit. He would ask her to fix spaghetti and Maltese cheese cakes and he would stop by and join the family for dinner. Father Solanus was able to assist Father Michael Cefai at St. Paul's parish from 1938 to 1945.

While serving at St. Bonaventure, Father Solanus was often taken on sick calls by his friend, William Tremblay. On one occasion, they visited a sick woman in Windsor, Ontario named Eva Dugall. Eva, who was in her late thirties, had tuberculosis and had been critically ill for many months. She could not bear the thought of leaving her two small children and was clinging to life because of them.

When Father Solanus walked in to Eva's house, she told him that he reminded her of Jesus Christ. "I was sent here by him," Father Solanus said. "I came here to tell you that the Lord has a crown waiting for you. Why don't you resign yourself to the fact that you are going to heaven and forget about your children. The Lord has a lot of good mothers and the Virgin Mary is the best of all. She is going to take care of your children."

Father Solanus' words had a marvelous effect on Eva. "I feel so different now," she said to him. "We want to pray for you and we would like you to pray with us," Father Solanus said to Eva. Everyone at Eva's house knelt down as Father Solanus led a decade of the Rosary. "I promise you that the Lord will help you today," Father Solanus said to Eva before he and William left. Eva passed away later that evening.

Once William Tremblay and Father Solanus were out together in the car and passed a bar. Father Solanus said that the man who owned the bar was a friend of his and he would like to stop and say hello to him. This was not his usual practice. If he was going out to dinner with a friend and the restaurant had a bar attached, he would not eat there.

The man who owned the bar had great admiration for Father Solanus. When he saw Father Solanus walk into his bar, he was shocked. He became quite flustered and hurried to set up a table and chairs so that they could sit and talk together. Father Solanus told him not to go to any trouble as he would be more than happy to sit at the bar. As surprised as the man was by the visit, he was even more surprised when Father Solanus ordered a beer. They had time to enjoy a friendly conversation together and when Father Solanus was getting ready to leave, the man said to him, "You will never know how proud I feel at this moment and what an honor it has been for me to have you come to visit me. I have many customers who regularly come to this bar, but not one of them has meant as much to me as you have. I am hoping you will come again."

Like so many others, William Tremblay had the greatest esteem for Father Solanus and often told his friends about him. One of William's friends was in an extremely difficult situation and asked William for advice. He told William that he had been having an affair and wanted to break it off but his girlfriend threatened to tell his wife if he left her. William advised his friend to tell his wife the truth about what he had done. He also encouraged him to take his wife to see Father Solanus and to seek his advice. His friend agreed to do so.

Both the husband and wife were angry and extremely upset when they walked into Father Solanus' office. While talking with him, they both shed many tears. After Father Solanus heard their story, he urged the wife to forgive her husband. He went on to tell her that the situation was not nearly as bad as it could be. "Your husband is repentant," Father Solanus said. "He loves you and he is sorry for what he has done. He is asking for your forgiveness. Remember that Jesus forgave Mary Magdalene." Father Solanus went on to tell the woman that she and her husband were blessed to have beautiful children and it would be a tragedy to break up the family by divorcing. He asked the woman to walk over to where her husband was sitting, to kiss him and to tell him that she loved him and that she forgave him. She did what Father Solanus asked her to do. Their marriage became happy once again and remained strong from that time forward.

Edward Karber, a successful business man from Detroit, was a generous donor to the soup kitchen. For Edward, meeting Father Solanus proved to be life changing. When his wife's sister died, Edward and his wife adopted the sister's four children - two boys and two girls. Edward was a wonderful father to the children and loved them as his own. The children were Catholic just like his wife. Edward had deep-seated prejudices against the Catholic Church. He agreed that the children could attend Catholic school but did not want them to change their last name to Karber due to the fact that they were Catholics. He would not allow crucifixes, religious pictures, or religious articles to be in his home.

Edward was a wonderful husband and father. He would drive his wife and four children to church every Sunday but always dropped them off a block away. He could not bring himself to stop in front of a Catholic Church. It was the same when he drove the children to St. Brigid's school. He dropped them off one block away since he was uncomfortable even looking at a Catholic school.

When Edward's oldest adopted daughter Catherine told him that she wanted to become a nun of the Immaculate Heart of Mary Congregation, he refused to give permission. He told her that she was free to do anything she wanted when she turned twenty-one years of age but until that time, he would not give his consent. He was secretly hoping that she would change her mind.

Catherine was accepted into the Immaculate Heart of Mary Congregation and entered St. Mary's convent in Monroe, Michigan in 1930. After completing the first year of postulancy, she was asked to choose a new name. In honor of her father whom she dearly loved, she took the name Sister Edward Marie. Every day she prayed for Edward's conversion.

Edward worked in management at the Crowley-Milner Company in Detroit. The Company regularly made charitable donations to the Capuchin soup kitchen. On one occasion, Edward visited the monastery regarding a matter involving his Company's financial support of the soup kitchen and it was there that he met Father Solanus for the first time. Edward felt drawn to Father Solanus from the first moment they met.

Sometime later, Father Solanus called Edward and asked him to drive him to the hospital to visit a sick man and he agreed to do so. Edward asked Father Solanus to promise that he would not talk about religion during the trip. "I will talk about sports, politics, or current events, but never religion," Edward explained. That was not a problem for Father Solanus. He could easily talk on a variety of subjects and he did so on many occasions. He loved baseball and was a big fan of the Detroit Tigers. He enjoyed discussing his favorite baseball team with friends and acquaintances. He promised Edward that he would not say a word about religion.

Edward asked Father Solanus to sit in the back seat rather than the front seat. Father Solanus would be less conspicuous that way since Edward did not want anyone to see him with a brown-robed member of the clergy.

True to his word, Father Solanus never brought up the subject of religion, but during the drive to the hospital Edward began thinking about some questions he had about the Catholic Church and posed the questions to Father Solanus. Father Solanus answered each one of the questions to Edward's satisfaction. From time to time, Edward would drive Father Solanus to the hospital and Edward always seemed to have more questions about Catholicism. After giving it a lot of thought, he finally decided to take instructions in the Catholic faith but did not tell anyone that he was doing so.

Later, Edward told his daughter Ann that he was about to enter the Catholic Church. She couldn't have been more surprised. "How did it happen?" Ann asked. "It is all because of Father Solanus," Edward replied. He explained how he had felt drawn to Father Solanus from their very first meeting and how talking to him sparked his interest in Catholicism. Edward received his first Holy Communion from Father Solanus and thereafter became a daily communicant.

Another individual whose encounter with Father Solanus proved to be a life-changing experience was Luke Leonard. Luke, who was an alcoholic, felt that his days were numbered because of his uncontrollable drinking. He was living in a run-down motel in Detroit, addicted and hopeless. Some of his friends urged him to make a spiritual retreat with them and he decided to do so. Father Solanus spoke at the retreat.

Luke was captivated by Father Solanus' simple, loving message. He had a gentle way of speaking and also told humorous stories to get his point across. Luke attended more of Father Solanus' talks and was always inspired by his words. Luke began to reflect on his life and he decided that he wanted to stop drinking yet at the same time, he knew that he would not be able to do so. He had already tried in the past but had failed.

Luke gave it more thought and finally decided to quit drinking cold turkey. For several days, he walked the streets of Detroit, trying to keep his mind off of drinking. Suffering the tortures of alcohol withdrawal, he experienced delirium tremens and uncontrollable shaking. Frightful hallucinations taking the form of monsters appeared before his eyes. When he stopped at a small refreshment stand and ordered a soda, his hands were shaking so badly that he could not raise the glass to his lips. Another customer who noticed his predicament, held the glass for him so that he could take a drink.

With a desire to speak to Father Solanus, Luke knocked on the door of St. Bonaventure monastery. When Father Solanus answered the door, he saw that Luke was in distress. He quickly said goodbye to a couple that he was speaking to and then asked Luke to come into his office. Luke told Father Solanus that he needed to speak to him confidentially. Father Solanus led him to a private room and closed the door.

Luke poured out his heart to Father Solanus, telling him how his life had taken a downward spiral into darkness. He had a long story to tell of pain and heartbreak. Two or three times while Luke was speaking, Brother Francis knocked on the door and told Father Solanus that other people were waiting to speak to him. Father Solanus told him to tell those who were waiting to wait just a little longer. Finally, Father Solanus said to Luke, "When did you get over your sickness?" The words seemed strange to Luke. He had never considered that his alcoholism was a sickness. It was 1941 and it would be many years before society would consider alcoholism to be a sickness or disease.

In order to be clear about the question Father Solanus asked him, Luke said to him, "Do you mean when did I get over my drinking problem?" At that, Father Solanus began to laugh. Luke knew that he had not gotten over his drinking problem. When he left the monastery, he had a great sense of peace. He felt free, as though he had just been released from the grip of something terrible. He never took another drink again.

One evening about ten o'clock p.m. Father Ralph Diederichs noticed the light on in the front office. He assumed that Father Solanus was answering his mail as he usually did late into the evening. When he walked in to the office, he was surprised to see that Father Solanus was playing his violin. He also noticed that the receiver of the phone was off the hook. The next day, he asked Father Solanus about it. Father Solanus explained that he was playing his violin for a Methodist minister who was ill and bedridden. The minister told his wife to call Father Solanus and ask him to play several hymns for him on his violin. Father Solanus set the telephone receiver close by and was happy to grant the sick man's request.

Every Wednesday at St. Bonaventure's, at three o'clock in the afternoon, a special devotional healing service was held in the chapel. It was a tradition that had been observed for many years. Shortly after Father Solanus was transferred to St. Bonaventure's, he was asked to preside at the Wednesday healing service. Attendance grew rapidly after that. People of all faiths and no faith at all attended.

During the healing service, Father Solanus always gave an inspirational sermon. His message was very simple. He spoke about trust in God, the importance of faith, fidelity to prayer and other spiritual topics. One of the Capuchins said, "Solanus' way of talking about God revolved around love." He spoke about God in a way that even non-believers could appreciate.

Because Father Solanus spoke in a soft and wispy voice, people came early so that they could get a good seat close to the front. They wanted to make sure they would be able to hear his message. He then blessed everyone with the relic of the True Cross. Following that, all those assembled would kneel at the altar rail for an individual blessing by Father Solanus.

Father Solanus was often late for the Wednesday healing service. He became so involved with counseling at the front office that he lost track of time. Usually, Brother Francis would have to remind him when it was time to go to the chapel. Fifteen minutes before the start of the Wednesday service, Brother Francis would give Father Solanus a reminder. Every five minutes after that, he would remind him again. Brother Francis, who was always punctual, found the situation more than a little annoying.

On one occasion, a woman named Bernadette Nowak was waiting at the front office to speak to Father Solanus about a personal matter. It was the first time she had been to the monastery. As it approached three o'clock in the afternoon, Father Solanus told everyone who was waiting that he needed to hurry over to the chapel for the Wednesday healing service.

Bernadette was disappointed that she didn't get to speak to Father Solanus and decided to follow him over to the chapel. Before the service ended, she knelt at the Communion rail with the others to receive a blessing. When Father Solanus approached Bernadette, he said to her, "Stop worrying. You are going to be all right." She noticed that he did not speak to any of the other people at the Communion rail. That night, Bernadette had the first sound sleep in many weeks. From that time forward, her health began to improve.

Casimira Scott was another individual who was blessed by attending the Wednesday afternoon healing services at St. Bonaventure. She attended the services every week for thirteen weeks but remained skeptical. She did not believe that individuals could be healed through the power of prayer. When a Rabbi was healed in front of her eyes and was able to walk out of the service without his cane, she became a believer.

Casimira said that Father Solanus helped her in countless ways. She said, "I don't know how I can put it into words, but you just had the feeling when you were with him that he believed very strongly in God and he passed on that same feeling to you. He always spoke of God when you were with him. . . He made you feel the presence of God in your life. He is the only person in my life who made me feel that way. By that I mean that I felt that God was with Father Solanus and that he was transmitting that same presence of God to me." Another person said, "When I was with Father Solanus, I felt that God was all around us."

In addition to the gift of healing, Father Solanus also had the gift of prophecy, miracles, reading of hearts, supernatural knowledge and discernment. On numerous occasions, people observed that he possessed knowledge about the outcome of many future events.

In Detroit, the Sisters of St. Agnes had great faith in Father Solanus and they also had first-hand experience regarding Father Solanus' gift of knowledge. They noticed that in the summer time when they were getting ready to go back to the Motherhouse in Wisconsin, if Father Solanus said, "I will see you in September," it meant that they would be returning to Detroit. However, if he simply said "Goodbye," it meant that their superiors would be transferring them to another convent.

Brother Ignatius Milne said that one could often discover the outcome of a particular situation by listening very carefully to Father Solanus' words. If he gave specific instructions to a person who was asking for help, it was a sign that his or her prayer request was going to be granted. At times he would say, "By nine o'clock this evening, your temperature will return to normal. Or he might say, "By tomorrow morning, all of your painful symptoms will have vanished." On the other hand, if Father Solanus said simply, "I will pray," it was often a sign that the favor would not be granted.

Naturally, not all prayers were answered according to a person's desire. Whether one received an answer to their prayers or not, Father Solanus asked everyone to give thanks to God and to accept everything as coming from the hand of Divine Providence. Whenever Father Solanus was sick or in pain, he thanked God for it.

On one occasion, a woman brought her three-year-old daughter to Father Solanus. The little girl was suffering from a kidney disease. Father Solanus said, "Why don't we pray for a while." He then closed his eyes and became completely still.

After a time, Father Solanus said to the little girl, "The Lord loves little angels just like you!" The mother knew then that her daughter was not going to live. Nevertheless, the mother felt a great sense of peace and believed it was Father Solanus' prayers that was giving her strength. The little girl passed away three days later.

On Christmas Eve in 1929, Patrick Egan, a tow truck driver, had a terrible accident. Patrick as well as the entire Egan family knew Father Solanus well. Patrick's sister Kathleen, called Father Solanus on the telephone and told him about the accident and asked him to pray that Patrick would survive. Father Solanus was quiet for a moment and then said, "Well, let's see what the good God wants." Patrick's mother was at the hospital waiting to find out what Father Solanus had said. The minute Kathleen got off the phone with Father Solanus, she called her mother. "Mama, Patrick is not going to live. Father Solanus said, 'Let's see what the good God wants.' Mama, Patrick is going to die." Kathleen knew Father Solanus well enough to understand what his words meant. Patrick died later that night.

Father Solanus' gifts of knowledge were evident when he met Margaret Ann Ryan for the first time. The official name on her birth certificate was Anna Marguerite and it was the name that she actually preferred. However, there was not a single person who called her Anna Marguerite because no one knew that she had any other name other than Margaret Ann.

She introduced herself to Father Solanus as Margaret Ann but was very surprised that he called her Anna Marguerite during their conversation together. He had no way of knowing that information about her. He invited her to enroll in the Seraphic Mass Association which she was happy to do. When he filled out the small enrollment card and handed it to her, she was astonished to see that he had written Anna Marguerite on the card.

Father Solanus' gift of knowledge and his ability to read hearts was evidenced in the testimony of a young man named Michael who was trying to help his elderly father. Michael's father had a great desire to talk to Father Solanus and asked Michael to take him to the monastery and he agreed to do so. Connie, Michael's landlady, asked if she could go with the two of them to see Father Solanus and they were happy to have her come along.

Michael introduced himself to Father Solanus and told him that his father was worried because he was elderly and was no longer able to get to church. He was hoping that Father Solanus would talk to his father and tell him not to worry anymore because he had been strong in his faith throughout his life and had already done his part. "Yes, he has done his part," Father Solanus said, "but when are you going to start doing your part?"

Connie then interrupted the conversation and told Father Solanus that Michael was a person of faith and attended Mass every Sunday. He was "doing his part," she was sure of it. "Do not be so sure of it," Father Solanus replied. He has not been to Mass in more than five years." Michael then admitted that it was true. On Sundays, when Connie thought he was going to church, he was actually going to a bar. Father Solanus had never met Michael before and had no way of knowing anything about him. Through the gifts God gave him, he was often able to penetrate into the hearts and minds of his visitors.

In 1939, John Joseph Tighe went to the Mayo Clinic in Rochester, Minnesota and was diagnosed with terminal cancer. His doctor estimated that he had two months to live. The doctor explained that surgery was an option but it would not heal him. At best, it would only buy him a little more time. John remembered that he had talked to Father Solanus about his health and Father Solanus told him that he would get well. John had complete faith in Father Solanus' words. He insisted on having the surgery. In the operating room, the doctor, as well as the other doctors in attendance, were very surprised to find that there was no cancer but instead a blockage of a bile duct. After the blockage was removed, John recovered quickly.

When assisting people who were sick, Father Solanus made use of all of the sacramentals, including relics, holy water, blessed medals and more. On one occasion, a man named Steve Gergely asked Father Solanus to go to the hospital and bless his wife, Leona who was in critical condition. Father Solanus explained that he would not be able to since he was on his way out to say Mass. He took off a medal of St. Therese and asked Steve to pin it on Leona. The nurses on duty as well as Leona's family saw an immediate improvement in her condition after the medal was pinned on her.

In Detroit, a woman named Mrs. Bette spoke to Father Solanus and told him about a nineteen-year-old girl she knew who had eaten contaminated corn. Her condition was growing worse by the day. Father Solanus gave Mrs. Bette a small bottle of holy water that had been blessed in the name of Blessed Ignatius. He wanted the girl's mother to give her the blessed water by the spoonful. He also asked that the mother make a novena to St. Fidelis for her daughter's recovery. Mrs. Bette was very surprised at his words and told him that their family belonged to St. Fidelis parish. Father Solanus had no way of knowing that. He assured her that the girl would get better very soon and his words proved to be true.

During World War II, a man and his wife visited Father Solanus and asked him to pray for their son. He was serving in the military and his ship was in a war-zone at the time. Father Solanus asked the couple how many men were serving on the ship and they told him that there were twenty altogether. Father Solanus suggested that they enroll all twenty members of the crew in the Seraphic Mass Association. As it happened, the ship was torpedoed and destroyed but all twenty members of the crew survived.

In June 1945, Father Solanus' nephew, John McCluskey was going to be ordained in Seattle, Washington. John was the son of Father Solanus' sister Genevieve. Three of Father Solanus' brothers, Owen, Patrick, and Monsignor Edward visited Father Solanus in Detroit and urged him to attend the ordination with them. It would also be the occasion of a large Casey family reunion. Father Solanus asked if their brother Maurice had been invited and his brothers told him that he had not. Maurice was in Mt. Hope Sanitarium in Baltimore, Maryland. He had become increasingly despondent and depressed. Everyone in the family was aware of his emotional instability. Father Solanus told his brothers that he would not attend the ordination or the large family reunion unless Maurice was invited. He would not want his brother to feel rejected, knowing that he was the only member of the family who had been left out. His brothers agreed to it and went to pick up Maurice in Baltimore.

As soon as people in the Seattle area learned that Father Solanus was in town, his family members were bombarded with telephone calls from people wanting to speak with him or better yet, visit him. He had a kind of celebrity status in a city he had only visited twice in his life. Priests in the area wanted Father Solanus to come to their parishes to say Mass. Nuns in various religious congregations wanted Father Solanus to visit their convents. The phone rang constantly, at all hours of the day and night and during Father Solanus' time in Seattle, the house was packed with visitors and well-wishers. It was the same when he traveled to Spokane to visit his cousin, Euphrasia Casey. So many people came to the house that Euphrasia had little time to spend with her famous cousin.

The trip that Father Solanus made in 1945 for his nephew's ordination in Seattle was one of only three vacations that he took in his lifetime. In 1911, he traveled to St. Paul, Minnesota to celebrate his brother Maurice's ordination to the priesthood and in 1913 he traveled to Seattle for his parents' fiftieth wedding anniversary. In the Capuchin province, a vacation was allowed seven years after a friar had made his first profession and after that, two weeks of vacation could be taken every five years.

Father Solanus dearly loved his family and he kept up an active correspondence with them throughout his life. Because of the strict rules of the Capuchin Order, family visits were rare but he kept in touch by phone calls and letters. It was not unusual for him to write fifteen-page letters or longer to his family and to his extended family. He took great interest in his many nieces and nephews and would call them on the telephone saying, "This is your uncle who is just checking in with you to say hello and to make sure you are ok."

When Father Solanus got back from his trip to Seattle, he was told that he was being transferred to St. Michael's parish in Brooklyn. He had been at St. Bonaventure in Detroit for twenty-one years and was now seventy-five years old. The change in his priestly assignment was due to an effort by his superiors to give him a well-earned rest. They also wanted to relieve him from the pressure of almost constant contact with visitors.

The news that Father Solanus was leaving was devastating to many of his friends in Detroit who depended on him but it was not devastating to Father Solanus. He seemed to be content with wherever his superiors decided to send him and happy to obey.

One Sunday morning, Father Solanus was asked to give a talk to the Capuchin novices. In the talk, he said that he had noticed that some of the novices seemed overly preoccupied regarding which parish they would be assigned to after they were ordained. There were certain parishes that they definitely wanted to steer clear of and there were others that they found highly desirable and hoped to be assigned to.

Father Solanus advised the novices not to be concerned about such matters and to try not to allow such thoughts to enter their minds. He said to them, "It does not matter where our Order sends us or which parish we serve at or what city we serve in. Wherever we are sent we will be serving God and we will be in the presence of the Blessed Sacrament. Isn't that enough to make us happy?"

Father Solanus felt a certain relief to be moving to his new assignment at St. Michael's parish. He confided to a friend that he was exhausted from his crushing workload at St. Bonaventure's and was glad for the change. He was looking forward to having a little more time to rest. Hundreds of people in and around the Detroit area who depended on him for counseling were both shocked and devastated when they learned of his transfer. They were more than willing to travel the six hundred miles to Brooklyn in order to see him.

Father Solanus' friends and acquaintances from Detroit were soon visiting him in Brooklyn. They were also calling him on the telephone and writing letters to him. His days were almost as long as they had been in Detroit but there was not as much strain and stress. He had more letters to answer but less people coming in to the office for counseling.

Father Solanus had a number of health problems, but he never spoke about them. Even his closest friends did not know any of the details of his health issues. Friends and acquaintances who drove him to his doctor's appointments never knew why he was going to the doctor. Some had heard that he was bothered by varicose veins in his legs, but he never mentioned it to anyone.

One lady, Mrs. Edward Wolfe of Brighton, Michigan called Father Solanus at St. Michael's parish and told him that she wanted to make the trip to Brooklyn to see him. Her baby daughter, Kathleen Ann, was seriously ill with celiac disease. Father Solanus told Mrs. Wolfe not to make the trip but to kneel down beside the telephone and hold her baby in her arms. He then prayed and gave the baby a blessing over the telephone. He told Mrs. Wolfe to use the money she would have spent on the trip to Brooklyn to help the poor. Kathleen Ann recovered quickly after the blessing.

While at St. Michael's, Father Solanus made an effort to reconnect with friends and acquaintances from his former parish assignments. He had a wonderful time revisiting the annual

Labor Day Festival at Sacred Heart parish in Yonkers. He still enjoyed eating the hot dogs with mustard as well as participating in the many festivities and games. However, the number of people coming for counseling to Father Solanus at St. Michael's parish kept increasing as the months passed. His superiors realized that he was not getting the rest he needed and would never be able to find relief from his hectic schedule in a large city like Brooklyn.

Father Solanus' superiors wanted to transfer him to one of the Capuchin monasteries where he would be protected from the endless visitors. After serving at St. Michael's for nine months, he was transferred to St. Felix Friary in the small town of Huntington, Indiana and put on full retirement status.

St. Felix Friary was the Capuchin novitiate for the province and boasted thirty acres of beautiful grounds in the Indiana countryside. There was an abundance of pear, peach and plum trees on the property. In addition, the Capuchins had planted 170 apple trees right behind the monastery. There was also a huge vegetable garden, vineyards and a multitude of beautiful flowering shrubs. The Capuchins maintained beehives that provided excellent honey for the entire friary. The bees also proved to be very useful by pollinating the many fruit trees that were on the property.

Father Solanus enjoyed the peaceful surroundings at St. Felix Friary and loved to take walks in the countryside. The wide-open spaces reminded him of his happy boyhood days on the family farm in Wisconsin. At St. Felix, he spent time hoeing in the vegetable garden, trimming the trees in the orchard, pulling weeds, and cultivating his strawberry patch. There were a variety of birds in the area and he delighted in listening to their beautiful warbles, whistles and trills. He would usually jog a little each day in order to stay fit and also joined the novices in their games of volleyball and tennis.

Shortly after Father Solanus arrived at St. Felix Friary, he heard talk that he might be transferred once again to another monastery. He loved his new assignment at St. Felix but remained detached and unconcerned about his future. He wrote to his brother, Monsignor Edward saying, "I have not the least worry about whether I remain here at St. Felix or am transferred. It is after all, essentially quite the same." Father Solanus had enjoyed every one of his assignments during his many years as a priest. Once, when he was asked his feelings regarding his Capuchin vocation he said, "It is like starting heaven here on earth."

One of Father Solanus' classmates from the seminary, Father Damasus Wickland, lived at St. Felix Friary in the infirmary and was blind. Father Solanus often visited him there and would pray the Little Office of the Blessed Virgin with him. He would also play Irish tunes for Father Damasus on his violin. They loved to reminisce about their early days together in the seminary. Father Solanus and Father Damasus sat next to each other in the refectory. Every day, Father Solanus would cut up the meat and potatoes on Father Damasus' plate into small pieces to make it easy for him to eat.

Father Solanus loved to sit outside near the beehives and watch the bees at their work. While the bees crawled about his hands and arms, he talked to them. He called them "God's little innocent creatures." Once in a while he was stung, but not often.

Father Solanus was so relaxed around the bees and took such an interest in them that the head bee keeper, Father Elmer Stoffel asked him to be the assistant bee keeper. It was an assignment that Father Solanus loved. A year or more after arriving at St. Felix, Father Solanus ordered a queen bee for one of the hives, as the hive was growing larger and needed to be split.

When Father Elmer had work to do inside the hive, he sometimes set up his bee smoker since the smoke proved effective in keeping the bees calm. At those times, Father Solanus played his harmonica for the bees. More than one person observed that his harmonica playing seemed to have a soothing effect on the bees, especially if they were about to swarm.

The bees were ordered from a company in Illinois and upon arrival, Father Elmer and Father Solanus put them in their new home. One day a bee flew in to Father Solanus' cell. He carefully picked it up and took it to Brother Leon, telling him the little bee was lost. "Please take this little bee outside so that she can find her way back home," Father Solanus said.

The novices who resided at St. Felix were aware that Father Solanus had a remarkable rapport with birds, bees, and many other creatures. On one occasion, several of the novices were taking a walk on the grounds and saw a wild robin sitting on Father Solanus' hand.

Once, the superior at St. Felix asked the novices to help with a problem concerning the bees. A huge and angry swarm of bees had formed and was growing angrier and larger by the minute. The novices put on their bee protection suits and got their nets. Although the head and body gear protected them completely, a number of the novices were still very much afraid. They were told to make an effort to calm the bees down.

Soon, Father Solanus was called to help. As he walked toward the bees, he told all of the novices to remain calm. The bees started to swarm around him. He then spoke quietly to the bees, telling them to calm down. He reached into the hive with his bare hands and inspected it. He quickly discovered the problem. There were two queen bees inside the hive and one needed to be removed. He did not have any protective gear on. He found the queen and put it in his handkerchief and then put it in his pocket. By this time, his arm was covered with bees and bees were clinging to his long white beard as well. Not one of the bees stung Father Solanus. He reached inside the long sleeve of his habit and removed a large handful of bees and then got out his harmonica and played an Irish tune, "Mother Machree," to calm them down. From that point on, the bees settled down completely and the problem was resolved.

Regarding the bee incident, Father Solanus did not seem to think that anything extraordinary had occurred but many of the novices who were there and had witnessed the entire incident were awestruck. One of the novices said, "The event was surreal, seemingly impossible, but I witnessed it. No one could have done what Father Solanus did, but it happened, and what's more, Father Solanus didn't think there was anything particularly special about it."

On one occasion, Father Elmer was working with the hives on a day when the bees were agitated. He had been negligent in taking the customary precautions and had not tightened up his clothing. Consequently, three bees crawled up his pant leg and stung him. Having an immediate allergic reaction, he fell to the ground in great pain and felt his air passages closing off, preventing him from breathing. Father Solanus immediately ran over to Father Elmer and blessed him saying, "God will make you well." The painful symptoms vanished instantly as though he had never been stung.

Years later, when the tribunal of judges was assembled to consider Father Solanus' Cause for sainthood, they interviewed many people who had known him personally. Father Elmer was interviewed and recounted the story of how he was instantly healed when Father Solanus blessed him. Father Elmer referred to the incident as "my miracle." Some of the Capuchins spoke of Father Elmer's immediate recovery from the bee sting to Father Solanus and said, "When you blessed Father Elmer, he got well. Why don't you help us in our ailments?" Father Solanus said in reply, "But Father Elmer was dying."

In general, Father Solanus believed that the Capuchins were called to patiently endure the physical sufferings that came into their lives. He once said, "In the crosses of life that come to us, Jesus offers us opportunities to help Him redeem the world. Let us profit by His generosity. If we try to show the Dear Lord our good will and if we ask him for resignation to the crosses he sends or permits to come our way, we may be sure that sooner or later they will turn out to have been just so many blessings in disguise."

One of the only other cases of Father Solanus' help to a fellow Capuchin suffering a physical ailment was his assistance to Brother Daniel Brady, a student in the Capuchin novitiate at St. Bonaventure monastery. On one occasion, Brother Daniel had an infected tooth which was causing him a great deal of pain. When he went to the dentist, he was told that the infection had spread to his jawbone. Brother Daniel went every week so that the dentist could drain the infected area but the treatment proved futile. The dentist informed Brother Daniel that there was no other option but surgery. Unfortunately, it would be major surgery because part of his jaw bone would have to be removed.

One day, Father Solanus saw Brother Daniel in the sacristy and noticed that he looked sad. He asked him why he looked so downcast. Brother Daniel explained that it was possible that he would have to leave the novitiate. He would be having surgery very soon because of his dental problems. There was a chance that the malady could put a halt to his religious vocation.

Father Solanus asked him to kneel down for a blessing. He told Brother Daniel that when he went back to the dentist, the dentist would be very surprised. Then he touched Brother Daniel's cheek. At Father Solanus' touch, Brother Daniel felt his cheek tighten up and knew at that moment that he had been healed.

The next time the dentist saw Brother Daniel, he assumed that he was there in order to make an appointment for the surgery. When the dentist examined him, he was truly amazed to find that the infection was gone. No operation would be necessary. To be sure, he had Brother Daniel come back five more times. The dentist told him to come in immediately if he had any pain but he never had any more trouble.

Like Brother Daniel, Nettie Dearbin of Detroit, also received a healing on one occasion at Father Solanus' touch. At the time, Nettie had an unsightly dark spot on her check caused by a skin infection which the doctors had not been able to cure. She did not mention it to Father Solanus, but when he reached out his hand to greet Nettie, she quickly touched the back of his hand to the sore on her cheek. From that time forward, the infection began to heal until the dark blemish disappeared completely.

Not long after Father Solanus arrived at St. Felix Friary, heavy frost warnings were broadcast on the radio as well as in the newspaper. The Capuchins knew the frost could severely damage the apples in the apple orchard. They were trying to decide what course of action they should take. They considered placing an orchard heater between the trees. The burning oil in the heater would then create smoke, heat and water vapor that would protect the apples from the frost.

Father Solanus was doubtful about the effectiveness of the orchard heater. He offered to bless the orchard with a special blessing and a prayer invoking the intercession of Blessed Ignatius of Laconi, a Capuchin Brother. The superior was in favor of the idea and told Father Solanus to give the special blessing to the apple trees. It happened to be May 11, the Feast Day of Blessed Ignatius who had passed away on May 11, 1781. That season, all of the apple trees on the nearby farms suffered from the frost damage. St. Felix Friary had the only apple orchard in the vicinity whose apples were not harmed.

On January 25, 1947, the *Detroit News* wrote that Father Solanus was traveling from St. Felix Friary in Huntington to St. Bonaventure's in Detroit to celebrate his Golden Jubilee of fifty years as a Capuchin. Most people did not know that Father Solanus had been transferred to St. Felix, and that was how his superiors wanted it. When the article was printed, everyone suddenly knew Father Solanus' whereabouts. His superiors were disappointed that the information had been printed in the newspaper and they continued to make a real effort to try to protect Father Solanus from the crowds.

Father Solanus' three brothers, Monsignor Edward, Father Maurice and Owen as well as his sister Grace were present at his Golden Jubilee in Detroit. A special Mass was celebrated in the chapel at St. Bonaventure's and after the Mass, more than two thousand people walked through the reception line in order to greet and congratulate him. Even then, people were trying to give him a quick update on their various personal problems and difficulties and hopefully receive a word from him. Obviously, it was not the appropriate time to be talking to him in confidence, but the people seemed oblivious to that fact.

Father Solanus returned to St. Felix with many lovely gifts, vestments, and generous checks. One of the gifts was a beautiful chalice. While he deeply appreciated the kindness and generosity of his friends, he did not want to keep the gifts for himself. He received permission to give the chalice to a visiting missionary priest who was serving in India.

Father Solanus spent many quiet hours in deep prayer in the chapel at St. Felix Friary. On one occasion, one of the novices went into the chapel in the middle of the night because he could not sleep. He turned on the lights in the church and saw Father Solanus kneeling on the top step of the altar. He was staring intently at the tabernacle with his arms raised. He was completely still and did not even notice that the bright overhead lights had been turned on. The young novice did not completely understand, but he felt like he had witnessed something very sacred and after just a few minutes he turned the lights off and quietly left the church.

A similar incident happened when Father Solanus visited his niece Mildred Conley and her husband Dean and spent the night at their house. In the middle of the night Dean saw a light on in the living room and thinking that he had left it on, he went to check. He saw Father Solanus on his knees, with a small prayer book close by. He was motionless with his hands raised and seemed to be in a deep state of prayer. Father Solanus did not notice that Dean had come into the room. Dean left the room quietly so as not to disturb him.

The next morning when Dean came into the living room at 5:45 a.m. Father Solanus was still kneeling in the same position with his arms outstretched. To Dean, it did not appear that he had slept at all during the night. Dean told Father Solanus when they would all be leaving the house and Father Solanus said to Dean, "Let me just finish up my prayers and I will be ready to go in a minute."

On one occasion, the superior of the friary, Father Francis Heidenreich mentioned that the community car had seen better days. He asked all the Capuchins to keep on the lookout for a reliable car to purchase. Father Solanus put a call in to his friend Jerry McCarthy. Jerry was the owner of the largest Chevrolet dealership in Detroit. Jerry, who had a great admiration for Father Solanus, told him that he would like to give the Capuchins a brand-new car.

Father Francis Heidenreich, Father Gorden Garske and Father Solanus drove down from Huntington to Jerry's car dealership in Detroit. Father Gordon and Father Francis were truly amazed to see the reverence and awe of each of the employees when Father Solanus walked onto the car lot. They were beaming with joy when they greeted him. He always seemed to be unaware of his immense popularity or of the esteem that so many had for him.

On another occasion, Father Francis mentioned that the friary was in need of laundry equipment. Father Solanus told a friend and in a short time, a gift was delivered to the monastery, a brand-new washer and dryer.

While Father Solanus was always grateful for the needed items that his friends and benefactors gave to the monastery, for his own part, he had few wants and few needs. On one occasion, when Father Solanus' regular confessor was away, Father Cyril Langheim went to his cell to hear his confession. Father Cyril was surprised to see how plain and empty his cell was. Most of the Capuchins had a few keepsakes in their cell - personal mementos from the past, perhaps gifts and books that had been given to them, but not Father Solanus. Other than one book on his desk and a small sign that said," Blessed be God in all his designs," his cell was free of personal possessions. If he did receive gifts from people, it was his habit to give them away.

Not long after Father Solanus arrived at St. Felix Friary, he began to regularly receive boxes of candy in the mail. It was not just one box or two boxes but many, many boxes. A number of people were aware that he loved to give candy to the children who came to see him and they wanted to make sure he always had a good supply.

On one occasion, Father Solanus' superior came in his cell and saw that he had his feet propped up on an orange crate because his doctor had advised him to keep his feet elevated. The superior wanted to find something more suitable than a simple orange crate for him to use but Father Solanus was content. He said that he did not need or want anything fancy. He was perfectly happy with the orange crate.

Father Solanus possessed only one habit and it was threadbare. Many times, he used safety pins to hold it together. On one occasion, he asked Father Pius Cotter if he could borrow his habit. Father Pius had the impression that someone was waiting for Father Solanus in the office and he was embarrassed to be seen in his tattered old habit. Like his habit, Father Solanus' shoes were also old and weather-beaten. When he traveled, his suitcase was nothing more than a cardboard box.

Once, a couple visited Father Solanus at St. Felix Friary in order to ask him for his prayers. The woman had a diabetic sore on her arm that wasn't healing and she was very worried about it. During their visit, Father Solanus talked to them about other matters and it almost seemed like he was ignoring the woman's problem. However, as the couple was leaving, Father Solanus said to the woman, "When you reach the Michigan border, it would be a good idea to take the bandage off your arm." When they got to the border, the woman took the bandage off and to her great surprise, the sore on her arm had completely disappeared. At first, she thought she was looking at the wrong arm. She and her husband were truly amazed and very grateful.

It was a challenge for the superior at St. Felix Friary to deal with the people who were coming to see Father Solanus in increasing numbers. Caravans of chartered busses began to arrive regularly from Detroit. Visitors were calling on the telephone and coming to the friary at all hours of the day and night. The cars in the monastery parking lot revealed license plates from all parts of the United States as well as Canada. Finally, the superior told the people not to come to St. Felix by chartered bus. At Father Solanus' advanced age and with his serious health problems, it was too taxing for him to see so many people.

One day, two busloads of people arrived at St. Felix Friary from Detroit. The superior would not allow Father Solanus to go out and meet them. Instead of going home, the people stayed on the grounds near the busses for the entire day. Finally, about five o'clock in the afternoon, the superior told Father Solanus that he could go out and greet the people for ten minutes maximum. When he walked out to the busses, the entire group of people got down on their knees to receive a blessing. In addition to the group blessing, he also gave each person an individual blessing. He did not waste any time and was finished in the ten minutes his superior had allotted to him.

At St. Felix Friary, the number of letters that Father Solanus received continually increased with the passage of time. Finally, a secretary was assigned to help him with the task. The postman delivered the mail each morning at 9:30 a.m. and Father Solanus usually got to work right away on it. He could have easily spent ten or twelve hours a day answering the letters. Because of the painful arthritis in his hands, he often used a typewriter. Brother Leon occupied the cell next to Father Solanus. Late into the night, Brother Leon could hear Father Solanus typing, making an attempt to answer the letters.

Every day after having lunch with the community, Father Solanus would join the other Capuchins in the priests' recreation room. He often joined Father Blase Gitzen in a game of pool. None of the other Capuchins were interested in the game. Actually, Father Solanus wasn't interested in pool either. The only reason he played was because he knew how much Father Blase enjoyed it.

Father Cosmas Niedhammer used to watch Father Solanus and Father Blase playing pool together during recreation time. He often observed that shortly after the game began, Father Solanus' call bell would ring. That meant that someone was asking for him at the front office. He would immediately put the pool cue back in the rack without the slightest sign of impatience or annoyance and hurry over to the office. It meant that Father Solanus had to cut his recreation time short and in all likelihood, would be in the office until dinner time, or even later. Yet, there was never a word of protest. Father Cosmas thought it was remarkable.

Father Solanus had a wonderful sense of humor and delighted in telling jokes to his fellow Capuchins. He was a great storyteller and often during recreation, he shared anecdotes from his past, embellishing the stories with great detail. He loved music and would frequently play a tune on his violin for the other Capuchins. He took some teasing for it because he was by no means an accomplished player. Brother Agathangelus, who knew Father Solanus very well, described him as a "good community man, a man of great charity." Brother Agathangelus stated that he never once heard him utter an unkind word about anyone. He had no enemies.

During the ten years that Father Solanus was at St. Felix Friary in Huntington he went back from time to time to Detroit for special occasions and celebrations. On one occasion, a Franciscan brother named Brother Rumold and his friend James Maher, offered to drive Father Solanus on the return trip from Detroit back to Huntington in James' car. Father Solanus told Brother Rumold that a very nice couple had already offered to drive him to Huntington. However, he wanted to say the Rosary in the car on the way back to the friary and he knew it would be awkward since the couple were not Catholics. He decided to go with Brother Rumold and James.

As it turned out, Brother Rumold's superior would not let him take the day off, so James was the designated driver. James was supposed to pick Father Solanus up at ten o'clock in the morning but the trip was delayed by five hours because James had to unexpectedly take his car to the shop for a repair. A friend drove Father Solanus to the car repair shop at three o'clock in the afternoon so that he and James could leave from there.

Because they were leaving later than expected, James assumed that Father Solanus would be anxious to get on the road as soon as possible but that was not the case. Instead, Father Solanus asked James if he would be willing to take him to a nearby Catholic church so that he could say a few prayers. James was happy to do so. He took Father Solanus to his own Presentation parish in Detroit. They prayed five decades of the Rosary as well as other prayers and got on the road for Huntington an hour later. Father Solanus said that he hoped to get back to Huntington by midnight.

On the way home, Father Solanus noticed a man hitchhiking by the roadside and asked James to stop and pick him up. Because of the way the roads intersected, James was unable to pull over. Father Solanus told James that if they happened to see another man hitchhiking, they must try to stop for him. Soon they came upon another hitchhiker and this time they were able to pick him up. The hitchhiker said that he had lost his job and was on his way to Chicago to look for work. Father Solanus asked the man if he was hungry and he said he had not eaten in two days. When they got to Niles, Michigan, Father Solanus asked James to stop at a restaurant for dinner. Father Solanus had a cardboard box and a briefcase in the back seat so James made sure he locked the car.

At the restaurant, the man ate his meal very quickly. James noticed that Father Solanus was eating slowly, moving the fish around on his plate with his fork. Father Solanus asked the man if he was still hungry and he said that he was. Father Solanus gave him about half of his own plate of fish. After they had finished eating, Father Solanus said they would have to part ways since the man would have to take a different route to get to Chicago. Father Solanus asked the man if he had any money and he said that he did not. Father Solanus gave him five dollars. "I wish I could repay you for what you have done for me," the man said. "Well, there is something you can do for me," Father Solanus replied. "When you get to Chicago, please stop for a moment in a Catholic Church and pray for poor sinners." The man promised that he would and said he would be very happy to do so.

When James and Father Solanus were walking back to the car, Father Solanus was a few steps in front of him and reached out and opened the locked door. Needless to say, James was shocked. "But I locked the car door! How were you able to open it?" James asked. Father Solanus made no reply. James thought about the strange incident and wondered about it for years.

On the return trip to Huntington, Father Solanus and James prayed ten more decades of the Rosary. They also had a chance to talk together. James told Father Solanus that he had heard that many people had been healed through his prayers. "That is not true," Father Solanus replied. "I have never healed a soul. I do not have the ability to. Only God heals." It was after midnight when they arrived at St. Felix Friary and Father Solanus went straight to the chapel to pray in thanksgiving for a safe trip home before going to bed.

Another incident of Father Solanus opening a locked door took place when he was serving at St. Bonaventure's monastery in Detroit. Mrs. Thomas V. Egan and her sister, Mrs. Vincent Kelly stopped one afternoon to pray in the chapel at St. Bonaventure's. When they came out of the chapel, they saw Father Solanus walking on the path in front of the monastery and they greeted him. When Mrs. Egan walked to her car, she looked in the window and saw her keys inside the ignition. She and her sister tried the two doors but they were both locked. Mrs. Egan realized she was going to have to call a locksmith. When she saw

Father Solanus walking back toward the monastery, she told him about being locked out of her car. He said to her, "That is not a problem." He walked over to the car and opened the door. The two women were at a total loss as to how he was able to do it.

Once, a lady name Mrs. William Evison, in desperation, used the long-distance operator to call Father Solanus at St. Felix Friary in Huntington. She had heard many wonderful things about him and hoped that he could help her. Her baby daughter, Cynthia, had been hospitalized with heart problems and was not expected to live.

A Capuchin Brother answered the telephone when Mrs. Evison called. She was weeping when she told him that her baby was ill and that she needed to speak to Father Solanus. The Brother ran as fast as he could to try to find Father Solanus.

The long-distance operator who put the call through had listened on the line to the conversation between Mrs. Evison and the Brother. While Mrs. Evison was waiting to speak to Father Solanus, the operator broke in on the line and said to her, "I hope you don't mind if I speak to you but I have heard that Father Solanus is a very gifted priest. I feel sure he will be able to help your daughter!" Mrs. Evison was happy to hear the words of encouragement.

Father Solanus then got on the telephone and talked to Mrs. Evison. He told her that as soon as they got off the phone, he would go to the chapel and pray for her baby. "You will be bringing your baby home from the hospital in just a few days," he said. His words proved true and the baby made a complete recovery.

Father Solanus' nephew, Father John McCluskey, once visited Father Solanus at St. Felix Friary. After the visit, he was going to return by air to his home in Seattle. When he read a report of an airplane crash in New York, he became afraid and decided to cancel his airplane reservation. He purchased a train ticket instead. During his visit, Father John asked Father Solanus if he was afraid of flying. Father Solanus had actually just flown back to Huntington from Detroit. Father Solanus told him that he was not the least bit afraid of flying. "We are all in the hands of God. God will take care of everything," he said. John felt his own fears subsiding as Father Solanus talked. He was so impressed by his uncle's faith that he returned the train ticket and got an airplane ticket instead for his trip back to Seattle.

On January 12, 1949, Father Solanus received the sad news that his brother Maurice had died. Father Solanus had tried for many years to help his brother whom he dearly loved. He wrote him countless letters, had many long phone conversations with him, and visited him when he was able to. Maurice had entered the seminary as a young man and then left after three years. After Father Solanus was ordained, Maurice felt inspired to reenter the seminary. Later, feeling misunderstood and disillusioned, he left the diocesan priesthood and at the age of sixty-two and joined the Capuchin Order. Even that did not work out for him. He had suffered from psychological problems and depression for many years. Sadly, Father Solanus' brother Jim passed away on the same day as Maurice.

Father Solanus presided at the funeral for Maurice at Holy Rosary Church in Graceville, Minnesota. During the funeral homily, he spoke on the meaning of death and said that to the Christian, death should be considered a blessing from God. "Death is the last of the blessings God showers upon our earthly journey toward Home," he said.

The same year, Father Solanus had to be hospitalized at St. Joseph's Hospital in Fort Wayne, Indiana. He was diagnosed with weeping eczema, sometimes called psoriasis. It was a painful skin disease that caused scaling, itching and burning of the skin. Because he was allergic to antibiotics, there was little that could be done to help him. His legs were turning black and were covered with painful sores complicated by a serious lack of circulation. The doctor said that if his condition did not improve, his legs might have to be amputated. Nurses monitored his circulation by checking the pulse in his legs every three minutes.

In order to protect Father Solanus from numerous visitors, the Capuchins made it a point to keep his hospitalization a strict secret. At St. John's Hospital, a very large "Do Not Disturb" sign was put on his door. When Father Blase came to the hospital to visit him, he was very surprised to find fifteen people inside his room. Father Blase had no idea how they found out about his hospitalization.

Father Blase noticed that Father Solanus did not appear to be worried or anxious about his condition but instead showed a complete lack of concern. Thinking that he possibly had not been given the full report, he asked Father Solanus if he knew how serious his condition was. Father Solanus said that he did. Father Blase also spoke to him about the possible amputation that the doctor had been discussing. Father Solanus said that if he had to lose his legs, it would be all right. He would accept it. Most of all, he was looking forward to getting out of the hospital and was hoping to get back to his beekeeping and gardening work if his health improved. He also thought about the mail that was surely piling up at the monastery and he was anxious to get to work on it. He stayed in the hospital for sixteen days.

The following year, Father Solanus traveled regularly to his doctors in Fort Wayne to be treated for the painful sores and skin eruptions on his legs. In 1952, he was admitted to Grace Hospital in Detroit where he made a great impression on the staff. It soon became evident that he did not like to be fussed over. He even insisted on making his own bed every day. Among the many patients in the hospital, that was a first. He was so popular that on the day he was discharged, doctors, nurses, patients and visitors formed two lines, each asking for a blessing.

In 1956, Father Solanus' general health was growing worse. The doctors at St. Joseph's Hospital in Fort Wayne, Indiana had done all they could do for him. Brother Gabriel Badalamenti, the infirmarian at St. Bonaventure monastery, drove Father Solanus to Detroit for further medical treatment. Father Bernard Burke, the superior, felt it best for Father Solanus to remain at St. Bonaventure's permanently.

As soon as Father Solanus arrived in Detroit, he was hospitalized for a brief period. Once back at St. Bonaventure monastery, he was told by Father Bernard Burke, that in order to protect his health, he would not be allowed to go to the front office or to take phone calls or receive visitors without permission. He was too weak and too feeble to deal with the demands of the public and Father Bernard wanted to make sure that he got the rest he needed. Father Solanus was not happy about the restrictions but as always, he obeyed. Father Bernard also told the Capuchins that Father Solanus' move to St. Bonaventure's was to be kept a strict secret. Absolutely no one was to know.

With very little work to do, Father Solanus spent much of his time in the chapel. Often when the other Capuchins visited the chapel, they found him standing near the tabernacle, playing hymns on his violin. He loved to go to the chapel in the quiet of the night to kneel before the Blessed Sacrament.

On May 15, 1957, Father Solanus was taken by ambulance to St. John's Hospital in Detroit. The skin disease that had afflicted his legs for many years had now spread over his entire body. His doctor, Dr. William McIntyre, diagnosed him as having severe erysipelas, a rare bacterial infection of the upper layers of the skin. Due to his labored breathing, he was placed in an oxygen tent. When he improved, he was discharged and a short time later was readmitted. Again, he improved and was able to go home. On July 2, 1957, he went back to the hospital where he remained until his death.

He was admitted to the hospital under the name Father Casey rather than Father Solanus Casey in the hopes that people would not discover his whereabouts as easily. Only his fellow Capuchins, relatives, and closest friends were allowed to visit him. His skin was so red from his skin disease that it looked like an extreme sunburn.

Father Solanus' illness brought him intense suffering but he never complained or asked for anything to aleve his pain. Brother Gabriel watched over him constantly and never left his bedside. Father Solanus talked about his approaching death in a joyful way and said that he was looking forward to heaven. "Death can be beautiful – like a wedding, if we make it so," he said.

One woman who was desperate to speak to Father Solanus, snuck up the back stairs of the hospital to the floor that Father Solanus was on. When she entered his room, she blurted out that she had always wanted his blessing. Just as she was about to be ushered out of his room, she spoke quickly and said, "I have never been able to conceive a child. Will you pray for me?" "You will have a boy and a girl," Father Solanus said to her. The following year she had a son and one year later, a daughter.

The Sisters of St. Joseph served at St. John's Hospital in Detroit. Sister Arthur Ann, who was on the nursing staff, was assigned to assist Father Solanus. She observed that although he was very weak, he was always in good humor, even telling jokes to friends and acquaintances. When the Sisters asked him what he would like them to bring him to eat he would say, "Whatever the good Lord wants me to have." The Sisters understood then that he did not really care what he was served.

When Father Solanus had the strength, he liked to be wheeled to the hospital chapel. People were always on the lookout for his wheelchair passing through the corridor. The patients, their relatives and members of the hospital staff would stand in the hallway and ask Father Solanus to bless them as he passed.

In the chapel, Father Solanus loved to sing the *Ave Maria* in Latin and to pray the Rosary. He often asked Sister Arthur Ann to read to him from *The Mystical City of God* by Mary of Agreda. The Sisters observed that as sick as he was, he possessed an interior joy and serenity. When he had the strength, he celebrated Mass in the hospital chapel. His superior had him say Mass at different times of the day in order to avoid large numbers of people attending. Although the time of his Mass was never announced, there were always numerous people in attendance.

A few days before Father Solanus' death, Father Gerald Walker, the provincial superior, visited him in the hospital. The two priests had been the best of friends for many years. Father Solanus reflected on his life as a Capuchin and said to Father Gerald, "I have looked on my whole life as giving and I want to give until there is nothing left of me to give. I have prayed that when I come to die, I might be perfectly conscious, so that with a deliberate act I can give my last breath to God." Before Father Gerald left, Father Solanus said, "Tomorrow will be a beautiful day."

At eleven o'clock in the morning on July 31, 1957, a hospital nurse stepped into Father Solanus' room. She heard him whispering but was not able to catch the words. Suddenly he sat up in the bed, opened his eyes very wide, stretched out both of his arms and said, "I give my soul to Jesus Christ." He laid his head back on the pillow and with that, he died. He was eighty-six years old. The time of his death was auspicious for at eleven o'clock on July 31, exactly fifty-three years before and to the very hour, he had celebrated his first Mass in Appleton, Wisconsin.

Father Solanus' body was taken to the Van Lerberghe Funeral Home in Detroit. Father Solanus had been friends with the Van Leberghe family and used to regularly stop in to say hello when their funeral home was located just two blocks from St. Bonaventure monastery.

Arthur Van Lerberghe felt especially devoted to Father Solanus because of a grace he had received many years before. In 1937, Arthur wanted to build a new funeral home but was unable to find financing. He told Father Solanus about his predicament and asked him to pray and he agreed to do so. The very next day, Arthur received a call from a man who was willing to co-sign on the loan. Arthur was so grateful that he started the practice of waiving all funeral and burial expenses whenever one of the Capuchins passed away.

At the Van Lerberghe Funeral Home, the viewing was scheduled for ten o'clock in the morning on Thursday, August 1. The particulars were announced on both radio and television. People began knocking on the door of the funeral home and lining up as early as 5:00 a.m. Everyone wanted to view Father Solanus one last time. All day long and into the evening the crowds came, pausing at the casket and touching their Rosaries and religious articles to Father Solanus' body. At 10:30 p.m. everyone was told to go home as the funeral home had to close.

On Friday, Father Solanus' body had been moved to St. Bonaventure monastery where he lay in state in the chapel. A total of twenty thousand people filed by Father Solanus' casket in order to pay their last respects.

The funeral Mass was held on Saturday, August 2, at ten o'clock in the morning. The chapel was full to overflowing. Loud speakers were set up so that the hundreds of people who lined both sides of the street outside the chapel could hear the service. The street in the front of the monastery was closed to traffic and a police squad was present to maintain order but the crowd was peaceful, reverent and orderly. Father Solanus was buried in the small cemetery behind St. Bonaventure monastery where seventeen other Capuchins had already been laid to rest.

We become transfigured by becoming little, humble, poor, dependent, powerless. How do we empty ourselves? How do we become little? By accepting all the sufferings that God permits to come into our lives. By seeking to serve others rather than to be served. By taking the last place. By never seeking recognition or applause. By making charity the foundation of our lives. By forgiving and loving our enemies.

–Father Frederick Miller

Bibliography

Ball, Ann, *Modern Saints: Their Lives and Faces - Book One*, TAN Books, Charlotte, North Carolina, 1983.

Ball, Ann, *Modern Saints: Their Lives and Faces - Book Two*, TAN Books, Charlotte, North Carolina, 1983.

Bergeron, Henri-Paul C.S.C., *Brother André: The Wonder Man of Mount Royal*, St. Joseph's Oratory, Montreal, Canada, 1997.

Bernardo, Antonio, *Bernadette Recounts her Apparitions*, Andre Doucet Publications, Lourdes, France, 1998.

Brocker, James H., *The Lands of Father Damien*, James H. Brocker Publisher, Molokai, Hawaii, 1997.

Bunson, Margaret R., *Father Damien - The Man and His Era*, Our Sunday Visitor, Huntington, Indiana, 1989.

Burton, Katherine, *Blessed André of Mount Royal*, Roman Catholic Books, Ft. Collins, Colorado, 1952.

Casey, Sister Bernadine SNJM (editor), *Letters from Solanus Casey OFM. Cap.*, The Father Solanus Casey Guild, Detroit, Michigan, 2000.

Crosby, Michael H. O.F.M. Cap., *Solanus Casey: The Official Account of a Virtuous American Life*, The Crossroad Publishing Company, New York, New York, 2000.

Crosby, Michael H. O.F.M. Cap., *Thank God Ahead of Time: The Life and Spirituality of Solanus Casey*, Franciscan Herald Press, Chicago, Illinois, 1985.

Derum, James Patrick, *The Porter of Saint Bonaventure's*, The Fidelity Press, Detroit, Michigan, 1968.

De Volder, Jan, *The Spirit of Father Damien – The Leper Priest – A Saint of Our Times*, Ignatius Press, San Francisco, California, 2010.

Doucet, Andre, *Lourdes: The Life of Bernadette – The Apparitions – The Shrines*, Andre Doucet Publications, Lourdes, France, 1998.

Dubuc, Jean-Guy, *Brother André*, Editions Fides, Quebec, Canada, 1999.

Englebert, Omer, *The Hero of Molokai*, Daughters of St. Paul, Derby, New York, 1955.

Farrow, John, *Damien the Leper*, Doubleday, New York, New York, 1937.

Ghéon, Henri, *The Secret of the Curé d'Ars*, Sheed and Ward, London, England, 1987.

Groeshel, Benedict J., CFR, *Travelers Along the Way*, Servant Books, Cincinatti, Ohio, 2010.

Hanley, Boniface O.F.M., *Ten Christians*, Ave Maria Press, Notre Dame, Indiana, 1979.

Hanley, Sister Mary Laurence O.S.F. and Oswald A. Bushnell, *Pilgrimage & Exile: Mother Marianne of Molokai*, Mutual Publishing, Honolulu, Hawaii, 2009.

Hatch, Alden, *The Miracle of the Mountain*, Hawthorne Books Inc., New York, New York, 1959.

Jourdain, Vital, SS.CC., *The Heart of Father Damien*, The Bruce Publishing Company, Milwaukee, Wisconsin, 1955.

Korson, Gerald (editor), *The Wonders of Lourdes*, Magnificat, Yonkers, New York, 2008.

LaFreniere, Bernard, C.S.C., *Brother André According to Witnesses*, St. Joseph's Oratory, Montreal, Canada, 1997.

McEachern, Patricia, PhD., *A Holy Life – The Writings of Saint Bernadette of Lourdes*, Ignatius Press, San Francisco, CA, 2005.

Milsome, John, *Damien: Father to the Lepers*, Servant Publications, Ann Arbor, Michigan, 1989.

Monnin, Alfred, *The Spirit of the Curé of Ars*, Burns, Lambert, and Oates, London, England, 1865.

O'Brien, Father Bartholomew J., *The Curé of Ars*, Tan Books and Publishers, Rockford, Illinois, 1987.

Odell, Catherine M., *Father Solanus: The Story of Solanus Casey, OFM CAP.*, Our Sunday Visitor, Huntington, Indiana, 1988.

Pezeril, Daniel, *Blessed and Poor*, Pantheon Books, New York, New York, 1961.

Ruffin, C. Bernard, *The Life of Brother André: The Miracle Worker of St. Joseph*, Our Sunday Visitor, Huntington, Indiana, 1988.

Rutler, George William, *The Curé d'Ars Today*, Ignatius Press, San Francisco, California, 1988.

Schorn, Joel R., *God's Doorkeepers: Padre Pio, Solanus Casey and André Bessette*, Servant Books, Cincinnati, Ohio, 2006.

Stewart, Richard, *Leper Priest of Molokai: The Father Damien Story*, University of Hawaii Press, Honolulu, Hawaii, 2000.

Treece, Patricia, *Nothing Short of a Miracle*, Our Sunday Visitor, Huntington, Indiana, 1988.

Trochu, Abbé Francois, *Saint Bernadette Soubirous*, Tan Books and Publishers, Rockford, Illinois, 1985.

Trochu, Abbé Francois, *The Curé D'Ars – St. Jean-Marie-Baptiste Vianney*, Tan Books and Publishers, Rockford, Illinois, 1977.

Trouncer, Margaret, *Saint Jean Marie Vianney: Curé of Ars*, Sheed and Ward, New York, New York, 1959.

Wisniewski, Richard, *Kalaupapa and the Legacy of Father Damien*, Pacific Basin Enterprises, Honolulu, Hawaii, 1988.

Wollenweber, Brother Leo OFM. Cap., *Meet Solanus Casey: Spiritual Counselor and Wonder Worker*, Servant Publications, Ann Arbor, Michigan, 2002.

Made in the USA
Middletown, DE
01 September 2024